Engaging
the neighbours

AUSTRALIA AND ASEAN
SINCE 1974

Engaging
the neighbours

AUSTRALIA AND ASEAN
SINCE 1974

FRANK FROST

Australian
National
University

PRESS

ANU PRESS

Published by ANU Press
The Australian National University
Acton ACT 2601, Australia
Email: anupress@anu.edu.au
This title is also available online at press.anu.edu.au

National Library of Australia Cataloguing-in-Publication entry

Creator:	Frost, Frank, 1947- author.
Title:	Engaging the neighbours : Australia and ASEAN since 1974 / Frank Frost.
ISBN:	9781760460174 (paperback) 9781760460181 (ebook)
Subjects:	ASEAN. Australia--Foreign relations--Southeast Asia. Southeast Asia--Foreign relations--Australia.
Dewey Number:	327.94059

Cover design and layout by ANU Press.

Contents

Chronology

1945   Declaration of independent Republic of Indonesia (August);
        after armed struggle against Dutch forces, sovereignty is
        transferred formally in December 1949

1945   Declaration of independent Democratic Republic of
        Vietnam (September); armed struggle against French forces
        pursued until 1954

1946   The Philippines independent from the US (July)

1948   Burma independent from Britain (January)

1953   Cambodia and Laos independent from France
        (October–November)

1954   Geneva Accords end French involvement in Vietnam (July);
        the Democratic Republic of Vietnam governs north of the
        Demilitarised Zone and the State (later Republic) of Vietnam
        in the south

1954   Manila Treaty establishes the Southeast Asia Treaty
        Organization, SEATO (September)

1955   Asian–African Conference, Bandung (April)

1957   Malaya independent from Britain (August)

1959   Prime Minister Tunku Abdul Rahman of Malaya proposes
        a Southeast Asian Friendship and Economic Treaty,
        SEAFET (February)

1961   Association of Southeast Asia (ASA) formed by Malaya,
        the Philippines and Thailand (July)

1963   Indonesia declares policy of *Konfrontasi* (Confrontation)
        of proposed Federation of Malaysia (January)

1963	Indonesia, Malaya and the Philippines initiate dialogue under the banner of 'Maphilindo' (June); the effort is abandoned amid tensions over the formation of the Federation of Malaysia
1963	Federation of Malaysia incorporating Malaya, North Borneo (Sabah), Sarawak and Singapore inaugurated (September)
1965	Singapore expelled from Malaysia and becomes independent state (August)
1966	*Konfrontasi* ends formally between Indonesia and Malaysia (August)
1967	Association of Southeast Asian Nations (ASEAN) established by Indonesia, Malaysia, the Philippines, Singapore and Thailand, Bangkok (August)
1971	ASEAN members issue declaration on Southeast Asian Zone of Peace, Freedom and Neutrality, ZOPFAN (November)
1974	Australia and ASEAN initiate multilateral relations, Canberra (April)
1975	Communist forces assume control of southern Vietnam and Cambodia (April) and Laos (December)
1975	Indonesian forces invade East Timor (December)
1976	ASEAN holds first heads of government meeting, the 'Bali Summit'; ASEAN Treaty of Amity and Cooperation signed (February)
1976	Vietnam reunified as Socialist Republic of Vietnam (July)
1977	SEATO dissolved (June)
1977	First meeting between Australian and ASEAN heads of government, Kuala Lumpur (August)
1978	Vietnam invades Cambodia; Khmer Rouge (Democratic Kampuchea) regime ejected (December)
1979	People's Republic of Kampuchea inaugurated in Cambodia, aligned with Soviet Union and Vietnam (January)
1979	Chinese invasion of northern Vietnam (February–March)
1980	Australia announces withdrawal of diplomatic recognition from ousted Democratic Kampuchea regime (October)
1984	Brunei independent from Britain; joins ASEAN (January)

1989	Asia-Pacific Economic Cooperation (APEC) group inaugurated in Canberra (November)
1990	Australia releases proposals to facilitate a peace agreement for Cambodia, the 'Red Book' (February)
1991	Paris Agreements on Cambodia concluded (October)
1992	ASEAN commitment to develop the ASEAN Free Trade Area (January)
1992	United Nations Transitional Authority in Cambodia, UNTAC, deployed (February)
1992	ASEAN joint declaration on the South China Sea (July)
1993	Elections in Cambodia followed by inauguration of Royal Government of Cambodia (May)
1994	ASEAN Regional Forum established (July)
1995	Vietnam joins ASEAN (July)
1997	Laos and Myanmar join ASEAN (July)
1997	Asian financial crisis adversely affects a number of regional economies (from July)
1997	ASEAN Plus Three cooperation inaugurated by ASEAN and China, Japan and South Korea (December)
1999	Cambodia joins ASEAN (April)
1999	Ballot in East Timor results in vote for independence from Indonesia (August)
1999	International Force for East Timor, INTERFET, deployed after substantial violence in the territory (September)
2002	East Timor independent (May)
2002	ASEAN and China sign Declaration on the Conduct of Parties in the South China Sea (November)
2003	ASEAN Summit in Bali issues commitment to establish an ASEAN Community (October)
2004	Heads of government meeting between ASEAN, Australia and New Zealand, Vientiane (November)
2005	Australia accedes to ASEAN Treaty of Amity and Cooperation (December)
2005	East Asia Summit inaugurated in Kuala Lumpur with Australia as a member (December)

2007	ASEAN adopts a Charter that provides a legal identity and reaffirms the Association's values and goals (November)
2008	Agreement reached on ASEAN–Australia–New Zealand Free Trade Agreement, AANZFTA (August)
2008	Australia appoints non-resident ambassador to ASEAN (September)
2010	ASEAN Defence Ministers' Meeting (ADMM) Plus process initiated, Hanoi (October)
2010	ASEAN–Australia heads of government summit, Hanoi (October)
2011	Russia and the US join the East Asia Summit (November)
2012	ASEAN foreign ministers unable to agree to a communiqué because of divisions over South China Sea issues, Phnom Penh (July)
2012	ASEAN commences negotiations with six major trading partners to develop the Regional Comprehensive Economic Partnership, RCEP (November)
2013	Australia appoints resident ambassador to ASEAN, based in Jakarta (September)
2014	ASEAN–Australia fortieth anniversary Commemorative Summit, Nay Pyi Taw (November)

Preface

In Australia's foreign relations with Southeast Asia, the Association of Southeast Asian Nations (ASEAN) has been of significant interest since its inauguration in 1967. Australia was the first country to establish a formal multilateral relationship with ASEAN (in 1974) and interactions have since expanded to include a wide range of dialogues and cooperation.

This monograph has arisen from interests I developed in ASEAN and Australian policies towards it in the aftermath of the wars in Indochina and my work as a PhD student on Australia's involvement in the war in Vietnam. I first wrote about ASEAN and its significance for Australia in the late 1970s. The work that follows seeks to contribute to the subject by providing a concise history of the origins and evolution of Australia's multilateral relations with ASEAN since 1974.

In preparing this work, I was fortunate to have been a Visiting Fellow in the Department of International Relations in the Coral Bell School of Asia Pacific Affairs in the College of Asia and the Pacific at The Australian National University. I want to express my great appreciation to Bill Tow for supporting me as a Visiting Fellow and for welcoming me as a guest in the department.

I would like to thank a number of people who have helped me greatly in my work on ASEAN and Australia and in the preparation of this manuscript. Anthony Milner and Graeme Dobell provided advice on the project overall and gave me most valuable comments on the full draft manuscript. I also benefited greatly from comments on the draft by Stephen Henningham and from Allan Gyngell, Stephen Sherlock and Carlyle Thayer on specific sections. For their help and advice during my work on this project, I would also like to express my appreciation to Kavi Chongkittavorn, Ralf Emmers, Tim Huxley, Paul Kelly, Andrew MacIntyre, Christopher B. Roberts, Daljit Singh, Tan See Seng, Tang Siew Mun, the late Barry Wain and Sally Percival Wood.

I want to express my special thanks to Mary-Louise Hickey in the Department of International Relations for her extensive advice and outstanding editorial contribution to the preparation and completion of the manuscript. I also want to express my deep gratitude to my brother-in-law Peter van der Vlies and to my friends for their support and encouragement while I was preparing the project. I would especially like to thank Andrew Chin, Minh Davis, Gayle Deel, Peter and Umi Freeman, Susan Geason, Averil Ginn, Carol Kempner, Eleanor Lawson, Cathy Madden, John Mandryk, Stephen O'Neill, Michael Ong and Effi Tomaras.

I would like to dedicate this book to my late parents, Dr John Norbert and Doreen Eveleen Frost.

Frank Frost
February 2016

Abbreviations

AACM	ASEAN–Australia Consultative Meeting
AANZFTA	ASEAN–Australia–New Zealand Free Trade Agreement
ADMM	ASEAN Defence Ministers' Meeting
AEC	ASEAN Economic Community
AFP	Australian Federal Police
AFTA	ASEAN Free Trade Agreement
ALP	Australian Labor Party
ANZ	Australia and New Zealand
ANZUS	Australia, New Zealand, United States
APEC	Asia-Pacific Economic Cooperation
ARF	ASEAN Regional Forum
ASA	Association of Southeast Asia
ASEAN	Association of Southeast Asian Nations
ASEM	Asia–Europe Meeting
ASPAC	Asian and Pacific Council
CER	Closer Economic Relations
CGDK	Coalition Government of Democratic Kampuchea
CSCA	Conference on Security and Cooperation in Asia
CSCAP	Council for Security Cooperation in the Asia Pacific
DFAT	Department of Foreign Affairs and Trade
DK	Democratic Kampuchea
EAEG	East Asian Economic Group
EAS	East Asia Summit
EEC	European Economic Community

EPG	Eminent Persons' Group
EU	European Union
FUNCINPEC	National United Front for an Independent, Neutral, Peaceful and Cooperative Cambodia
G20	Group of Twenty
GATT	General Agreement on Tariffs and Trade
ICAP	International Civil Aviation Policy
IMF	International Monetary Fund
INTERFET	International Force for East Timor
ISEAS	Institute of Southeast Asian Studies
JSCOT	Joint Standing Committee on Treaties
KPNLF	Khmer People's National Liberation Front
OECD	Organisation for Economic Co-operation and Development
PECC	Pacific Economic Cooperation Council
PKI	*Partai Komunis Indonesia*
PMC	Post-Ministerial Conference
PRK	People's Republic of Kampuchea
RCEP	Regional Comprehensive Economic Partnership
SEAFET	Southeast Asian Friendship and Economic Treaty
SEATO	Southeast Asia Treaty Organization
SIA	Singapore Airlines
TAC	Treaty of Amity and Cooperation
TPP	Trans-Pacific Partnership
UN	United Nations
UNTAC	United Nations Transitional Authority in Cambodia
ZOPFAN	Zone of Peace, Freedom and Neutrality

Introduction

On 8 August 1967, Indonesia, Malaysia, the Philippines, Singapore and Thailand formed the Association of Southeast Asian Nations (ASEAN). The Australian Government and Opposition responded promptly. The next day, Paul Hasluck, the Minister for External Affairs, endorsed ASEAN's aims of accelerating 'the economic growth, social progress and cultural development of the region', and of promoting 'regional peace and stability'. These objectives, he said, 'had Australia's full support'.[1] For his part, Opposition leader Gough Whitlam, speaking on 17 August, said that the formation of ASEAN was a 'natural development'. In addition, it had historical significance because it 'was the first occasion on which Indonesia has been associated with all her immediate neighbours' and because it was 'the first occasion on which Singapore, a Chinese State ... has been associated with Malay nations or other peoples in the region'.[2]

Despite these favourable remarks, there was at that time good reason to doubt whether ASEAN would become a durable regional organisation. Its founding members, as Whitlam noted, were highly diverse. They were rivals and in some cases recent enemies. Previous efforts at indigenous regional cooperation and organisation in Southeast Asia had not succeeded. In the event, however, while ASEAN has gone through some difficult times, it has gained in profile and significance. It has developed traditions of and mechanisms for consultation and cooperation, which have helped it to maintain peace among its members. Its style of cooperation has been attractive to all the states in Southeast Asia and its membership has accordingly expanded from

1   Paul Hasluck, 'Statement', in *Current Notes on International Affairs*, 38(8) August 1967: 328–9.
2   Gough Whitlam, in *Commonwealth of Australia Parliamentary Debates*, House of Representatives, Official Hansard, No. 33, 17 August 1967, p. 220.

the original five to 10. An additional neighbouring state, Timor-Leste, is interested to join. ASEAN has become essential to political and economic cooperation in Southeast Asia and has developed a broader regional and international significance.

ASEAN has also become central to Australia's relations with Southeast Asia. In 1974, Australia became the first external country to develop a formal multilateral relationship with ASEAN. Australia as a dialogue partner has, since 1980, taken part in consultations at the time of ASEAN's annual foreign ministers' meetings and has many other sectoral consultations. Australia has also participated in other ASEAN-sponsored institutions, including the ASEAN Regional Forum (ARF) (at foreign minister level) and the East Asia Summit (of heads of government), which provide dialogues that include the ASEAN members and the major powers, including the United States, China, Japan and India.

Australia's economic and people-to-people linkages with the ASEAN region are very extensive in many areas. The ASEAN countries, with a total population of over 620 million people and an estimated combined gross domestic product in 2014 of US$2.5 trillion, are important economic partners for Australia. Australia's total merchandise trade with ASEAN in 2013–14 was over A$100 billion, about 15 per cent of Australia's trade overall, making the ASEAN members collectively Australia's second largest trade partner. Australia's services trade with the ASEAN group was valued at over A$20 billion. The two-way investment relationship was, in 2014, valued at about A$140 billion, with ASEAN investment in Australia at A$111 billion and Australia's investment in ASEAN members at A$29 billion.[3] Economic relationships are supported by the ASEAN–Australia–New Zealand Free Trade Agreement, which was inaugurated in 2010 and is Australia's largest multilateral regional trade agreement. Development assistance has also been significant, with Australia in 2015–16 providing over A$770 million in bilateral and multilateral contributions.[4]

---

3   Australian Department of Foreign Affairs and Trade and Austrade, 'Why ASEAN and Why Now? Insights for Australian Business', Canberra: Australian Department of Foreign Affairs and Trade and Austrade, August 2015, p. 7.
4   Australia's bilateral aid in 2015–16 was provided to Cambodia, Indonesia, Laos, Myanmar, the Philippines and Vietnam. See Australian Department of Foreign Affairs and Trade, 'Where We Give Aid', dfat.gov.au/aid/where-we-give-aid/Pages/where-we-give-aid.aspx (accessed 1 October 2015).

People-to-people associations enmesh Australia and ASEAN. There were, in 2011, over 650,000 people in Australia who were born in ASEAN countries. Education has been a particularly important element in the relationship and constitutes Australia's largest services export to ASEAN members. There were 614,327 enrolments by students from ASEAN countries in higher education in Australia in the decade from 2002 to 2012, and over 100,000 students from ASEAN members study in Australia each year.[5] Australians are also gaining increased interactions with ASEAN members through education; the Australian Government's 'New Colombo Plan' (inaugurated in 2013) will increase the number of Australians who will study for at least part of their degrees in ASEAN member (as well as other Asian) countries.

Australia's ASEAN relationship has attracted some increased attention from analysts. Jiro Okamoto has provided a detailed account of the economic relationship between the two sides.[6] Sally Percival Wood and Baogang He have edited a valuable collection of papers on a number of aspects of relations.[7] The relationship has also been evaluated in a study edited by Anthony Milner and Percival Wood for Asialink at the University of Melbourne.[8]

This monograph seeks to contribute to the subject by providing a concise account of the origins and phases of development of Australia's relations with ASEAN, the role ASEAN has played in Australian foreign relations since the 1970s, and the ways in which the two sides have collaborated, and at times disagreed, in the pursuit of regional security and stability. Chapter 1 begins with a review of Australia's engagement with Southeast Asia in the years immediately before the formation of ASEAN and then discusses the origins of ASEAN and the first phase of Australian policies towards it with the inauguration of multilateral relations in April 1974. Chapter 2 covers relations between 1976 and 1983 under Malcolm Fraser's government when interactions were dominated by trade and economic issues

---

5   Bob Carr, 'Southeast Asia: At the Crossroads of the Asian Century', IISS-Fullerton Lecture, Singapore, 9 July 2013.
6   Jiro Okamoto, *Australia's Foreign Economic Policy and ASEAN*, Singapore: Institute of Southeast Asian Studies, 2010.
7   Sally Percival Wood and Baogang He, eds, *The Australia–ASEAN Dialogue: Tracing 40 Years of Partnership*, New York: Palgrave Macmillan, 2014.
8   Anthony Milner and Sally Percival Wood, eds, 'Our Place in the Asian Century: Southeast Asia as "The Third Way"', Melbourne: Asialink, University of Melbourne, 2012.

(which involved considerable discord) and then after 1979 by the regional and international conflict over Cambodia. Chapter 3 assesses relations during the Bob Hawke and Paul Keating governments from 1983 to 1996, when the initial focus was on efforts to alleviate conflict over Cambodia. From the late 1980s, in the context of the decline of Cold War confrontation, relations with ASEAN were central in Australia's contributions to the Cambodian peace process and to the development of two new regional groups to enhance economic and security cooperation, the Asia-Pacific Economic Cooperation (APEC) grouping and the ARF. Chapter 4 reviews developments between 1996 and 2007 under John Howard's government, when ASEAN relations experienced strain in the aftermath of the Asian financial crisis and the separation of East Timor from Indonesia. Relations were then redeveloped by both sides after 2001 with the advent of cooperation over multilateral economic relations and the inauguration of the East Asia Summit, which Australia joined as a founding member. Chapter 5 considers relations from 2007 onwards, when Kevin Rudd's government sought to advance proposals for a wider Asia Pacific Community but met with ASEAN resistance. The chapter discusses efforts to extend Australia's institutional relations under Julia Gillard's government amid rising major power tensions after 2009, especially in relation to the South China Sea; the chapter then considers the approaches of Tony Abbott's government and the ASEAN–Australia Commemorative Summit in November 2014. Chapter 6 in conclusion reviews major issues and patterns in relations since 1974 and outlines key issues that are likely to affect the relationship in the future.

In assessing the evolution of multilateral relations since 1974, the work considers and explores four major themes that are especially relevant:

- the impact of major power relations in East Asia and how they have influenced the context and course of Australia's interactions with ASEAN;
- the interest which successive Australian governments have expressed since the 1970s in regional communication and détente between the original participants in ASEAN (from 1967) and the states of Indochina and Myanmar;

- the diversity and pluralism in both Australia and Southeast Asia in relation to how to delineate and define an appropriate 'region' for cooperation and how this has impacted on the course of Australia's multilateral relations with ASEAN; and
- the special significance for the multilateral ASEAN connection of relations between Australia and ASEAN's largest member, Indonesia.

Three additional points should be noted about the monograph and its scope and coverage. In discussing the development of Australia's ASEAN relations, the work refers at a number of points to major developments in ASEAN itself. This work, however, is not seeking to provide a comprehensive account of ASEAN's evolution and character. Those issues have been addressed by many other studies, including a comprehensive account of ASEAN by Christopher B. Roberts, and a paper on these issues in 2013 by this author.[9]

The focus in this monograph is on ASEAN as a grouping and on how Australia has interacted with ASEAN as an association of regional states. The work is accordingly not seeking to cover in detail each of the bilateral relationships that Australia has with the 10 ASEAN members. It will, however, discuss how major individual Australian relationships, particularly with Indonesia, Malaysia and Singapore, have at times had particular significance for the course of the multilateral relationship with ASEAN overall.

A key issue in the discussion below on regional cooperation is that differing conceptions of how to delineate and define 'region' have been significant for Australia and for ASEAN members in the pursuit of regional cooperation. It is therefore important to note at the outset that 'regions' in international politics are often not only geographically defined but socially constructed entities, and appropriate definitions of them can be contested. For the purposes of this work, the term 'Southeast Asia' refers to the 10 member countries of ASEAN and Timor-Leste. The term 'East Asia' refers to the states of Southeast Asia

---

9   Christopher B. Roberts, *ASEAN Regionalism: Cooperation, Values and Institutionalization*, Abingdon: Routledge, 2012; Frank Frost, 'ASEAN and Regional Cooperation: Recent Developments and Australia's Interests', Parliamentary Library Research Paper Series, 2013–14, Canberra: Department of Parliamentary Services, 8 November 2013, www.aph.gov.au/About_Parliament/Parliamentary_Departments/Parliamentary_Library/pubs/rp/rp1314/ASEAN (accessed 1 October 2015).

along with China, Japan, the two Korean states and Taiwan. The term 'Asia-Pacific' is a broad concept that refers to the East Asian states just mentioned, along with other interested countries including the United States, Russia, Canada, Australia, New Zealand, the Pacific Islands and some states in Latin America that have declared significant identities in this wider region. A further regional term, 'Indo-Pacific', has been given increasing reference in discussions about regional cooperation in Australia in recent years; this associates the states of East Asia and the Western Pacific (including the US, Australia and New Zealand) with India and the other states of South Asia. The development of these multiple conceptions of 'region' reflects the diversity of the states and peoples involved in international relations in Asia and the Pacific and has been a significant part of the context in which Australia's relationship with ASEAN has developed and evolved since 1974.

It is hoped that this monograph (which was completed in October 2015) will be informative for the reader and that it can contribute to further debate and research on Australia's interactions with ASEAN and on the long-term significance of ASEAN in Australia's policies towards Southeast Asia overall.

1

Australia and the origins of ASEAN (1967–1975)

The origins of the Association of Southeast Asian Nations (ASEAN) and of Australia's relations with it are bound up in the period of the Cold War in East Asia from the late 1940s, and the serious internal and inter-state conflicts that developed in Southeast Asia in the 1950s and early 1960s. Vietnam and Laos were engulfed in internal wars with external involvement, and conflict ultimately spread to Cambodia. Further conflicts revolved around Indonesia's unstable internal political order and its opposition to Britain's efforts to secure the positions of its colonial territories in the region by fostering a federation that could include Malaya, Singapore and the states of North Borneo. The Federation of Malaysia was inaugurated in September 1963, but Singapore was forced to depart in August 1965 and became a separate state. ASEAN was established in August 1967 in an effort to ameliorate the serious tensions among the states that formed it, and to make a contribution towards a more stable regional environment. Australia was intensely interested in all these developments. To discuss these issues, this chapter covers in turn the background to the emergence of interest in regional cooperation in Southeast Asia after the Second World War, the period of Indonesia's *Konfrontasi* of Malaysia, the formation of ASEAN and the inauguration of multilateral relations with ASEAN in 1974 by Gough Whitlam's government, and Australia's early interactions with ASEAN in the period 1974–75.

The Cold War era and early approaches towards regional cooperation

The conception of 'Southeast Asia' as a distinct region in which states might wish to engage in regional cooperation emerged in an environment of international conflict and the end of the era of Western colonialism.[1] Extensive communication and interactions developed in the pre-colonial era, but these were disrupted thoroughly by the arrival of Western powers. In the era of colonial intervention, all of the territories of Southeast Asia except Thailand were dominated by six different external countries (Britain, France, Holland, Portugal, Spain and the United States), and most administrative and commercial activities were oriented towards those external authorities. As Amitav Acharya has observed, the colonial authorities had no interest in fostering the development of any regional diplomatic framework.[2] Japan's invasion and occupation of much of the region interrupted and undermined Western colonial domination and attempted to replace it with a new form of external control.[3] In the aftermath of the Second World War, most areas of Southeast Asia were preoccupied with the challenges of seeking independence (either through peaceful negotiation or violent struggle), and then of attempting to establish new states and political orders. In this environment, not surprisingly, notions of regional cooperation took time to emerge.

In the period immediately after the Second World War nonetheless, some independence leaders displayed interest in the potential for regional associations, including Ho Chi Minh in Vietnam and Aung San in Burma. The idea of cooperation was also stimulated by conferences held in India, whose own transition to independence in 1947 was an inspiration for other peoples still under colonial rule. India sought to take a leading role. An unofficial Asian relations conference, chaired by Jawaharlal Nehru, was held in New Delhi in March–April 1947, and the 31 delegations included representatives from all of the states of Southeast Asia. The tone of the meeting

---

1   Amitav Acharya, *The Making of Southeast Asia: International Relations of a Region*, Singapore: ISEAS Publishing, 2012, pp. 1–104; Nicholas Tarling, *Regionalism in Southeast Asia: To Foster the Political Will*, London: Routledge, 2006, pp. 35–92.
2   Acharya, *The Making of Southeast Asia*, pp. 80–1.
3   Tarling, *Regionalism in Southeast Asia*, pp. 49–68.

was anti-European, pro-liberation and pro-neutrality. The conference provided a platform for subsequent protests against Dutch intervention in Indonesia, but no regional machinery emerged from the meeting. A subsequent conference in New Delhi in January 1949 (the second Asian relations conference) was again sponsored by Nehru (now prime minister).[4] At the conference, Nehru declared that it would be natural that the 'free countries of Asia' should look towards developing an arrangement for consultation and the pursuit of common goals. However, as Acharya has argued, 'prospects for a Pan-Asian grouping were plagued by differences among the pro-communist, pro-Western and neutrality-minded delegations. They had little to agree upon apart from the end to direct colonial rule'.[5]

The conferences in India did however stimulate Southeast Asian nationalists to consider that a form of cooperation focusing on Southeast Asia was preferable to a 'Pan-Asian' model which would be dominated by China or India. At the 1947 meeting, delegates from Burma, Indonesia, Malaya, the Philippines, Thailand and Vietnam discussed a cooperation group that could focus first on economic and cultural issues and, later on, political cooperation. However, no grouping followed from either the 1947 or the 1949 New Delhi conferences.[6]

An indigenous mode of institutional cooperation did not emerge in Southeast Asia in the 1950s. The states and territories of the area were divided by several factors. While some leaders and peoples were able to pursue independence through negotiation (as in the Philippines and Malaya), Vietnam and Laos were enmeshed in a revolutionary armed struggle against the French. In Indonesia, which had achieved independence after armed struggle and was the largest state in Southeast Asia, President Sukarno had little interest in cooperation with a regional Southeast Asian focus and had wider foreign policy ambitions.[7]

---

4   Acharya, *The Making of Southeast Asia*, pp. 105–10.
5   Ibid., p. 109.
6   Ibid.
7   Ibid., pp. 116–17; see also Anthony Milner, 'Regionalism in Asia', in Juliet Love, ed., *The Far East and Australasia 2014*, 45th edn, Abingdon: Routledge, 2013.

President Sukarno hosted a major conference of Asian and African countries in Bandung in April 1955.[8] The Bandung communiqué condemned colonialism in all its forms and set out a number of principles for cooperation and peace including:

> respect for the right of each nation to defend itself singly or collectively, in conformity with the Charter of the United Nations ... abstention from the use of arrangements of collective defence to serve particular interests of any of the big powers and ... from the exertion of pressure by one country on another ... refraining from acts or threats of aggression or force against the territorial integrity or political independence of any country ... settlement of disputes by peaceful means ... promotion of mutual interest and cooperation; and ... respect for justice and international obligation.[9]

No specific 'Southeast Asian view' on possible cooperation emerged at the Bandung meeting but it had an important long-term significance in the evolution of regionalism.[10] Acharya and See Seng Tan have commented that:

> [T]he Bandung conference did not end the Cold War polarisation of Asia, nor did it create a standing regional organisation for the management of intra-regional conflict. But it articulated the basis for a normative regional and international order marked by tolerance of diversity, mutual accommodation, and the softening of ideological conflicts and rivalries. This approach to international order subsequently influenced the outlook and approach of ASEAN and could well be the basis for an emerging Asian security community.[11]

Interest in a more distinctly Southeast Asian focus for cooperation increased after Malaya gained independence in 1957. In February 1958, Prime Minister Tunku Abdul Rahman said at a press conference that Southeast Asian countries were:

---

8   Jamie Mackie, *Bandung 1955: Non-Alignment and Afro-Asian Solidarity*, Singapore: Editions Didier Millet, 2005.
9   Tarling, *Regionalism in Southeast Asia*, p. 92.
10   Acharya, *The Making of Southeast Asia*, pp. 116–17.
11   Amitav Acharya and See Seng Tan, 'The Normative Relevance of the Bandung Conference for Contemporary Asian and International Order', in See Seng Tan and Amitav Acharya, eds, *Bandung Revisited: The Legacy of the 1955 Asian–African Conference for International Order*, Singapore: NUS Press, 2008, p. 14.

[t]oo much inclined to dance to the tune of bigger nations. They should not concern themselves unduly with the world and Afro-Asian politics when they had problems of their own nearer at hand. An effort should be made to build up their own unity and understanding. If they did not do this, they would have to look outside the area for protection and the full meaning of independence would be lost.[12]

In February 1959, the Tunku sought to advance these ideas by proposing a Southeast Asian Friendship and Economic Treaty (SEAFET), which could foster regional consultation and cultural and economic cooperation. The proposal attracted some interest from the Philippines, but Indonesia indicated that such a treaty would be contrary to the spirit of Afro–Asian cooperation.[13] The SEAFET proposal, however, was an early example of interest in Southeast Asian-focused dialogue, a mode of cooperation that would emerge again in the next decade with the formation of ASEAN.

Australia's emphasis in the first two decades of the period after the Second World War was directed principally towards the consolidation of its relationships with its two major power allies, the United States and Britain, and in developing bilateral relations with the emerging non-communist states in Southeast and Northeast Asia. Australia under Ben Chifley's Labor Government adopted a supportive attitude towards the Indonesian struggle for independence against the Dutch. This approach was in contrast to the policies of the US and Britain; Australia's support was a strong element in its subsequent relationship with Indonesia.[14] The Chifley Government was interested in the 1947 New Delhi conference and provided financial support for the attendance of representatives from two Australian non-governmental organisations: the Australian Institute of International Affairs and the Australian Institute of Political Science. Australia was represented

---

12   Quoted in Tarling, *Regionalism in Southeast Asia*, p. 96.
13   Ibid., pp. 98–108.
14   David Lee, 'Indonesia's Independence', in David Goldsworthy, ed., *Facing North: A Century of Australian Engagement with Asia, Volume 1: 1901 to the 1970s*, Carlton, Vic.: Melbourne University Press, 2001; Christopher Waters, 'Creating a Tradition: The Foreign Policy of the Curtin and Chifley Labor Governments', in David Lee and Christopher Waters, eds, *Evatt to Evans: The Labor Tradition in Australian Foreign Policy*, St Leonards, NSW: Allen & Unwin, in association with the Department of International Relations, The Australian National University, 1997.

officially at the 1949 New Delhi conference by the Secretary of the Department of External Affairs, John Burton, and the government affirmed Australia's support for Indonesia's independence.[15]

After the victory of the communist forces in China and inauguration of the People's Republic of China (in October 1949), Australia's foreign policy approaches under the newly elected Coalition Government led by Robert Menzies (in office from December 1949) emphasised support for Australia's major power allies and opposition to communist movements and armed struggle in regional states. Australia thus gave backing to the British Government in opposing the Malayan Communist Party (which included a military commitment from 1955) and also supported the position of the non-communist regime in southern Vietnam. In this context of Cold War tensions, the Menzies Government did not support the Bandung conference of Afro–Asian nations, which it saw as presenting a challenge to Australian and Western interests, and made it clear that it did not wish Australia to be invited.[16] Later in the decade, Australian officials were sympathetic towards the Tunku's SEAFET proposal but (as noted above) this did not move beyond the discussion stage.[17]

Australia and regional cooperation: SEATO and ASPAC

In the environment of Cold War competition and tensions in the early 1950s, the first phase of multilateral institutional cooperation was initiated by external powers. A conference in Manila in September 1954 led to the adoption of the Southeast Asia Collective Defence Treaty (known widely as the Manila Treaty), which was followed by

---

15 Julie Suares, 'Engaging with Asia: The Chifley Government and the New Delhi Conferences of 1947 and 1949', *Australian Journal of Politics and History*, 57(4) 2011.

16 The Menzies Government feared that the conference could see an increase in Chinese influence in East Asia, that it might encourage opposition to the military presence of the US and Britain in East Asia (which Australia strongly favoured), and that it might increase resistance to the newly formed Southeast Asia Treaty Organization. A senior official from the Department of External Affairs, Keith Shann, attended as an observer and Dr Burton, his wife and Professor C. P. Fitzgerald participated on a non-official basis. See Christopher Waters, 'Lost Opportunity: Australia and the Bandung Conference', in Derek McDougall and Antonia Finnane, eds, *Bandung 1955: Little Histories*, Caulfield, Vic.: Monash University Press, 2010; and David Walker, 'Nervous Outsiders: Australia and the 1955 Asia–Africa Conference in Bandung', *Australian Historical Studies*, 36(125) 2005.

17 Tarling, *Regionalism in Southeast Asia*, p. 103.

the establishment of the Southeast Asia Treaty Organization (SEATO).[18] The Manila Treaty was signed by eight states (Australia, New Zealand, France, the United Kingdom, Pakistan, the Philippines, Thailand and the United States). While the treaty did not explicitly cite communism as a core concern, the US attached a unilateral statement at the time of signature limiting its commitment to instances of 'communist aggression'. The specifically anti-communist orientation of the treaty precluded support from non-aligned states such as Indonesia. While SEATO was established as a 'Southeast Asian' grouping, its concept of 'region' was loose and it in fact included only two Southeast Asian states.[19]

SEATO did not establish a strong presence as a 'regional' grouping. It did not attract any further members from Southeast Asia. Its potential relevance to states in Southeast Asia was reduced by the fact that it did not have any mechanism for conflict resolution. A SEATO headquarters was established in Bangkok and some contingency planning pursued, but the US did not commit forces especially to SEATO in advance of a specific requirement. SEATO continued in existence for two decades, but did not maintain coherence and was abandoned formally in 1977.[20]

In the mid-1960s another grouping developed, which from the Australian Government's perspective seemed to offer some promise as a vehicle for multilateral dialogue and with a scope that encompassed both Southeast and Northeast Asia. The Asian and Pacific Council (ASPAC) was formed in 1966 by the Republic of Korea, the Republic of China, Japan, the Republic of Vietnam, Malaysia, the Philippines, Thailand, Australia and New Zealand.[21] ASPAC was intended to reflect the 'urgent need for continuing consultations among participating countries with a view to forging better international understanding, promoting closer and more fruitful regional cooperation and further

---

18   For a comprehensive assessment of the Manila Treaty and SEATO, see Leszek Buszynski, *SEATO – The Failure of an Alliance Strategy*, Singapore: Singapore University Press, 1983.

19   Ibid., p. 38.

20   Acharya, *The Making of Southeast Asia*, p. 136.

21   C. W. Braddick, 'Japan, Australia and ASPAC: The Rise and Fall of an Asia-Pacific Cooperative Security Framework', in Brad Williams and Andrew Newman, eds, *Japan, Australia and Asia-Pacific Security*, Abingdon: Routledge, 2006.

strengthening Asian and Pacific solidarity'.[22] The first ASPAC meeting established a standing committee that met in Canberra and advised and made preparations for the main Council.

As its membership suggested, ASPAC was an explicitly anti-communist grouping. Political and security topics were discussed freely in the Council's meetings. In 1968 the US, under Lyndon B. Johnson's administration, expressed some interest in ASPAC as a potential vehicle for regional security cooperation. ASPAC's members, however, did not have an agreed approach towards security issues or on how the Council might serve these. The representatives from the Republic of Korea and the Republic of Vietnam advocated harder-line positions on international issues.[23] However, the Council's largest member, Japan, was not willing to support any shift for ASPAC towards a more explicit security role. Australia did not favour this either: an official statement in July 1968 said that 'ASPAC is in no sense a security organisation and in the view of the Australian Government it should not attempt to become one'.[24] ASPAC never attained any major significance as a regional grouping and its relevance declined in the early 1970s in the context of the opening of communications between the United States and China. ASPAC was discontinued in May 1975.[25]

Regional conflict and Indonesia's *Konfrontasi* of Malaysia

The period of serious conflict in Southeast Asia in the early 1960s, particularly that surrounding Indonesia's *Konfrontasi*, or 'confrontation' of the new Federation of Malaysia, led to the development of a new regional grouping, ASEAN, but this did not emerge quickly or easily. Southeast Asia at the beginning of the 1960s had several serious political and security problems. In Vietnam, the insurgency in the south against the regime of Ngo Dinh Diem was gathering strength under the national direction of the

---

22   'Asian and Pacific Council: Joint Communiqué on Establishment of Asian and Pacific Council', *International Legal Materials*, 5(5) 1966: 985.
23   Henry S. Albinski, *Australia in Southeast Asia: Interests, Capacity, and Acceptability*, Springfield, VA: National Technical Information Service, December 1970, p. 21.
24   Ibid.
25   Braddick, 'Japan, Australia and ASPAC', pp. 40–1.

communist leadership based in the north, but also with substantial support within the south. Several other states faced challenges from insurgent communist movements, including Burma, the Philippines and Thailand. Indonesia had recently experienced secessionist revolts in Sulawesi, which had included some external support. Malaya had gained independence in 1957 and Singapore had secured internal self-government in 1959, but Britain retained authority over the external relations of Singapore and over the North Borneo territories of Brunei, Sarawak and Sabah. The process of the final decolonisation of the British-controlled territories was to prove highly contentious.

Britain and the newly independent state of Malaya had agreed on a plan for a federation that would encompass Malaya along with Singapore, the British territories of North Borneo (Sabah and Sarawak) and the British protectorate of Brunei. In Malaya, the government led by the Tunku had from 1961 supported the concept of including Singapore into a federation with Malaya. In Singapore, the state's Prime Minister, Lee Kuan Yew, considered that a union with Malaya was essential to the future economic viability of the island and it had been the policy of his People's Action Party since 1954. Britain saw the incorporation of the North Borneo territories into a federation both as a way of alleviating concerns in Malaya about a possible dominant position for Chinese citizens, and as a way of facilitating the decolonisation process for the Borneo territories. Britain accordingly sponsored a process of consultation in the North Borneo states that concluded (in a report in August 1962) that the majority of peoples in the territories generally supported the federation proposal.[26]

For its part, Australia had supported the merger of Singapore with Malaya since the mid-1950s. Australian policymakers feared that if Singapore became fully independent it might gravitate towards China and then become a focus for subversion in Malaya and in the region overall. The Australian Government did not have a strong opinion in relation to the Borneo territories, but it supported Britain's preference that they be included in a new federation. Australia's Minister for External Affairs, Garfield Barwick, summarised the government's position in a conversation with President Diosdado Macapagal of the Philippines in March 1963 when he said that '[a]s far as we could see,

---

26   J. A. C. Mackie, *Konfrontasi: The Indonesia–Malaysia Dispute, 1963–1966*, Kuala Lumpur: Oxford University Press, 1974, pp. 36–78.

there was no alternative to Malaysia. The British could not remain in Singapore and the Borneo Territories. An independent Singapore would fall easy prey to the Communists, while separate British Borneo states had little chance of survival.'[27]

Indonesia under President Sukarno had a number of reservations about the proposed Federation of Malaysia. It thought that Malaysia might be used as a base by external powers, that Malaysia would be a venue for Britain to continue its influence in the Southeast Asian region to the detriment of Indonesia's aspiration to regional leadership and that a federation would be susceptible to potential dominance by its Chinese communities, given their numbers, education and economic significance. In January 1963, President Sukarno rejected the Malaysian federation proposal as an artificial construct that was unacceptable to Indonesia. In the same month, Foreign Minister Subandrio characterised Indonesia's attitude as one of 'confrontation'. Britain in turn rejected Indonesia's criticism and portrayed Indonesia's approach as indicating a desire to dominate Malaya and the Philippines; Britain asked Australia and the US for assistance to help support and defend the federation.[28] Australia was thus involved in a potentially serious emerging regional conflict. Some of Australia's diplomatic efforts in relation to these tensions were to be of relevance to emerging approaches towards regional dialogue in Southeast Asia.

Australia, along with Britain and New Zealand, held talks in Washington with the US Government in February 1963. The US made it clear that the protection of Malaysia was exclusively the responsibility of the British Commonwealth: the US declined to assume any responsibility towards Malaysia beyond attempting to persuade Indonesia and the Philippines to accept the proposed new state. After the Washington talks, the Australian Government adopted a cautious approach towards the Malaysian issue, supporting the concept of Malaysia without as yet making a commitment to defend it, and seeking regional, and particularly Indonesian, endorsement of the new federation.[29]

---

27   Quoted in David Lee and Moreen Dee, 'Southeast Asian Conflicts', in David Goldsworthy, ed., *Facing North: A Century of Australian Engagement with Asia, Volume 1: 1901 to the 1970s*, Carlton, Vic.: Melbourne University Press, 2001, p. 265.
28   Mackie, *Konfrontasi*, pp. 111–99.
29   Lee and Dee, 'Southeast Asian Conflicts', p. 267.

In the first half of 1963, Barwick sought to promote reconciliation among Indonesia, Malaya and the Philippines. These efforts were pursued against Britain's wishes and in the face of US scepticism. Barwick sought to advance his policy at a meeting in Manila in March 1963. In talks with Subandrio, he encouraged Indonesia to accept a proposal by the Philippines for a three-way meeting with Malaya. Barwick also offered to use his contacts with the Tunku to advance this proposal with Malaya. Tensions were rising within the region, and in April 1963 Indonesian 'volunteers' crossed the border from Indonesia into Sarawak. Nonetheless, in June 1963 a meeting of the foreign ministers of Indonesia, Malaya and the Philippines took place in Manila and the ministers decided to set up a loose grouping called 'Maphilindo'.[30] The Indonesian Government agreed to accept the establishment of Malaysia if an authority such as the United Nations Secretary-General 'ascertained' that the Malaysia proposal was supported by the peoples of North Borneo. The leaders of the three states went on to issue a joint statement in which they declared that foreign bases should not be allowed to subvert the independence of any of the three countries. They also agreed to '[a]bstention from the use of arrangements of collective defence to serve any particular interests of the big powers'. These declarations were a significant precursor to the viewpoints that would be included in ASEAN's foundation declaration in 1967.[31] David Lee and Moreen Dee have argued that this period marked a significant phase in Australia's policies towards Southeast Asia:

> Barwick's initiative was important both in the history of Australia's engagement with Asia and for the history of Southeast Asia itself. It resonated with the earlier Australian approach to Indonesian independence in the 1940s since Barwick, in pursuing a negotiated solution to a regional dispute, acted against the inclinations of the United States and Britain. The importance, in historical terms, of Barwick's initiative was that it encouraged the process of regional Southeast Asian dialogue that would culminate some four years later in the establishment of ASEAN.[32]

---

30   Acharya, *The Making of Southeast Asia*, pp. 154–5; Tarling, *Regionalism in Southeast Asia*, pp. 115–23.
31   Christopher B. Roberts, *ASEAN Regionalism: Cooperation, Values and Institutionalization*, Abingdon: Routledge, 2012, pp. 38, 39–41.
32   Lee and Dee, 'Southeast Asian Conflicts', p. 268.

The discussions between the Maphilindo states did not succeed in alleviating the rising crisis over the Malaysia proposal. The new federation was inaugurated formally on 16 September 1963. On 25 September, President Sukarno stated that he would 'gobble Malaysia raw'.[33] By the end of the year, Australia was committed to supporting Malaysia in the face of Indonesia's *Konfrontasi*. In 1964, tensions rose further as Indonesian forces staged some incursions into Malaysian territory and Britain contemplated the potential for strikes against Indonesia. In February 1965, Australia deployed military forces to Borneo to support Malaysia and Britain.[34]

In August 1965, an additional focus for stress in Southeast Asia emerged when Singapore was abruptly expelled from the Malaysian federation. Pressures had been rising between Singapore and the leadership of the federation over differing priorities for the future of the country, communal strains in Malaya and ethnic riots in Singapore. With tensions rising, the Tunku and Lee met secretly on 7 August and it was then announced the next day that Singapore would leave the federation and become an independent state: Australia and Britain learned of the decision only a few hours before the formal announcement. When publicly announcing the news of Singapore's departure, the normally controlled Lee shed tears. The region now had another independent state, whose economic and political future seemed highly uncertain.[35]

The establishment of ASEAN

The regional impasse involving Indonesia and Malaysia was transformed by events within Indonesia. A period of conflict between the Indonesian army and the Indonesian Communist Party (*Partai Komunis Indonesia* or PKI) from September to October 1965 was followed by mass killings of PKI members and alleged supporters by military units and vigilante groups. By March 1966, Sukarno was replaced as the dominant figure in Indonesia by General Suharto, who assumed the office of president in March 1967. Indonesia's new

---

33   Quoted in ibid., p. 270.
34   Ibid., p. 276.
35   Mackie, *Konfrontasi*, pp. 292–7.

Foreign Minister, Adam Malik, and Malaysia's Deputy Prime Minister, Tun Abdul Razak, negotiated an end to *Konfrontasi* in Bangkok in May 1966 and a formal agreement was signed in Jakarta in August.[36]

The ending of *Konfrontasi* saw interest in establishing a new multilateral group that might help ease inter-state relations, although the prospects for a new cooperative association were not necessarily favourable. Two recent attempts at regional association had not succeeded. In 1961, Malaya, the Philippines and Thailand had come together to form the Association of Southeast Asia (ASA). The proposal for ASA had come from Malaya's Tunku Abdul Rahman in the wake of his efforts to seek support for SEAFET: he envisaged a grouping to help combat communist insurgency by targeting what he considered to be its major cause, poverty. While Malaya gained support from the Philippines and Thailand, Indonesia refused to join a grouping it considered pro-Western and a front for SEATO. Rising tensions over the Malaysia proposal and the Philippines' claim to North Borneo (Sabah) and then Indonesia's declaration of *Konfrontasi* rendered ASA unviable.[37] The Maphilindo grouping had provided another precedent for Southeast Asian cooperation, but it too had failed in the face of intense disputes over Malaysia and *Konfrontasi*.

While these efforts had not succeeded, by 1966 there was renewed interest and increased motivation for another attempt at regional cooperation. The period of *Konfrontasi* had left Southeast Asia with a high degree of inter-state tension, particularly among Indonesia, Malaysia, Singapore and the Philippines. Thailand had not been involved in any of these conflicts but felt vulnerable to other threats, including the conflicts in neighbouring Vietnam, Laos and Cambodia; Thailand also faced an internal communist insurgency. At the same time, as Rodolfo Severino has commented:

> China posed a broader strategic threat, with the convulsions of the Great Proletarian Cultural Revolution, the Chinese propaganda organs' strident denunciations of the non-communist Southeast Asian regimes, and China's at least verbal support for the communist insurgencies.[38]

---

36   Ibid., pp. 308–24.
37   Acharya, *The Making of Southeast Asia*, pp. 150–5; Tarling, *Regionalism in Southeast Asia*, pp. 110–18.
38   Rodolfo C. Severino, *Southeast Asia in Search of an ASEAN Community: Insights from the Former ASEAN Secretary-General*, Singapore: Institute of Southeast Asian Studies, 2006, p. 3.

In this highly uncertain environment, the foreign ministers of Indonesia, the Philippines, Singapore and Thailand and the deputy prime minister of Malaysia met in Bangkok to make a new attempt at regional cooperation. Rather than try to adapt ASA, it was felt desirable to establish a new grouping, because Indonesia preferred to join a new association as a founding member rather than enter an existing group consisting entirely of Western-aligned states. As a result, ASEAN was inaugurated on 8 August 1967. The Bangkok Declaration called for joint efforts to 'accelerate the economic growth, social progress and cultural development' of members; to promote 'regional peace and stability through abiding respect for justice and the rule of law'; to advance 'collaboration and mutual assistance … in the economic, social, cultural, technical, scientific and administrative fields'; to foster 'educational, professional, technical and administrative spheres'; and to 'promote South-East Asian studies'.[39] To carry out these goals, the Declaration set up what Severino has called a 'rudimentary mechanism'. The member foreign ministers would meet annually and ASEAN would be managed by a Standing Committee comprising the foreign minister of the country chairing ASEAN in that particular year along with the ambassadors of the other members in that country. Committees of 'specialists and officials on specific subjects' would operate as necessary.[40]

The formation of ASEAN did not initially attract substantial international attention. However, Australia, as an interested neighbouring state, immediately welcomed the inauguration of the new Association. In a statement on 9 August, a day after the Bangkok Declaration, the Minister for External Affairs Paul Hasluck:

> expressed satisfaction at the announcement from Bangkok [and] … noted that the member nations of the new Association, who have a number of special interests in common and with all of whom Australia enjoys close and friendly relations, had undertaken to cooperate to accelerate the economic growth, social progress and cultural development of the region, and to promote regional peace and stability. These were objectives which had Australia's full support.[41]

---

39   ASEAN Secretariat, 'The ASEAN Declaration (Bangkok Declaration)', Bangkok, 8 August 1967.
40   Severino, *Southeast Asia*, p. 3; see also Roberts, *ASEAN Regionalism*, pp. 41–6.
41   Paul Hasluck, 'Statement', in *Current Notes on International Affairs*, 38(8) August 1967: 328–9.

ASEAN's inauguration was also noted favourably by Whitlam, the Leader of the Opposition. In a speech on 17 August 1967, Whitlam stated:

> All these countries are neighbours. With four of them we have political and defence arrangements. With all of them we have trade arrangements. Quite clearly, looking at the map, it is the most natural development in our part of the world. It is the first occasion on which Indonesia has been associated with all her immediate neighbours. It is the first occasion on which Singapore, a Chinese State as we are a British State, has been associated with Malay nations or other people in the region.[42]

At the time of ASEAN's formation, there was some discussion about the possibility of Australian membership in the new group. The Bangkok Declaration had stated that '[t]he Association is open for participation to all States in the South-East Asian region subscribing to the aforementioned aims, principles and purposes'. While this implied that the membership would include the five participants and, potentially, the Indochina states and Burma, Ceylon made a short-lived effort to be considered as a member but this did not lead to a formal application.[43] At the time of ASEAN's formation, Malaysian officials raised with Australian Government representatives the possibility of Australia joining. Some elements in the Indonesian Government were also considered by the Department of External Affairs to favour the participation of Australia and New Zealand in ASEAN, but others 'perceived Australia as too closely aligned with Britain and the United States and as needing to make up its mind about whether it wished to become part of the Southeast Asian area before it could join a Southeast Asian regional organisation'.[44] Lee and Dee have noted that:

> There are no indications that the Australian government sought membership of ASEAN, whose future might not have seemed to Australian policy-makers at the time to be especially promising. For one thing, it was a strange mixture of aligned and non-aligned states. For another, two of its signatories, Malaysia and Indonesia,

---

42 Gough Whitlam, in *Commonwealth of Australia Parliamentary Debates*, House of Representatives, Official Hansard, No. 33, 17 August 1967, p. 220.

43 Severino, *Southeast Asia*, pp. 41–7.

44 Lee and Dee, 'Southeast Asian Conflicts', p. 280.

had recently ended a bitter three-year-long confrontation and another, Singapore, had undergone a difficult separation only two years earlier from Malaysia.[45]

As ASEAN consolidated its identity, it became clear that Australia was not likely to be considered to be a potential member. In 1971, at the time of the ASEAN foreign ministers' meeting in Kuala Lumpur, Malaysian officials indicated that membership for either Australia or New Zealand in the Association was out of the question, and also that neither country would be welcome as observers.[46]

ASEAN of necessity developed in a cautious manner and its first priority was to try to develop contacts and communication among its members in the uneasy aftermath of *Konfrontasi*. The Association faced some major difficulties in its early phase of existence. Sensitivities continued to be high between Singapore and both Indonesia and Malaysia, with the former keen to demonstrate its capacity for independent decision-making.[47] Relations were also tense between Malaysia and the Philippines, given that the latter had not renounced its claim to the state of Sabah. The Sabah issue was a particular focus for contention after April 1968 until tensions were eased at the end of 1969. ASEAN concentrated on attempting to develop cohesion and to assert the desirability of minimising the influence of external powers.[48]

While in ASEAN's early years there was little scope for any formal interaction on the part of Australia, the Australian Government continued to express support for the Association and its cooperation efforts. In November 1971, ASEAN sought to increase its profile by declaring that Southeast Asia should be a Zone of Peace, Freedom and Neutrality (ZOPFAN). The ZOPFAN Declaration represented a desire by ASEAN to affirm the goal of a regional order free from outside interference and it included an aspiration for the removal of foreign bases from the soil of ASEAN members. The Declaration, however,

45   Ibid.

46   David Goldsworthy et al., 'Reorientation', in David Goldsworthy, ed., *Facing North: A Century of Australian Engagement with Asia, Volume 1: 1901 to the 1970s*, Carlton, Vic.: Melbourne University Press, 2001, p. 345.

47   For example, tensions in Singapore–Indonesia relations were raised in October 1968 when Singapore executed two Indonesian marines who had been convicted of sabotage and murder for actions during *Konfrontasi*; see Tarling, *Regionalism in Southeast Asia*, p. 142.

48   Roberts, *ASEAN Regionalism*, pp. 46–8.

was limited in scope: ASEAN did not move beyond an expression of interest in the concept, it was not binding on members, and it did not involve any timetable for implementation.[49]

With Australia committed firmly to its alliance with the US and to an ongoing association with the UK in Southeast Asia (which was formalised through the Five Power Defence Arrangements in 1971),[50] the Liberal–Country Party Coalition Government led by Prime Minister William McMahon was initially concerned about the ZOPFAN concept, which was seen as an unwelcome endorsement of neutralism and as a potential challenge to Australia's defence relations with Malaysia. However, in 1972, with a greater awareness of the long-term nature of the proposal, the government endorsed the ZOPFAN Declaration.[51] The Minister for Foreign Affairs, Nigel Bowen, in an annex to his statement on foreign affairs on 9 May 1972 entitled 'ASEAN and the Declaration on Neutralisation of Southeast Asia', said:

> All five signatories made it clear subsequently that they would retain present security arrangements until the neutralisation proposal became a reality ... The Declaration does not ask the Great Powers to guarantee the proposed neutralised zone. Rather it seeks to secure recognition and respect for the concept of neutrality and freedom from interference by outside powers ... Despite the practical difficulties involved in working for neutrality as a long-term solution for stability in South-East Asia, Australia welcomes the Declaration as a regional initiative directed toward peace, and stability in Asia.[52]

At the conclusion of the visit to Malaysia by Prime Minister McMahon in June 1972, in a joint communiqué between McMahon and Tun Razak, McMahon reaffirmed that Australia 'welcomed the declaration as a regional initiative directed towards peace and stability in Asia'.[53]

---

49   Tarling, *Regionalism in Southeast Asia*, pp. 141–74; Roberts, *ASEAN Regionalism*, pp. 48–50.
50   The Five Power Defence Arrangements brought together Australia, Britain, New Zealand, Malaysia and Singapore and provided an ongoing framework for Australian defence associations with Malaysia and Singapore which have involved extensive cooperation; see John Blaxland, 'Australia, Indonesia and Southeast Asia', in Peter J. Dean, Stephan Frühling and Brendan Taylor, eds, *Australia's Defence: Towards A New Era?* Carlton, Vic.: Melbourne University Press, 2014, pp. 119–24.
51   John Rowland, 'Two Transitions: Indochina 1952–1955, Malaysia, 1969–1972', Australians in Asia Series No. 8, Nathan, Qld: Centre for the Study of Australian–Asian Relations, Griffith University, 1992, pp. 47–8.
52   'South-East Asia: The Neutralisation Proposal', *Current Notes on International Affairs*, 43(10) October 1972, p. 503.
53   Ibid., p. 504.

The Whitlam Government and the inauguration of multilateral relations with ASEAN

The election of the government led by Gough Whitlam in December 1972 brought a new phase of Australian interest in regional cooperation and in ASEAN. Whitlam came to office at a time of substantial change in the international and regional environment for Australian foreign policy. At the international level, the United States had begun a process of détente with China, which had included President Richard Nixon's historic visit in February 1972. The period of direct US military involvement in the conflict in Vietnam was drawing to an end and a US withdrawal from Vietnam followed the signing of the Paris Agreements in February 1973. These developments created a climate in which Whitlam was able to change the emphasis and direction of Australian foreign policy.[54]

In a statement just after his election, Whitlam noted that:

> the general direction of my thinking is towards a more independent Australian stance in international affairs, an Australia which will be less militarily oriented and not open to suggestions of racism; an Australia which will enjoy a growing standing as a distinctive, tolerant, co-operative and well regarded nation not only in the Asian and Pacific region, but in the world at large.[55]

Whitlam pursued this overall direction in a number of ways. Australia established diplomatic relations with the People's Republic of China. The government also moved to deepen relations with Japan, including through negotiation of a friendship treaty. In Southeast Asia, as well as emphasising relations with ASEAN and its members, Australia also extended recognition to the Democratic Republic of Vietnam (in February 1973). Australia's policies towards Asia overall were

---

54   Nancy Viviani, 'The Whitlam Government's Policy Towards Asia', in David Lee and Christopher Waters, eds, *Evatt to Evans: The Labor Tradition in Australian Foreign Policy*, St Leonards, NSW: Allen & Unwin, in association with the Department of International Relations, The Australian National University, 1997.
55   Quoted in ibid., p. 103.

enhanced by the final official termination of racial discrimination in Australia's immigration policies, thus removing a long-standing focus of discord in Australia's international and regional relationships.[56]

After assuming office, Whitlam moved quickly to assert the importance for his government of Southeast Asian relations and multilateral cooperation. In a speech on 27 January 1973, Whitlam stated that the government in its approach to Southeast Asia wished to look beyond the former emphasis on 'forward defence'. Australia did not see Southeast Asia as a frontier 'where we might fight nameless Asian enemies as far to the north of our own shores as possible – in other people's backyards'. Whitlam said that '[t]o meet the new realities and our perception of them we shall be seeking new forms of regional co-operation.' Regional cooperation, he said, 'will be one of the keystones of Australia's foreign policy for the 70s'.[57] Whitlam argued that ASPAC in its present form no longer reflected the new realities in the region and that Australia was interested in exploring bases for a new and wider cooperation forum in the Asia-Pacific (see below).[58]

In his first overseas visit as prime minister, to Indonesia in February 1973, Whitlam said that his government regarded ASEAN as 'a model of regional co-operation'. He also reaffirmed that Australia supported ASEAN's concept of ZOPFAN for Southeast Asia.[59] Whitlam continued to praise ASEAN's value and relevance for Australia. In an interview with the *New York Times* in March 1973, he said he considered the SEATO pact to be moribund and irrelevant and that the ANZUS (Australia, New Zealand, United States) alliance and ASEAN were the only groupings which were still vital: 'All other arrangements are either transitory or belong in the past.'[60]

---

56   Ibid., pp. 102–3. The Whitlam Government's actions followed important steps taken by the Coalition Government led by Prime Minister Harold Holt (1966–67) which had liberalised access to residence and citizenship rights for non-Europeans and provided for an increased intake of skilled migrants from non-European backgrounds; see Tom Frame, *The Life and Death of Harold Holt*, St Leonards, NSW: Allen & Unwin, 2005, pp. 158–61.

57   Gough Whitlam, 'Opening Address', delivered to the Australian Institute of Political Science Summer School, Canberra, 27 January 1973.

58   'Whitlam Sets New Policy on Asia', *The Herald* (Melbourne), 29 January 1973.

59   'Indonesia Tells Whitlam, Aust Welcomed in SE-Asian Defence', *Sydney Morning Herald*, 22 February 1973.

60   C. L. Sulzberger, 'New Look, Not New Reality', *New York Times*, 11 March 1973.

Whitlam gave further emphasis to ASEAN in February 1974, during a regional visit that included Malaysia, Singapore, the Philippines and Thailand, along with Burma and Laos. Brian Johns noted at the time that:

> The present tour, taking in as it does four of the five ASEAN nations, points to Mr Whitlam's emphasis on the importance of this regional grouping ... [I]n his speeches Mr Whitlam has lauded ASEAN as had no other Australian Prime Minister. The previous Australian Government gave ASEAN attention but did not show Mr Whitlam's positive enthusiasm for it.[61]

In a speech in Bangkok, for example, Whitlam described ASEAN as 'unquestionably the most important, the most relevant, the most natural of the regional organisations'.[62]

After returning from this regional visit, Whitlam indicated that he saw ASEAN as likely to be of long-term interest and significance for Australia and said that as the Association consolidated, Australia might develop political links with the ASEAN Secretariat. He said in March 1974 in a prescient comment: 'Looking ahead and depending on the views of the ASEAN countries, we could consider the accreditation in the future of an ambassador to ASEAN as an organisation, as we have done with the European Economic Community and the OECD.'[63]

At the time of this heightened interest on Australia's part, the ASEAN members were moving to advance their own cooperative activities with other states. ASEAN's decision in 1973 to establish a small secretariat to be based in Jakarta enhanced the potential for joint cooperation with external parties. In 1973, ASEAN engaged in discussion with Japan about economic issues, particularly on the problems perceived

---

61   Brian Johns, 'Whitlam: Some Rabbits Out of the Hat', *Sydney Morning Herald*, 25 February 1974.

62   Ibid.

63   Quoted in John Ingleson, 'Southeast Asia', in W. J. Hudson, ed., *Australia in World Affairs 1971–1975*, Sydney: Allen & Unwin and Australian Institute of International Affairs, 1980, p. 301. Australia ultimately did nominate an ambassador to ASEAN, but not until 2008; see Chapter 5.

to be posed by Japan's production of synthetic rubber.[64] ASEAN also took steps to develop discussions with the European Economic Community, particularly on economic issues.[65]

In this environment, discussion began in the latter part of 1973 between ASEAN and Australia on the possibility of Australian assistance to ASEAN joint economic cooperation projects, and the Australian Government supported this idea strongly.[66] In December 1973, ASEAN issued an invitation for Australia to participate in consultations in Thailand in the next year.[67] Talks duly took place in Bangkok in January 1974 to advance these proposals and led to an invitation by Australia for ASEAN representatives to meet in Canberra.[68]

On 15 April 1974, talks were held between the ASEAN members' secretaries-general and Australian officials. The meeting was notable as the first gathering of the ASEAN national secretaries-general to be held outside an ASEAN member.[69] Australia's Minister for Foreign Affairs, Don Willesee, announced that Australia would provide A$5 million for joint ASEAN–Australia economic projects. Richard Woolcott, Deputy Secretary of the Department of Foreign Affairs, in addressing the opening of the talks, said that the forging of a new link with ASEAN was 'novel' and 'an appropriate new step in terms of our joint aims and interests'. Woolcott said that the Australian Government:

> welcomes the possibility of forging a cooperative link between Australia and ASEAN … Australia is conscious that there are differences in character between itself and the ASEAN countries. For that reason we do not think of ourselves as potential members of ASEAN. On the other hand, we see the success of ASEAN as very important to our hope for the future of South East Asia. We wish to make a practical contribution to its success in terms that are welcome to ASEAN.[70]

---

64 Michael Richardson, 'Asean Warns of Trade Reprisals', *The Age*, 23 April 1973.
65 Harvey Stockwin, 'The Europeans Lack Vision', *Financial Times* (London), 3 May 1973; see also Acharya, *The Making of Southeast Asia*, pp. 171–2. Severino notes that the European Economic Community can be considered to have become ASEAN's first dialogue partner (in 1973) but that Australia was the first individual country to become a dialogue partner (in 1974); see Severino, *Southeast Asia*, pp. 309–10.
66 Michael Richardson, 'Aust Hand of Friendship to South-East Asia', *Sydney Morning Herald*, 17 November 1973.
67 'A.S.E.A.N.', *Canberra Times*, 20 December 1973.
68 Henry S. Albinski, *Australian External Policy under Labor: Content, Process and the National Debate*, St Lucia: University of Queensland Press, 1977, p. 95.
69 Ibid., p. 95.
70 Richard Woolcott, 'Opening Remarks by Mr Richard Woolcott, Deputy Secretary, Department of Foreign Affairs, to Meeting with ASEAN Secretaries General', Canberra, 15 April 1974.

Willesee said after the meeting that 'Australia is honoured that ASEAN should have singled it out as the first country for discussions of this kind. We think that ASEAN's action denotes its confidence in Australia and the Australian Government will do what it can to justify that confidence'.[71] The inauguration of the multilateral relationship was given bipartisan support: just after the Canberra meeting, the Opposition's Shadow Minister for Foreign Affairs, Andrew Peacock, said that the Opposition supported the move.[72]

Whitlam, ASEAN and the 'Asia-Pacific forum' proposal

While the Whitlam Government pursued the enhancement of relations with ASEAN, it also had ambitions to try to develop a basis for wider cooperation in the Asia-Pacific. This effort was advanced with enthusiasm by the government but was met with some caution and disquiet by its neighbours in ASEAN. This proved to be an early example of ASEAN sensitivities over Australia's interest in pursuing a conception of 'region' encompassing countries beyond Southeast Asia.

The concept of a cooperative group or forum for the Asia-Pacific was advanced by Whitlam soon after his government came to office. The idea was discussed by Whitlam in meetings with New Zealand's Prime Minister Norman Kirk (also a newly elected leader of a Labour Government) in January 1973. In a speech on 27 January 1973, Whitlam said that he foresaw a grouping 'genuinely representative of the region, without ideological overtones'. Such a forum, he suggested, could 'help free the region of great power rivalries that have bedevilled its progress for decades and [was] designed to insulate the region against ideological interference from the great powers'.[73]

The proposal was not subsequently defined in any substantial detail. In comments in January 1974 in Kuala Lumpur, Whitlam suggested an analogy of the Commonwealth of Nations. His concept was 'not a body where decisions are made and then [made] binding, but where it is possible for heads of government regularly to exchange views

---

71   '$5m. to Aid Asian Ties', *Courier Mail*, 17 April 1974.
72   'Import Quality Control Sought by ASEAN', *Canberra Times*, 18 April 1974.
73   Whitlam, 'Opening Address'.

which are of mutual interest'.[74] No precise envisaged membership was provided by Australia – it was understood that Australia, New Zealand and the ASEAN members should be included, along with China, India and Japan, but probably neither the United States nor the Soviet Union.[75]

The Asia-Pacific forum proposal reflected the Whitlam Government's strong interest in regional multilateral cooperation as a potential contribution towards enhanced security and economic development. Henry Albinski has argued that '[t]he government's investment of time and energy in sponsoring the idea was demonstration that Australia under Labor was capable of initiatives, of exercising an "independent" foreign policy'.[76]

The Asia-Pacific forum concept, however, met with a cool response both from Australia's ally the US and among the ASEAN members. The US under the Nixon administration was unenthusiastic about the Whitlam concept, principally because it did not wish to see any disruption to the United States' existing pattern of bilateral relationships and alliances in the Asia-Pacific. The administration also felt that recent developments had shown that relationships between the US and its allies with China and the Soviet Union could be improved without altering regional multilateral arrangements.[77]

When Whitlam raised the proposal with President Suharto in February 1973, Suharto responded by saying that there were not sufficient common interests within Asia for such a grouping to be practicable. Suharto said, 'he doubted the usefulness of a formal conference or organisation. This would only aggravate conflicting interests. ASEAN also needed to be consolidated beforehand'. Suharto opposed participation by India and said there would be questions about China's participation.[78] Singapore's attitude was also negative:

---

74 Albinski, *Australian External Policy under Labor*, p. 92.

75 Ibid., p. 93.

76 Ibid.

77 James Curran, *Unholy Fury: Whitlam and Nixon at War*, Carlton, Vic.: Melbourne University Press, 2015, pp. 238–40.

78 Australian Department of Foreign Affairs, record of the meeting between Prime Minister Whitlam and President Suharto, 25 February 1973, quoted in Graeme Dobell, *Australia Finds Home: The Choices and Chances of an Asia Pacific Journey*, Sydney: ABC Books, 2000, p. 80.

Prime Minister Lee criticised the Whitlam proposal in May 1973 as 'lacking in sensitivity'.[79] The concept continued to be discussed by the Australian Government but did not gain any significant traction.

Part of the problem with the Whitlam proposal was the manner in which it was seen to have been advanced. The proposal was introduced in Whitlam's speech at the end of January 1973 and it was evident that there had been no substantial consultation in regional states (including among the ASEAN members) and that there was little supporting detail available on it. In a commentary written in 1974, David Solomon and Laurie Oakes argued that '[t]he flurry of activity was counter-productive given the lack of detail available. ASEAN ministers in mid-February informally discussed the proposal, but rejected it as it stood.'[80] Graeme Dobell later wrote:

> Whitlam's 1973 attempt to create an Asia Pacific forum was killed off by ASEAN's objection that such a body would be a threat to the Association's own importance. It was an early demonstration of the veto that ASEAN could wield in dealing with regional initiatives from Canberra.[81]

As Dobell suggested, the question of how Australia pursued ideas about regional cooperation could easily arouse some concerns and tensions in relations with ASEAN. This was later to be evident in discussion about the proposals at the end of the 1980s for economic cooperation in the Asia-Pacific and over regional security dialogues. There are also some notable parallels between the debate over Whitlam's Asia-Pacific forum concept and the 'Asia Pacific Community' proposal advanced by Kevin Rudd in 2008, as discussed in Chapter 5.

The changing security environment in 1975

The Whitlam Government had been pursuing its regional policies since 1973 with a substantial degree of optimism about the future prospects for Southeast Asia. However, two developments in 1975 had significant and potentially problematic implications for the politics

---

79   Curran, *Unholy Fury*, p. 239.
80   Quoted in Albinski, *Australian External Policy under Labor*, p. 97.
81   Dobell, *Australia Finds Home*, p. 79.

and security of the region and for Australia's relations with ASEAN. They were the end of the Second Indochina War and Indonesia's invasion and subsequent incorporation of East Timor.

The conflicts that had engulfed Indochina since the late 1950s culminated in 1975 with the collapse of the non-communist regimes in Cambodia and southern Vietnam in April 1975, and the assumption of full control by communist forces in Laos by the end of the year.[82] The developments in Cambodia and southern Vietnam in April 1975 were followed by new concerns about security, especially among the ASEAN members. In the immediate aftermath of April 1975, the prospects for détente between ASEAN and the new regimes in Indochina were not promising. Both Thailand and the Philippines had been involved militarily in the Vietnam War and the regime in Hanoi had made some highly critical comments about their roles in supporting US policies.[83] There were widespread concerns among ASEAN members about the capture of large supplies of arms by the victorious communist forces in Vietnam and at the potential that these could be deployed to assist communist-led resistance movements in ASEAN members.[84] The ASEAN members moved to take actions to consolidate their own coordination and began to prepare for their first heads of government summit meeting (held in Bali in February 1976, see Chapter 2).

In this new environment, the Whitlam Government expressed the hope that all states in Southeast Asia would be able to co-exist peacefully. In comments in Japan in June 1975, Minister for Foreign Affairs Willesee urged Southeast Asian governments to 'face up' to the existence of the new governments in Indochina and live together with them in 'peace, neutrality and friendship'. Willesee noted that Australia's approach towards Asia overall was to 'show our concern for developments in the region and to try at all times to be helpful, without ever becoming meddlesome'.[85] The issue of how Australia

---

82   William S. Turley, *The Second Indochina War: A Concise Political and Military History*, 2nd edn, Lanham, MD: Rowman & Littlefield, 2009, pp. 205–36.
83   Frank Frost, 'Vietnam's Foreign Relations: Dynamics of Change', Pacific Strategic Paper No. 6, Singapore: Institute of Southeast Asian Studies, 1993, pp. 58–9.
84   M. G. G. Pillai, 'Viet Hardware Now Going Cheap', *The Nation Review* (Melbourne), 19 June 1975; Peter Bathurst, 'Common Denominator: Captured Guns', *Far Eastern Economic Review*, 4 July 1975.
85   Eduardo Lachica, 'Australia Suggests Coexistence Talks', *The Australian*, 20 June 1975.

could approach the issue of relations and interactions between ASEAN and the regimes in Indochina, particularly Vietnam and Cambodia, was to be one of the dominant themes in Australian policy concerns over the next two decades.

A second set of political and security issues arose in late 1975 when Indonesia invaded and then assumed control of East Timor, a Portuguese colonial outpost. After securing independence in 1949, Indonesia had not pursued any claim in relation to the territory, which had been under Portuguese rather than Dutch control since the seventeenth century. However, the collapse of Marcelo Caetano's dictatorship amid political and economic turmoil in Portugal in April 1974 was followed by rapid change in Portugal's colonies, including in East Timor where there was a rise in pro-independence sentiment at a time when Portugal had lost the will and capacity to maintain its rule. The Suharto Government began to view developments in East Timor with increasing interest and concern. Against the background of Cold War global tensions, and with the fall of Saigon in April 1975 seeming to presage a possible rise in communist influence throughout Southeast Asia, the Suharto Government feared the establishment of a radical regime in East Timor.[86]

In this environment, the weight of opinion in Jakarta, particularly amongst the dominant military, was that East Timor should be integrated into Indonesia. To this end, Indonesia launched *Operasi Komodo*, which comprised a campaign to win international diplomatic support for its position, an intelligence and propaganda operation against pro-independence groups and, from mid-1975, a series of military actions in East Timor. After the pro-independence party Fretilin (Revolutionary Front for an Independent East Timor) gained dominance in the territory in September, Indonesian forces launched an invasion and seized control in Dili on 7 December 1975. Indonesia subsequently incorporated East Timor as a province.[87] While the state of Indonesia after 1949 had accommodated many different areas and peoples, it became clear over the following years that much of the population in East Timor did not accept the imposition of Indonesian rule, which resulted in prolonged internal conflict and the loss of as

86   James Cotton, *East Timor, Australia and Regional Order: Intervention and its Aftermath in Southeast Asia*, London: Routledge, 2004, pp. 4–48.
87   Ibid.

many as 200,000 lives.[88] The status of the territory continued to be an issue for Indonesia in its foreign relations for the next two and a half decades.[89]

The invasion and incorporation of East Timor into Indonesia became a highly sensitive and controversial issue in Australia. Controversy was heightened by the deaths of five Australian journalists at Balibo on 16 October 1975 and of another journalist in Dili on 8 December at the hands of Indonesian forces. The Whitlam Government had supported the right of the people of the territory to decide their own future but it had also supported its ultimate incorporation into Indonesia, while urging that this be done peacefully. Whitlam and his government came under substantial criticism over East Timor. Nancy Viviani has commented:

> Whitlam suffered continual attack for his policies on Timor – that he had helped foreclose the independence option, that he had not protested strongly enough on the use of force by the Indonesians before the invasion, and that he had not protested the journalists' deaths at Balibo.[90]

The incorporation of East Timor into Indonesia was subsequently granted *de facto* and *de jure* recognition by Malcolm Fraser's government, in 1978 and 1979 respectively (most states internationally did not recognise Indonesia's incorporation; 31 other governments did extend such recognition).[91] However the circumstances and direction of Australian policies in 1975 remained highly controversial in Australia, with many observers arguing that Australia had made insufficient efforts to affirm and protect the East Timorese people's right to self-determination.[92] In the years that followed, the status of

---

88   Ibid., p. 53.

89   Ibid.; Rawdon Dalrymple, *Continental Drift: Australia's Search for a Regional Identity*, Aldershot: Ashgate, 2003, pp. 185–210.

90   Viviani, 'The Whitlam Government's Policy', p. 106.

91   The 31 other countries recognised Indonesia's sovereignty, either expressly (through direct statements or by explanation of their votes in the United Nations General Assembly) or by implication (by signing treaties with Indonesia which contained clauses that defined Indonesia's territory as including East Timor); see Australian Department of Foreign Affairs and Trade, *East Timor in Transition 1998–2000: An Australian Policy Challenge*, Canberra: Australian Department of Foreign Affairs and Trade, 2001, p. 12.

92   Viviani, 'The Whitlam Government's Policy'; Cotton, *East Timor*.

East Timor continued to be a source of controversy and contention in Australia–Indonesia relations and this in turn affected the climate for Australia's ASEAN relations.

Conclusion

By 1975, ASEAN had gained a significant profile in Australia's policies towards Southeast Asia. After the highly disruptive period of *Konfrontasi*, the Coalition Government had shown interest in ASEAN's establishment and emerging role in Southeast Asia. Australia's interest had heightened after 1972 when the Whitlam Government saw ASEAN as an important indigenous effort at cooperation that could help stabilise relations among its members and could begin to contribute positively to regional security. This led to the inauguration of a direct multilateral connection in April 1974, ASEAN's first with an external partner. While the relationship had begun auspiciously, there had already been signs that Australia's interactions with ASEAN as a corporate identity would have elements of discord and tensions. The sensitivity shown by ASEAN from early 1973 over the Whitlam Government's proposal for a wider Asia-Pacific cooperative forum had indicated that ASEAN had the potential to be a factor to be reckoned with in Australia's regional diplomacy.

2

Economic disputes and the Third Indochina War (1976–1983)

The period after 1975 was marked by considerable uncertainty in Southeast Asia and in the Association of Southeast Asian Nations (ASEAN). The regimes in Indochina were estranged from the ASEAN members and ASEAN's concerns about regional security prompted it to undertake a major upgrade in its cooperation efforts at its conference in Bali in February 1976. In Australia, a new Coalition Government led by Prime Minister Malcolm Fraser (elected on 13 December 1975) expressed strong concerns about the potential expansion of Soviet influence, both internationally and in Southeast Asia. The Fraser Government was committed to continuing and advancing Australia's relations with ASEAN, but it soon encountered significant tensions in economic and trade relations. Later in the decade, major additional security problems arose as Southeast Asia experienced the traumatic impact of the outflows of refugees from the Indochina states. Southeast Asia then faced renewed conflict and major power involvements after Vietnam's invasion of Cambodia in December 1978 and China's subsequent invasion of northern Vietnam in February–March 1979, in the period of conflict known as the Third Indochina War.[1] Australia's interactions with ASEAN on regional security in this period were marked by both substantial cooperation and some discord, notably over the role of the ousted Khmer Rouge movement in ASEAN's

---

1   Odd Arne Westad and Sophie Quinn-Judge, eds, *The Third Indochina War: Conflict Between China, Vietnam and Cambodia, 1972–79*, London: Routledge, 2006.

strategies in opposing Vietnam's presence in Cambodia. This chapter discusses these issues by focusing in turn on ASEAN's Bali summit in 1976, the Fraser Government's approach towards Southeast Asia, the advent of disputes between Australia and ASEAN over trade and civil aviation policies, the impact of the Indochina refugee crisis, and ASEAN and Australian approaches to the conflict over Cambodia.

ASEAN's 1976 Bali summit

A key factor for Australia in its approaches towards Southeast Asia was ASEAN's efforts to upgrade its cooperation and raise its own profile. As noted in Chapter 1, there were widespread concerns amongst the ASEAN members in the aftermath of the communist victories in Indochina in 1975. The ASEAN members saw a need for greater foreign policy coordination and an increased emphasis on ASEAN as an institution.[2] ASEAN's first summit meeting of heads of government in Bali in February 1976 was a watershed for the Association, as has been widely observed. The members adopted two key documents – the Treaty of Amity and Cooperation and the Declaration of ASEAN Concord. The treaty set out basic norms of inter-state behaviour that ASEAN sought to advance for the conduct of relationships in the region, including the concept of sovereign equality, freedom from external coercion, the peaceful resolution of disputes and the renunciation of the use of force against one another. The treaty provided for a dispute resolution mechanism, a 'High Council' of ministers that could consider conflicts and, with the agreement of all participants, make recommendations on appropriate means of settlement; the Council has not so far been convened.[3] While the treaty was developed explicitly for ASEAN and for other states who might in the future be eligible to join ASEAN, it later became a key means by which ASEAN could seek recognition and endorsement from countries from outside Southeast

---

2   Amitav Acharya, *The Making of Southeast Asia: International Relations of a Region*, Singapore: ISEAS Publishing, 2012, pp. 164–79; Nicholas Tarling, *Regionalism in Southeast Asia: To Foster the Political Will*, London: Routledge, 2006, pp. 174–85.

3   ASEAN, 'Treaty of Amity and Cooperation in Southeast Asia', Indonesia, 24 February 1976; Christopher B. Roberts, *ASEAN Regionalism: Cooperation, Values and Institutionalization*, Abingdon: Routledge, 2012, pp. 53–5.

Asia who wanted to increase their interaction with ASEAN. In 2005, accession to this treaty was a key step by which Australia was able to join the ASEAN-initiated East Asia Summit (see Chapter 5).

The Bali summit reaffirmed ASEAN's distinctive approach to and 'norms' of cooperation, which have been referred to widely as the 'ASEAN way'.[4] This approach emphasised regular communication among the members' ministers and (after 1976) heads of government, often conducted in an informal manner and with the aim of building up familiarity and confidence. The values of respect for national sovereignty, non-interference in internal affairs, opposition to external interference, support for the peaceful resolution of disputes and renunciation of the threat or use of force continued to be emphasised. ASEAN's style was based on frequent meetings and the avoidance of 'top heavy' institutions. It maintained a Secretariat in Jakarta but its size and budget were modest. ASEAN also emphasised the value of dialogue with the major powers with interests in Southeast Asia.[5] It sought to express its cooperative norms in several ways, including its declaration in 1971 that Southeast Asia should be a Zone of Peace, Freedom and Neutrality (ZOPFAN, discussed in Chapter 1) and its sponsorship of wider forums such as the ASEAN Regional Forum and the East Asia Summit (discussed in Chapters 3 and 4). In 1997, ASEAN added to its norms of cooperation by adopting the Treaty on the Southeast Asia Nuclear-Weapon-Free Zone by which members reassured each other that they would not acquire, store, transport or test nuclear weapons.[6]

The 'ASEAN way' has continued to be emphasised by the Association in the years since 1976 as a focus for developing cooperation among highly diverse states with little previous bases for communication or accord.[7] ASEAN's emphasis on consensus-based decision-making,

---

4   On the 'ASEAN way', see Rodolfo C. Severino, *Southeast Asia in Search of an ASEAN Community: Insights from the Former ASEAN Secretary-General*, Singapore: Institute of Southeast Asian Studies, 2006, pp. 1–40.

5   This section draws from Frank Frost, 'ASEAN and Regional Cooperation: Recent Developments and Australia's Interests', Parliamentary Library Research Paper Series, 2013–14, Canberra: Department of Parliamentary Services, 8 November 2013, www.aph.gov.au/About_Parliament/Parliamentary_Departments/Parliamentary_Library/pubs/rp/rp1314/ASEAN (accessed 1 October 2015), pp. 5–19.

6   Roberts, *ASEAN Regionalism*, p. 59.

7   See also Amitav Acharya, *Constructing a Security Community in Southeast Asia: ASEAN and the Problem of Regional Order*, 3rd edn, Abingdon: Routledge, 2014, pp. 43–78.

informality and voluntary compliance in relation to agreements has been criticised for producing a cautious and slow pace of development. The Association has, for example, been described as 'making process not progress'.[8] ASEAN's style of cooperation has continued to be debated within and outside the Association since the 1970s, particularly in relation to approaches to the issues of national sovereignty and the principle of non-interference in internal affairs.[9] The directions set through the Bali summit have nonetheless continued to be highly influential, as subsequent chapters will suggest.

In addition to reaffirming ASEAN's identity and style of operation, the Bali summit sought to upgrade economic cooperation among the members. One avenue was to promote joint industrial projects by which a designated enterprise located in one of the member countries could gain preferential access to the whole five-country ASEAN market.[10] A second avenue was the endorsement of the desirability of joint cooperation to try to secure more favourable market access for ASEAN countries' exports to their major trading partners. In a significant comment, one section of the Declaration of ASEAN Concord stated that ASEAN members 'shall accelerate joint efforts to improve access to markets outside ASEAN for their raw materials and finished products by seeking the elimination of all trade barriers in those markets'.[11] This area of ASEAN cooperation was to figure prominently in the first phase of Australia's relationship with the Association from 1976 onwards.

The Fraser Government (December 1975 – March 1983) pursued Australian foreign policy with some different emphases from the preceding Gough Whitlam administration. Fraser was suspicious of and apprehensive about the role of the Soviet Union and re-emphasised Australia's commitment to the US alliance, while maintaining

---

8   David Martin Jones and Michael Smith, 'Making Process, not Progress', *International Security*, 32(1) 2007. See also David Martin Jones, Nicholas Khoo and M. L. R. Smith, *Asian Security and the Rise of China: International Relations in an Age of Insecurity*, Cheltenham: Edward Elgar, 2013, pp. 68–130.

9   Severino, *Southeast Asia*, pp. 372–85; Shaun Narine, 'Asia, ASEAN and the Question of Sovereignty', in Mark Beeson and Richard Stubbs, eds, *Routledge Handbook of Asian Regionalism*, London: Routledge, 2012.

10   Severino, *Southeast Asia*, pp. 212–22.

11   ASEAN, 'The Declaration of ASEAN Concord', Bali, Indonesia, February 1976; see also Michael Richardson, 'Asean Upset By Our Trade Curb', *The Age*, 27 February 1976.

a willingness to differentiate Australian policies from its ally, as was the case in approaches towards Vietnam after 1975 (see below). Stewart Firth has provided a concise summary of Fraser's policy approaches:

> Fraser dominated the making of Australian foreign policy in his time almost as much as Whitlam dominated it in his. The two men differed in outlook. Where Whitlam was an optimist in international affairs and inclined to a tolerant view of Soviet intentions, Fraser was a pessimist who saw Soviet expansion as a serious threat to world peace. Where Whitlam sought greater independence from the United States, Fraser reasserted the central importance to Australia's security of the American alliance. And where Whitlam welcomed détente between the two superpowers, Fraser believed the Soviets were exploiting it to build themselves a military advantage over the West.[12]

A further element in Fraser's approach to foreign policy was an interest in the challenges of relationships between the developed countries and the developing states (refered to widely as 'North–South relations'). The Fraser Government commissioned a report on 'Australia and the Third World' and expressed some interest in efforts by developing states to seek more equitable international economic relationships, although it was not always easy for the government to reconcile this overall attitude with specific policies, for example, in trade relations with ASEAN.[13]

Fraser's overall foreign policy emphasis was reflected in his government's approach towards Southeast Asia. In the period immediately after the defeat of the non-communist regimes in Indochina, the United States moved to reduce its military presence in Southeast Asia: it withdrew from its bases in Thailand although it retained a security relationship with that country and maintained its bases in the Philippines. The Fraser Government, from 1976, was concerned about a perceived decline of US interest in the region and sought to persuade the US Government of the region's continuing importance.[14]

---

12   Stewart Firth, *Australia in International Politics: An Introduction to Australian Foreign Policy*, 3rd edn, Crows Nest, NSW: Allen & Unwin, 2011, p. 22.
13   The government's report was written by Professor Owen Harries; see Owen Harries, *Australia and the Third World: Report of the Committee on Australia's Relations with the Third World*, Canberra: Australian Government Publishing Service, 1979.
14   David Goldsworthy et al., 'Reorientation', in David Goldsworthy, ed., *Facing North: A Century of Australian Engagement with Asia, Volume 1: 1901 to the 1970s*, Carlton, Vic.: Melbourne University Press, 2001, pp. 346–7.

The new Australian Government was also keen to pursue relations with the Southeast Asian region and its states. On 18 January 1976, shortly after his election to office and just before a visit to Malaysia to attend the funeral of Prime Minister Tun Abdul Razak, Fraser said that '[i]t is the intention of my government to concentrate its activities more in our own region. I think that in recent times, Australia's diplomatic effort have [sic] been scattered too far and wide around the world'. Fraser said that efforts should be made at two levels, country to country, and between Australia and ASEAN as a group. He noted, '[j]ust as Australia recognises the importance of Asean to Australia, the Asean countries for their part recognise the importance of Australia'.[15]

Fraser accordingly sought to maintain and extend the emphasis that had been given to ASEAN by the Whitlam Government. Soon after coming to office, he pursued his government's interest in ASEAN by seeking talks with the ASEAN leaders at their inaugural summit in Bali in February 1976.[16] Minister for Foreign Affairs Andrew Peacock told the Indonesian ambassador in Canberra in January 1976 that 'the Prime Minister was most anxious to receive an invitation' to visit Bali for discussions after the ASEAN summit the next month, but the response from Jakarta was that 'the timing is not correct' (a position that also applied to Japan and New Zealand).[17] A media report in February 1976 suggested that the timing of the Australian request had been an issue for some ASEAN members. A Malaysian official was quoted as saying that '[t]he proposal was too sudden. It came out of the blue without consultation. If we had been given three months' notice and time to prepare, there might have been no problem.'[18] While Australia was not able to gain representation at the Bali summit, ASEAN's approaches to cooperation soon became significant issues in Australia's regional relations.

15   'Improve Asean Relations – PM', *Courier Mail*, 19 January 1976.
16   Michael Richardson, 'PM Sought Invitation from ASEAN', *The Age*, 11 February 1976.
17   Goldsworthy et al., 'Reorientation', p. 347.
18   Michael Richardson, 'How Mr Fraser Got the Cold Shoulder', *Australian Financial Review*, 27 February 1976.

The politics of trade

As noted in Chapter 1, when Australia established its formal link with ASEAN after talks in Canberra in April 1974, the discussions had aroused no controversy; the major item agreed upon was a modest A$5 million multilateral aid program.[19] At this time, however, developments were already taking place in both the Australian economy and some ASEAN members' economies, which were soon to lead to significant problems in trade relations. After the events of early 1975 in Indochina, and the drive by the ASEAN members to find meaningful avenues for economic cooperation, a multilateral political framework was now established that enabled ASEAN members' complaints about Australian policies to be given sharp focus.

By the early 1970s, Australia had developed a trading relationship with the ASEAN members that was a relatively small part of Australia's overall trade (6.6 per cent of its exports in 1976–77 and 4.1 per cent of imports in the same period), but that was heavily in Australia's favour. ASEAN members were a useful market for Australian manufactures, minerals and primary products. For ASEAN, Australia was also a minor trading partner, supplying 4.6 per cent of imports and taking 2.4 per cent of exports in 1975.[20]

In the early 1970s, several ASEAN members (Malaysia, the Philippines and Thailand) had begun to follow the Singaporean example by developing export-oriented manufacturing sectors, and producing labour-intensive goods such as textiles, clothing and footwear. In this period the Australian economy was buoyant. In response to a strong balance of payments position and gathering inflationary pressure, the Whitlam Government revalued the Australian dollar several times in 1973, cut tariffs abruptly by 25 per cent and adopted a more extensive system of tariff preferences for developing countries. Exporters in Northeast and Southeast Asia were the immediate beneficiaries of these changes. In 1974, the Australian economy began to weaken, but imports were rapidly rising, putting pressure on manufacturing

---

19   The discussion below draws in part from Frank Frost, 'Political Issues in Australia–ASEAN Relations', *Asia Pacific Community* (Tokyo), 7(Winter) 1980; and Frank Frost, 'ASEAN and Australia', in Alison Broinowski, ed., *Understanding ASEAN*, London: Macmillan, 1982.
20   Clive T. Edwards, 'Current Issues in Australian–ASEAN Trade Relations', *Southeast Asian Affairs 1979*, Singapore: Institute of Southeast Asian Studies, 1979, pp. 30–1.

in Australia. In response, the Australian Government devalued the dollar and placed import restrictions on 'sensitive goods' including textiles, clothing and footwear. Most of these restrictions hit Northeast Asian exporters: China, Hong Kong, South Korea and Taiwan. When Australian importers, in response, turned to alternative suppliers from ASEAN members, the government imposed restraints on goods coming from Malaysia, the Philippines and Thailand.[21]

Not surprisingly, the Australian restrictions had an unfavourable psychological and political impact on states whose economic expectations in foreign trade were rapidly changing. Clive Edwards wrote of the ASEAN states:

> History had cast them in the role of raw material suppliers. The experience of the fifties and sixties seemed to indicate that, in the field of manufacturing, they could not be internationally competitive. The exhilarating experience of 1973–74 *permanently* changed this depressing scenario. The ASEAN countries realised that there were manufactures that they could export at highly competitive prices. Unfortunately, it was at this moment of euphoria that Australia struck.[22]

In this context, the ASEAN members took a significant new step in dealing with Australia. In line with their Declaration of ASEAN Concord, ASEAN formulated a 'joint approach', which was transmitted formally to Australia in November 1976, but quoted extensively in the *Australian Financial Review* on 27 July 1976, effectively beginning substantive debate in Australia on ASEAN relations.[23] The ASEAN 'aide-memoire' heavily criticised Australia's protection policies and indicated disappointment with Australia's system of tariff preferences for developing countries. The document stated that:

> For a developed country, Australia has one of the highest tariff rates, especially on labour-intensive light industrial goods exported by developing countries ... Although Australia was the first developed country to grant tariff preferences to the developing countries, the benefits derived therefrom have been far below the expectations of the ASEAN member countries.[24]

---

21   Ibid., pp. 34–7. See also Jiro Okamoto, *Australia's Foreign Economic Policy and ASEAN*, Singapore: Institute of Southeast Asian Studies, 2010, pp. 112–19.
22   Edwards, 'Current Issues', p. 36, emphasis in original.
23   Michael Richardson, 'ASEAN Takes Fraser to Task', *Australian Financial Review*, 27 July 1976.
24   Ibid.

The main reasons for ASEAN dissatisfaction with Australia's policy on tariff preferences were the scheme's limited product coverage, the low level of tariff reductions, the existence of a quota system and stringent definitions of handicrafts.[25] Malaysia and the Philippines followed up this move with informal delays to Australian exports.[26]

Debate about Australian trade policies with ASEAN was continued by contributions from Singapore's Prime Minister Lee Kuan Yew. In a notable statement in June 1977, Lee argued that trade liberalisation by Australia would:

> remove a source of considerable frustration and bitterness on the part of countries like the Philippines, Indonesia and Malaysia, which feel this is a one-sided business – of a very wealthy continent, sparsely populated, with enormous natural resources, not yet fully developed with an industrial capacity commensurate with those resources, yet wanting to make all the little things. It wants labour-intensive products like shirts and garments, knitwear, shoes and socks, all for itself, behind high tariff walls. Buying little and selling more. Of course, let me add that successive Australian governments have been conscious of this and have made up with dollops of aid – it's like giving toffees and chocolates away. That's not the kind of relationship which generates mutual esteem, respect and an adult mutual continuing inter-dependence which in the long term is the only sound relationship we can develop … And if that's the way the world is going to be – if the relationship between the countries of ASEAN and Australia is the relationship between the developed and underdeveloped world – then I see strife.[27]

ASEAN continued its approach on a joint basis. A further detailed critique of Australian policies was presented in an ASEAN paper in November 1978, which stated that 'Australia seems to regard developing countries only as a source of supply of certain materials for her industrial outputs'. The document called on Australia to liberalise tariffs, assist ASEAN export promotion efforts in the Australian market and promote ASEAN–Australia cooperation in industrial development in the region.[28]

---

25   Ibid.
26   Edwards, 'Current Issues', p. 40.
27   Michael Richardson, 'Lee Defines the ASEAN Blueprint', *Far Eastern Economic Review*, 10 June 1977.
28   John Short, 'ASEAN Hits Aust Policies on Tariffs, Aviation', *Australian Financial Review*, 22 November 1978.

The ASEAN challenge to Australian trade and economic policies had a significant impact in Australian Government, business and academic circles. There had been a long-standing debate in Australia about the structure of its economy and the question of protection for secondary industry.[29] While the challenge from ASEAN on this issue after 1976 was unexpected, it came from a region in which Australia had in recent years been closely interested, and the ASEAN criticism was thus given a credence that similar criticism from Europe or even Northeast Asia would probably not have received. Many Australian observers, including some businesspeople, academics and journalists, readily accepted the ASEAN claims and argued for Australian trade liberalisation.[30]

The Fraser Government in this period adopted a more reserved approach. It emphasised Australia's continuing interest in maximising political and economic relations with the ASEAN region and it initiated a series of joint projects and regular consultations. However, the government simultaneously continued to maintain policies of protection for endangered Australian labour-intensive industries, and it attempted to put the best possible face on the existing ASEAN–Australia economic relationship.[31]

Australian Government responses to the ASEAN criticism began in earnest in 1977. A Standing Interdepartmental Committee on Relations with ASEAN was established in January to bring together the many departments involved in ASEAN relations.[32] The government initiated efforts to secure an invitation for Fraser to attend ASEAN's planned second Heads of Government Meeting, to be held in Kuala Lumpur in August 1977, and this effort was successful.[33] Several Australian missions visited the region in the months leading up to the Kuala Lumpur meeting to prepare the ground for Fraser's visit.[34]

29   Okamoto, *Australia's Foreign Economic Policy*, pp. 34–95.
30   Joanna Lawe-Davies, 'The Politics of Protection: Australian–ASEAN Economic Relations 1975–1980', Research Paper No. 13, Nathan, Qld: Centre for the Study of Australian–Asian Relations, Griffith University, 1981.
31   'Fraser "No" to ASEAN Plea on Imports', *Sydney Morning Herald*, 18 January 1978.
32   Andrew Peacock, 'Australia–ASEAN Relations', news release, 19 January 1977.
33   'Fraser May Get ASEAN Invite', *Canberra Times*, 28 February 1977.
34   Michael Richardson, 'Asians Will Put Fraser to the Test', *The Age*, 14 July 1977.

At the ASEAN Kuala Lumpur summit in August 1977, Fraser held discussions on 7 August on a variety of issues, including global economic problems such as the need for stability in commodity prices and improved marketing facilities, Australian aid and consultative projects and trade problems.[35] Australia did not offer immediate concessions on trade issues, but did agree to increase its overall foreign aid commitment to the ASEAN members, and it offered to provide assistance to the ASEAN joint industrial projects. The discussions also resulted in an agreement on a series of meetings (including a trade fair and an industrial cooperation conference), a joint research project into the ASEAN–Australia economic relationship and an arrangement for regular consultation on trade matters.[36]

Considerable progress was subsequently made in establishing the pattern of relations agreed upon at Kuala Lumpur. Building on the original multilateral aid projects initiated in 1974, the ASEAN–Australian Economic Co-operation Program by 1980 involved a series of projects at a cost of A\$34.5 million in areas including the development of low-cost, protein-rich foods from locally available sources, studies on post-harvest handling, transportation and storing of grain, meat and cereals, and assistance to education and population programs and regional animal quarantine. The joint research project into economic relations was initiated in 1980. An Industrial Co-operation Conference was held in Melbourne in June 1978 and ASEAN Trade Fairs were mounted in Sydney (October 1978) and Melbourne (August 1980). Private business links were also developed on a multilateral basis; an ASEAN–Australia Business Conference was inaugurated in Kuala Lumpur in June 1980.[37] In November 1978, agreement was reached on the ASEAN–Australia Consultative Meeting (AACM) between the ASEAN Canberra Committee (comprising the head of ASEAN diplomatic missions in Canberra) and the Australian Interdepartmental Committee on Relations with ASEAN. Under the AACM, a working group on trade matters was set up to provide ASEAN members with 'early warning' of Australian policy changes.[38]

---

35   Malcolm Fraser, 'Post ASEAN Conference Talks', Ministerial Statement, in *Commonwealth of Australia Parliamentary Debates*, House of Representatives, Official Hansard, No. 33, 17 August 1977.
36   ASEAN, 'Joint Press Statement of the ASEAN Heads of Government and the Prime Minister of Australia', Kuala Lumpur, 7 August 1977.
37   Frost, 'Political Issues', pp. 131–2; 'ASEAN Talks End in Trade Pact', *The Age*, 22 June 1978.
38   Minister for Foreign Affairs, news release, M129, 13 November 1978.

The consultation and discussions provided by these forums were undoubtedly of some value to ASEAN. Since sudden and seemingly arbitrary changes in Australian tariff policy had been a major problem for some ASEAN producers in 1974 and 1975, the AACM was potentially useful. But while Australia was prepared to consult extensively, the Fraser Government made it clear in a number of statements and actions that in the domestic economic environment of the late 1970s in Australia, major liberalisation in areas of trade relevant to ASEAN would not occur.[39] On the same day as Prime Minister Fraser's report to the Australian Parliament on his successful talks with ASEAN leaders (17 August 1977), the Ministers of Industry and Commerce, and Business and Consumer Affairs announced that the government would attempt to maintain existing levels of employment in the textiles, clothing and footwear industries for the following three years. Further guarantees were given during the 1977 election campaign and, in August 1978, an additional tariff surcharge of 12.5 per cent was imposed for revenue purposes on a number of products of concern to ASEAN members. A commitment to attempt to maximise employment in the textiles, clothing and footwear industries was announced in August 1980.[40]

Although the substance of Australian external economic policy conceded little to ASEAN claims, Australian statements asserted consistently that ASEAN's market access in Australia was expanding rapidly, that Australia in fact imported considerably larger amounts of sensitive goods (such as textiles and footwear) per capita than ASEAN's other major markets, that ASEAN members should look at their problem of adverse balances of trade with Australia in a global context, and that as the Australian economy recovered and expanded, ASEAN exporters' opportunities would also further expand.[41]

By 1980, in a regional climate now dominated by concern over Sino-Vietnam relations and the ongoing problem of Cambodia (see below), ASEAN's criticism of Australian trade policies was no longer advanced with the stridency of 1976 and 1977. ASEAN's concern continued,

39   Michael Richardson, 'Govt Seeks a New Patsy on ASEAN Trade War', *Australian Financial Review*, 11 July 1977.

40   Okamoto, *Australia's Foreign Economic Policy*, pp. 117–19; Frost, 'ASEAN and Australia', p. 157; Senate Standing Committee on Foreign Affairs and Defence, *Australia and ASEAN*, Report, Canberra: Australian Government Publishing Service, 1980, pp. 31–4.

41   See Malcolm Fraser, 'Address to the Second ASEAN Trade Fair', Melbourne, 4 August 1980.

however, and it was illustrated in a speech delivered by Malaysia's Finance Minister Tengku Razaleigh Hamzah to the first ASEAN–Australia Business Conference in June 1980. Tengku Razaleigh reminded his audience of the link that ASEAN leaders saw between economic growth and political stability and said:

> Unfortunately there are many countries in the north which ironically are concerned with global security but which at the same time, adopt international economic and trade policies and practices, that in the longer-term erode the very foundation of security that they try to promote.

Razaleigh praised the steps that had been taken to develop and institutionalise ASEAN–Australia cooperation, but noted that protectionism was still a problem. He added:

> While ASEAN and other developing countries have strongly supported Australia's efforts in combating protectionist policies emanating from the United States, the EEC [European Economic Community] and OECD [Organisation for Economic Co-operation and Development] countries, it is understandably difficult for us simultaneously to experience the adverse effects of Australia's own protectionist policies.[42]

The tensions over trade relations were not resolved during the tenure of the Fraser Government. While that government supported close economic relations with the ASEAN members, it was not prepared to alter the basic pattern of protection for Australian industries.[43] Significant change in this area would have to wait for Bob Hawke's Labor Government, which did pursue major macroeconomic and trade policy reform.

Trade was not the only issue of contention to gain prominence in ASEAN–Australia relations in the late 1970s. The framework for discussion and negotiations set up by 1978 provided a ready avenue for consideration of additional ASEAN claims. Australia's civil aviation policies provided another source of ASEAN concern from 1978.

---

42 Tengku Razaleigh Hamzah, 'Speech', delivered to the first ASEAN–Australia Business Conference, 24 June 1980, pp. 7–8.

43 Rawdon Dalrymple, *Continental Drift: Australia's Search for a Regional Identity*, Aldershot: Ashgate, 2003, pp. 67–73.

The civil aviation dispute

The dispute that emerged over civil aviation in 1978 and 1979 did not necessarily fit easily into the context and framework of the ASEAN–Australia relationship.[44] The issue impinged directly on the interests of only one ASEAN member in a major way: Singapore. It was not automatically to be expected that Singapore would receive backing from its ASEAN partners. For a variety of interacting economic and political reasons, the civil aviation issue nonetheless became for a time a *cause celebre* in the relationship.

The genesis of the problem lay in an emerging conflict of interest between Australia and Singapore in the 1970s. Australia's national airline Qantas had steadily come under increasing competition on its most important air routes (Australia to Europe) from a number of other carriers, including Singapore Airlines (SIA). The financial position of Qantas came under pressure at a time when there was also a rising demand for cheaper fares from sections of the Australian public and travel industry. In order to secure cheaper fares and to ensure that a new arrangement to achieve these fares would safeguard Qantas's position, the Australian Government and Qantas devised a new approach – the International Civil Aviation Policy (ICAP) – which would limit foreign airlines' capacity on the Australia–Europe route, and guarantee high 'load factors' (that is, proportion of seats filled on flights) for the entire flight between Australian and European ports by discouraging (through a high-cost surcharge) 'stopovers' by passengers en route. This policy was justified on the grounds that it was in accord with the norms of international airline negotiating procedures, and that it was an assertion of legitimate Australian economic interests.[45] Singapore, however, was able to place the issue squarely in the ASEAN–Australia context.[46]

---

44   This section draws in part from Frost, 'ASEAN and Australia', pp. 159–62. On the civil aviation issue overall, see also Okamoto, *Australia's Foreign Economic Policy*, pp. 119–20; and Robyn Lim, 'Current Australian–ASEAN Relations', *Southeast Asian Affairs 1980*, Singapore: Institute of Southeast Asian Studies, 1980.

45   Peter Nixon, 'International Aviation Policy', Ministerial Statement, in *Commonwealth of Australia Parliamentary Debates*, House of Representatives, Official Hansard, No. 41, 11 October 1978.

46   Michael Richardson, 'ASEAN's Air Fare Threat', *Australian Financial Review*, 19 May 1978.

Singapore had a great deal to lose through the Australian policy. Its national airline had been operating under the SIA name only since 1972 (when Malaysia–Singapore Airlines was dissolved), but it had achieved by 1977 the highest passenger and freight load factors of any international airline. Singapore was understandably proud of its airline, which in 1978 accounted for over 3 per cent of the country's gross national product. Part of its successful growth had been based on the Australia–Europe route in which the airline had gained as much as 30 per cent of the traffic by 1978. ICAP threatened to reduce significantly SIA's participation in this traffic and the discouragement of stopovers threatened to damage Singapore's tourist industry, which was heavily dependent on this type of short-stay tourism. No other airline from an ASEAN member was as dependent on the Australia to Europe traffic to the same degree as SIA. Singapore's ASEAN partners were not automatically sympathetic towards its economic problems, and it had been involved in an acrimonious dispute with Malaysia over civil aviation.[47] Australian officials seem to have assumed that SIA could be isolated effectively through the initiation of favourable bilateral negotiations with other ASEAN members. Singapore, however, was able to successfully mobilise ASEAN support to challenge the Australian policy.[48]

Singapore depicted the dispute as one between Australia and ASEAN that was relevant to the wider issue of North–South economic relations. It was relatively easy for Singapore to attack the Australian policy as an act of discrimination against a successful airline from a rapidly developing Third World state, which was being penalised for its success in competing in the Western-dominated, technically sophisticated airline business.[49]

After preliminary complaints in early and mid-1978, ASEAN jointly criticised ICAP at the end of October, and in December the ASEAN economic ministers agreed that negotiations with Australia on ICAP would be broached on a group basis. Joint negotiations were held with Australia in January 1979, but the results were inconclusive. In February 1979, the economic ministers met again: their joint

47   Hamish McDonald, 'ASEAN Hostile to "Fly-Over" Air Fares', *Australian Financial Review*, 8 June 1978.
48   Lim, 'Current Australian–ASEAN Relations'; see also Frost, 'Political Issues', pp. 132–7.
49   Michael Richardson, 'Asean Aims to Fight Cheap Air Fares', *The Age*, 18 December 1978.

communiqué included the statement that 'ICAP would not be confined to ASEAN and Australia alone … ICAP is a manifestation of the tendency of developed countries to change the rules as soon as the developing countries have mastered the … rules and overcome the obstruction posed by them'.[50] ASEAN's major demands were that its airlines should be able to participate in the Australia–Europe low-fare scheme with or without stopovers, that stopovers should not be prohibitively costly for low-fare passengers, and that for ASEAN–Australia cheap fares, the cost per kilometre should be roughly equivalent to that charged between Australia and Europe.[51]

ASEAN pursued its case actively in early 1979, partly through negotiations with Australia and partly through a variety of comments and statements by Singaporean and other ASEAN spokespeople that gained extensive coverage in the Australian media. In May 1979, a preliminary agreement on the issue was reached and this agreement was subsequently accepted by the ASEAN economic ministers in September. The agreement did not meet all ASEAN demands, but it seemed to effectively defuse the issue as an ASEAN problem and much of the controversy on the question had subsided by the end of 1979.[52]

The ICAP dispute was significant in a variety of ways. The ASEAN members showed an impressive ability to coalesce on an issue that for them was potentially far more a divisive than a cohesive influence. They linked the dispute with Australia to the wider context of North–South relations. The framework for public and governmental discussions of ASEAN–Australia issues that had been developed initially to discuss trade relations could be used to consider other issues as they arose and used to exert pressure on Australia for concessions. While the ASEAN approach did not achieve all its aims, it did force significant Australian policy changes, and the ICAP challenge probably constituted ASEAN's single most influential external joint approach in economic relations up to 1979. The dispute showed that the ASEAN members had a considerable capacity both to advance their interests through

---

50 ASEAN, 'The Special ASEAN Economic Ministers Meeting', Kuala Lumpur, 22 February 1979.
51 Ibid.
52 Greg Hywood, 'ASEAN Cracks Australia's Air Fare Barriers', *Australian Financial Review*, 8 May 1979; Lim, 'Current Australian–ASEAN Relations', pp. 45–7.

the Australian domestic media, and to cause Australia considerable embarrassment by placing ASEAN–Australia issues in the context of the North–South dialogue.

The Indochina refugee crisis

While trade and economic issues had been sources of discord, Australia and ASEAN continued to have important interests in common, particularly in relation to security in the Southeast Asian region and the problem of great power interference. Towards the end of the 1970s, areas of long-term mutual interest for Australia and ASEAN were reaffirmed as the crisis stemming from the outflows of people from the three Indochina states and then the conflict that developed over Cambodia posed significant challenges to security and stability in Southeast Asia. These common concerns were a stimulus towards further important developments in the relationship that included both some extensive cooperation but also some discord, notably over the role of the radical Khmer Rouge movement in relation to the Cambodian conflict.

The refugee exodus from Vietnam and the other Indochina states from early 1975 had a profound impact on the ASEAN members, especially Thailand, Malaysia and Indonesia. Large numbers of people began to depart from Vietnam and Cambodia after the collapse of the non-communist regimes in April 1975 and substantial numbers also left Laos, where communist forces attained full control by the end of the year. There was a steady and large flow of people from 1975 to 1977, but from early 1977 several factors led to an increase in the pace of departures, particularly from Vietnam. While the departing people from Vietnam after 1975 had been principally ethnic Vietnamese, the government's decision to severely restrict the operations of private businesses in southern Vietnam in March 1978 led to a further exodus that included many Sino-Vietnamese. The deterioration of relations between Vietnam and China was heightened after Vietnam's invasion of Cambodia from 25 December 1978. China responded with a limited but highly damaging invasion of northern Vietnam in February–March 1979. From 1978, the Vietnamese Government pursued active policies of discrimination against the ethnic Chinese, which encouraged large numbers to try to flee by boat to both Hong Kong and Southeast Asia. Overall, between 1975 and 1982, about two million people left the three countries of Indochina and over 800,000 sought resettlement.[53]

The departures of people both by land and by sea posed major problems for the ASEAN member countries where they sought refuge. By 1977, Thailand had received over 200,000 people arriving by both land and sea. Up to the end of 1977, about 20,000 people had arrived by boat in ASEAN member countries, but the numbers escalated in 1978. By the end of 1978, 68,000 had arrived in Malaysia and only 31,000 had gained resettlement in third countries.[54] The people seeking asylum faced difficult and often dangerous journeys: many people perished at sea through accident or attacks from pirates operating from nearby countries, particularly Thailand. The refugees posed economic and administrative problems in the countries that gave them temporary entry, and were at times a source of some social and political tension.[55] In Malaysia, for example, there were social and political concerns about the impact of the arrival of large numbers of ethnic Chinese people on the east coast of the peninsula.[56]

The flows of asylum seekers, particularly the boat arrivals from Vietnam, were also of very real concern to Australia. In 1976, some refugee boats began arriving in northern Australia, having travelled onwards from Malaysia and Indonesia, and in November 1977 a number of boats arrived in Darwin. The boat arrivals provoked a hostile public reaction in Australia since they raised the spectre of an uncontrolled influx of Asian immigrants. The prospect of continued boat arrivals threatened to undermine support for the Australian Government's policy of accepting Indochinese refugees through organised channels

---

53   For an overview of the process and pattern of departures, see Nancy Viviani, *The Long Journey: Vietnamese Migration and Settlement in Australia*, Carlton, Vic.: Melbourne University Press, 1984, pp. 38–52. See also W. Courtland-Robinson, *Terms of Refuge: The Indochinese Exodus and the International Response*, London: Zed Books, 1998; and Frank Frost, 'Vietnam, ASEAN and the Indochina Refugee Crisis', *Southeast Asian Affairs 1980*, Singapore: Institute of Southeast Asian Studies, 1980.

54   Viviani, *The Long Journey*, p. 46; 'Refugee Talks Planned Monday', *Canberra Times*, 7 January 1979.

55   Peter Hastings, 'Price of the "Expel" Policy', *Sydney Morning Herald*, 6 July 1979; 'War Fears Over Flood of S-E Asian Refugees', *The Australian*, 31 July 1979; see also Barry Wain, *The Refused: The Agony of the Indochina Refugees*, New York: Simon and Schuster, 1982.

56   Viviani, *The Long Journey*, p. 74.

and it also threatened to reawaken controversy about the general question of Asian immigration. These issues provided a strong impetus for cooperation between Australia and ASEAN.[57]

The Australian Government adopted an active policy of gaining the cooperation of the ASEAN members, and it sought the assistance of Malaysia and Indonesia in preventing the onward passage of boats from their points of first asylum to Australia. The government moved actively to support the ASEAN members' efforts to 'internationalise' the refugee problem by gaining increased financial assistance and particularly increased resettlement commitments from Western states. Australia initiated the proposal that led to the first Geneva conference on Indochina refugees in December 1978. Australia played a major role in supporting the diplomacy of the ASEAN members in 1979, leading up to the ASEAN foreign ministers' meeting in Bali in early July, which Australia's Minister for Foreign Affairs attended, along with the foreign ministers of Japan and the US.[58] Australia also supported and took part in the second Geneva conference in July, which saw additional commitments of aid and offers of resettlement for refugees. By 1980, Australia was accepting 14,000 Indochinese refugees per year and by 1982 had accepted over 60,000 people from Indochinese countries since April 1975. Australia had now accepted more refugees per capita than any other country of asylum (only the British colony of Hong Kong accepted more) and the policy had maintained a high degree of public acceptance.[59]

The refugee crisis had posed substantial challenges for Australia and for its relations with the ASEAN members. The capacity and willingness of Australia to cooperate with its ASEAN neighbours was particularly important because it came against the backdrop of Australia's moves since 1966 to end the policies of restriction in immigration in relation to Asia. The significance of the issues raised for Australia in foreign relations from the refugee crisis were identified in a notable joint statement by the Australian Ministers for Foreign Affairs (Andrew Peacock) and Immigration and Multicultural Affairs (Michael MacKellar) on 29 November 1977:

---

57   Ibid., pp. 82–115.
58   'Peacock Goes to ASEAN Talks on Refugees', *The Australian*, 30 June 1979; Michael Richardson, 'Ease Curbs, Asean Asked', *The Age*, 4 July 1979.
59   Viviani, *The Long Journey*, pp. 82–115.

> The comparatively small countries of Southeast Asia have had to bear the brunt of the post-war exodus of refugees from Vietnam. It has presented them with serious problems. With rapidly growing populations, a shortage of employment opportunities, and very limited social services, they are ill-equipped to cope with the influx. The problem is a regional problem and the validity of Australia's credentials as a good neighbour will depend largely on a willingness to meet our regional obligations by bearing part of the burden. Our immigration policy has been misunderstood and misrepresented abroad in the past. It has taken a sustained effort to remove this misunderstanding. If we were now to respond to the Vietnamese refugee question in a narrow, ungenerous and emotive way, that effort would have gone for nothing.[60]

In its response to the refugee crisis, Australia had lent valuable support on an issue of major concern to all of the ASEAN members and it had demonstrated a capacity to make a contribution towards participating in the resolution of a serious regional problem. An official history of Australian–Asian relations has observed that '[i]t seems fair to say that ASEAN–Australian relations were enhanced by Australia's refugee policies in this period'.[61]

Australia, ASEAN and the Cambodia conflict

As ASEAN and Australia were responding to the refugee crisis, a further focus for regional disorder and conflict was emerging in Indochina as relations between the regimes in Vietnam and Cambodia deteriorated and a new phase of major power competition developed. The conflict over Cambodia was to be a major issue for the region and in Australian relations with ASEAN for the next 15 years.

A new phase of conflict emerged soon after the communist regimes took power in Vietnam and in Cambodia. The radical Khmer Rouge regime, which renamed the country Democratic Kampuchea (DK), pursued autarkic and nationalist policies that produced large-scale losses of life (of an estimated 1.7 million people) within the country and

---

60 Minister for Foreign Affairs, news release, M35/IEA 94/77, 28 November 1977.
61 Moreen Dee and Frank Frost, 'Indochina', in Peter Edwards and David Goldsworthy, eds, *Facing North: A Century of Australian Engagement with Asia, Volume 2: 1970s to 2000*, Carlton, Vic.: Melbourne University Press, 2003, p. 195; see also Viviani, *The Long Journey*, p. 114.

also involved substantial hostility towards Vietnam.[62] Armed conflict took place between the Khmer Rouge regime and Vietnamese forces from 1975, and fighting along their disputed border intensified in 1976 and 1977. During 1978, the Vietnamese leadership decided to launch an invasion. On 3 December 1978, a Kampuchean National Salvation Front was established with Vietnamese sponsorship and, three weeks later, a Vietnamese force, along with some dissident Cambodian allies, invaded the country. Phnom Penh was occupied on 7 January 1979 and the remnants of the Khmer Rouge regime fled to sanctuary in Thailand.[63]

Vietnam's invasion of Cambodia aroused strong concern in Southeast Asia and helped fuel a new phase of major power competition. The reaction in ASEAN members was strongly critical of Vietnam. Some progress had occurred in Vietnam's relations with ASEAN after 1975, in which a series of discussions had served to reduce the extensive mutual suspicions that had been a carry-over from the period of the Second Indochina War. The invasion of Cambodia, however, was seen as posing a considerable security threat to Thailand, and no Southeast Asian state was willing to accept the violation of the principle of territorial sovereignty that the invasion had represented.[64] The ASEAN reaction was also affected by the traumatic impact of the refugee crisis that was reaching a highpoint in late 1978, when over 200,000 people had already arrived in ASEAN member countries. The impact of the refugee arrivals intensified suspicion of Vietnam and bolstered the tendency within ASEAN to take a hard-line of opposition towards the invasion and Vietnam's presence in Cambodia. From 1979 and through the next decade, ASEAN's efforts to influence developments in relation to Cambodia and to secure a Vietnamese withdrawal were the centrepiece of its diplomatic activities and significantly increased the Association's international profile.[65]

---

62   Ben Kiernan, *The Pol Pot Regime: Race, Power, and Genocide in Cambodia under the Khmer Rouge, 1975–79*, 3rd edn, New Haven, CT: Yale University Press, 2008.
63   Huynh Kim Khanh, 'Into the Third Indochina War', *Southeast Asian Affairs 1980*, Singapore: Institute of Southeast Asian Studies, 1980, pp. 338–9. For a comprehensive analysis of the Cambodia conflict overall, see Nayan Chanda, *Brother Enemy: The War After the War*, New York: Free Press, 1988.
64   Sheldon Simon, 'Cambodia and Regional Diplomacy', *Southeast Asian Affairs 1982*, Singapore: Institute of Southeast Asian Studies, 1982; Carlyle A. Thayer, 'ASEAN and Indochina: The Dialogue', in Alison Broinoswki, ed., *ASEAN into the 1990s*, London: Macmillan, 1990.
65   Acharya, *Constructing a Security Community*, pp. 79–96.

The conflict fuelled major power competition and involvement. Vietnam had moved closer to the Soviet Union in the 1970s and concluded a treaty of friendship in November 1978. The Soviet Union and its allies supported Vietnam and the new regime it sponsored in Phnom Penh. For its part, China had supported the Khmer Rouge regime since 1975. A bilateral agreement had been concluded in August 1976 and China had provided substantial aid to DK. China denounced Vietnam's invasion and in February–March 1979 launched a limited invasion of northern Vietnam that failed to dissuade Vietnam from continuing its presence in Cambodia, but which caused substantial economic and social dislocation in Vietnam.[66]

For over a decade from 1979, the conflict over Cambodia became the dominant political, diplomatic and security problem in Southeast Asia. Within Cambodia, the Vietnamese-sponsored regime, the People's Republic of Kampuchea (PRK), whose dominant leader was Hun Sen, attempted to promote economic reconstruction and its own political consolidation. Vietnam and the PRK regime faced armed opposition from three Cambodian resistance movements, operating on and near the Thai border: the ousted Khmer Rouge (referred to widely as the 'Pol Pot regime' after its leading figure); the royalist FUNCINPEC (the National United Front for an Independent, Neutral, Peaceful and Cooperative Cambodia) led by Prince Norodom Sihanouk; and the republican KPNLF (Khmer People's National Liberation Front) led by Son Sann. Vietnam and the PRK faced opposition from ASEAN, which refused to accept the PRK regime's legitimacy and worked to deny acceptance of the regime internationally and to mobilise support for Vietnam's withdrawal. A key avenue for ASEAN's diplomacy was sponsorship of a resolution in the United Nations (UN) General Assembly calling for an immediate ceasefire and the withdrawal of Vietnam's forces – the first such resolution was adopted on 14 November 1979 and ASEAN continued to gain large majorities in support of similar resolutions for the next decade.[67] Cambodia furthermore became the focus of ongoing rivalry between the Soviet Union and China (which provided material aid to the resistance groups), while other major actors, including the US, Japan and the European Community also pursued an active

---

66   Simon, 'Cambodia and Regional Diplomacy'.
67   Ang Cheng Guan, *Singapore, ASEAN and the Cambodian Conflict 1978–1991*, Singapore: NUS Press, 2013, pp. 28–36.

although mostly less direct interest in the conflict. This pattern of conflict became a major issue for Australian policymakers and a focus for both cooperation and some tensions in relations with ASEAN.[68]

The Fraser Government, ASEAN and Cambodia

After coming to office in December 1975, the Fraser Government continued the orientation of the Whitlam Government towards Indochina, and this was maintained up until late 1978. Australian approaches towards ASEAN and the states of Indochina after 1975 were discussed in late 1976 in an internal Department of Foreign Affairs policy planning paper on Australia and Southeast Asia. The paper stated that 'in the next few years there will probably not be much scope for an activist Australian policy' towards Southeast Asia, but argued that Australia still had an interest in carefully seeking 'accommodations reached across the "fault-lines" separating Indochina from the ASEAN countries'. The paper argued that Australia's responsibilities under the ANZUS (Australia, New Zealand, United States) alliance 'do not necessarily entail an obligation to endorse or acquiesce in particular US policies that cut across important Australian interests in the area', such as the 'hostile attitude' of the US towards Vietnam, which the paper saw as obstructing 'Australia's important political interest in attempting to minimise the risk of polarisation and confrontation' in the region. The paper considered peaceful social and economic development in the ASEAN member countries as Australia's primary political interest, and observed that 'clearly, Australian political and strategic interests in South-East Asia are of major importance as compared with our economic interests there, which are still relatively minor, although with considerable potential for the future'. With Southeast Asia 'now likely to enjoy greater autonomy within the international political system', Australia 'should finally drop the concept of reliance on a particular major power protecting our interests in South-East Asia, and accept the implications of a self-reliant policy there'.[69]

The Fraser Government from 1976 pursued policies that were in line with this suggested approach and that differed significantly from those then being pursued by Australia's ally, the US. The government

---

68   Chanda, *Brother Enemy*; Frank Frost, 'The Cambodia Conflict: The Path Towards Peace', *Contemporary Southeast Asia*, 13(2) 1991.
69   Quoted in Goldsworthy et al., 'Reorientation', pp. 346–7.

emphasised the desirability of trying to prevent the isolation of the Indochinese states through cautious development of diplomatic contacts. Minister for Foreign Affairs Peacock stated in April 1977:

> We believe ... that nothing will be gained by either Australia or the region ostracising, ignoring, or setting out to alienate these governments. In the case of Vietnam in particular, it will be dangerous if it is placed in a position where it feels it can only maintain cordial relations with other Communist states.[70]

To support engagement, the government initiated a A$6 million aid program to Vietnam to be granted over three years. Facilities made available for Vietnamese students by the Whitlam Government in 1975 were continued, and in March 1978 the Fraser Government pledged to continue its support for the Mekong Committee of the UN Economic and Social Commission for Asia and the Pacific, a project of benefit to Vietnam. The Fraser Government supported Vietnam's entry into the UN (in contrast to prevailing US policy) and Australia received a visit from Vietnam's Deputy Foreign Minister Phan Hien in July 1978 at a time when no such visit would have been possible for a Vietnamese representative to Washington.[71]

When reports emerged of border clashes between Vietnam and Cambodia from late 1977, the Fraser Government was initially cautious. However, the deterioration of Vietnam–Cambodia relations in 1978, along with an intensification of Sino-Vietnamese tensions and the increased rate of refugee outflows from Vietnam from mid-1978, began to change the context of Australian policy. There was particular concern at the scale of the outflows from Vietnam and at reports of Vietnamese Government involvement.[72]

When Vietnam invaded Cambodia from 25 December 1978, the Fraser Government reacted sharply. On 23 January 1979, Cabinet suspended Australia's aid program to Vietnam and cancelled cultural exchanges.[73] The government denounced Vietnam's invasion and Australian policies quickly became aligned with those of ASEAN in demanding the withdrawal of all foreign forces from Cambodia and a halt to the

70   Carlyle A. Thayer, 'Australia and Vietnam, 1950–1980, Part II, From Conciliation to Condemnation, 1972–1980', *Dyason House Papers*, 6(3) 1980: 7.
71   Ibid., pp. 7–8.
72   Ibid.
73   Judith Hoare, 'Fraser Stops Aid to Vietnam', *Australian Financial Review*, 24 January 1979.

refugee exodus. When China launched a limited invasion of northern Vietnam on 17 February 1979, Australia's criticism of China's actions appeared less severe than its condemnation of Vietnam. At the height of China's invasion, Australia received Vice Premier Chen Muhua, the most senior Chinese official to visit Australia up to that time. Carlyle Thayer commented:

> Australian statements on China's invasion of Vietnam were always linked with a condemnation of Vietnam's actions, and, more significantly, with a satisfactory resolution of the Kampuchean situation. In brief, the Fraser Government gave the impression that while Vietnam had provoked the conflict, China had merely reacted to it.[74]

From early 1979, Australia supported ASEAN's diplomatic activity in the UN. A key part of ASEAN's strategy was to utilise its capacity to mobilise support in the General Assembly to maintain UN representation for the ousted Khmer Rouge DK regime and thus to gain explicit international backing for ASEAN's ongoing opposition to Vietnam's invasion through denial of recognition for the pro-Vietnam PRK in Phnom Penh. In keeping with ASEAN's approach, Australia at first maintained its recognition of the ousted Khmer Rouge DK regime, both bilaterally and in the UN, by voting in support of DK credentials in September 1979.[75] This aspect of Australian policy, however, became the subject of domestic controversy and a clash began to emerge between the policies supported by ASEAN and domestic attitudes within Australia.

The Pol Pot regime recognition issue

In Australia, the situation in Cambodia had become a matter of considerable public interest. The devastation during the Khmer Rouge period became even more clear after Vietnam's invasion and the need for humanitarian aid received considerable media attention. The Australian public contributed over A$10 million to relief programs. Pressure was exerted for the withdrawal of Australian recognition from the ousted Khmer Rouge regime by members of the public, the Australian Labor Party, and from within the government's

---

74   Thayer, 'Australia and Vietnam, 1950–1980', p. 10.
75   'Britain Drops Kampuchea's Pol Pot Government', *Sydney Morning Herald*, 8 December 1979.

ranks.[76] By July 1980, this pressure on the recognition issue had become significant enough for Peacock to say in an interview that 'the bestiality of that regime [DK] is such that there is no way I can allow a feeling of revulsion that exists in the Australian community to be simply swept aside'.[77]

The recognition issue fuelled tensions within the Fraser Government. Peacock strongly favoured the withdrawal of recognition from the DK regime, but Fraser and the rest of the Cabinet supported the existing policy, based on Australian support for ASEAN's stance on recognition as a source of political pressure in its campaign of opposing Vietnam's presence in Cambodia. Fraser stated to Parliament on 28 August 1980 that '[i]t is not possible to move away from Pol Pot without moving a distance towards that Vietnamese-supported regime [the PRK] ... There is no way of avoiding the fact that a move away from Pol Pot is in part an encouragement to the Vietnamese-supported aggression.'[78] After further debate within the government in September 1980 (particularly between Fraser and Peacock), during which Peacock threatened to resign over the issue, the government reached a decision on 23 September that recognition would be withdrawn from the DK regime in the near future. The issue was a notable case of a clash between the government's commitment to ASEAN's position on Cambodia and the pressures of Australian domestic concerns about the human rights issues raised by the record of the Pol Pot regime. As a result, Australia changed its position on the recognition issue by withdrawing recognition in October 1980.[79]

On 14 October 1980, Peacock announced that Australia had decided on a policy of 'de-recognition'; he stated that 'Australia cannot prolong its recognition of such a loathsome regime as that of Pol Pot'. Formalisation of de-recognition would be delayed for a limited time period. This announcement did not affect Australia's vote in the UN in 1980 on the issue of DK credentials; that vote took place just before the announcement and Australia voted in favour of DK's credentials.[80]

---

76   'Anti-Pol Pot "Group Grows"', *The Herald* (Melbourne), 27 August 1980.

77   Ali Cromie, 'Peacock Queries Policy on Pol Pot', *The Age*, 14 July 1980.

78   Malcolm Fraser and Margaret Simons, *Malcolm Fraser: The Political Memoirs*, Carlton, Vic.: Miegunyah Press, 2010, p. 479.

79   Ibid., pp. 480–1; Philip Ayres, *Malcolm Fraser: A Biography*, Richmond, Vic.: William Heinemann Australia, 1987, pp. 418–22.

80   Michael Richardson, 'Move Away from Pol Pot Disappoints Asean', *The Age*, 15 October 1980.

The formal bilateral 'de-recognition' was brought into effect by Australia on 14 February 1981 and, on 28 May 1981, a statement by Minister for Foreign Affairs Tony Street (who had replaced Peacock in this office) made it clear that in voting at international forums, Australia now recognised no Cambodian regime and thus would not support recognition of DK. Street added the proviso that if 'a coherent and effective regime truly representative of the Khmer people' emerged, Australia would reconsider its position.[81]

The Australian Government's change of policy on recognition had responded to domestic opinion but produced some critical reactions from ASEAN, and from China and the US, especially after the May 1981 announcement on recognition policy at international forums. In late May, the policy change was criticised by Singapore's Deputy Prime Minister Sinnathamby Rajaratnam, as one that 'will certainly damage the foreign-policy interests of Australia, seriously question its credentials as a reliable ally of those who have taken up the Soviet challenge in South-East Asia and bring comfort to the Vietnamese'.[82] At the time of the ASEAN foreign ministers' meeting in June 1981 in Manila, the Philippines foreign minister described Australia as being 'recalcitrant' on the issue, and reservations were also reported to have been expressed by US and Chinese officials.[83]

While Australia maintained support for ASEAN's policies of opposition to Vietnam's presence in Cambodia, some disagreement continued over the ongoing role of the Khmer Rouge. In 1982, ASEAN attempted to ameliorate the issue of the unpopularity of the Khmer Rouge by supporting the development of a coalition government in exile that included the Khmer Rouge along with the two non-communist resistance parties, FUNCINPEC and the KPNLF. This resulted in the inauguration of the Coalition Government of Democratic Kampuchea (CGDK) in June 1982. While the Fraser Government welcomed moves to establish a coalition, it continued to be concerned that such a process should not lead to a situation in which the Khmer Rouge could regain

---

81   Minister for Foreign Affairs, news release, M58, 28 May 1981.
82   'Our Stand on Kampuchea Criticised', *The Mercury* (Hobart), 1 June 1981.
83   Michael Richardson, 'Canberra Ruffles Asean Feathers over Kampuchea', *The Age*, 19 June 1981; Tony Walker, 'China Prods Australia Over its Policy on Kampuchea', *Sydney Morning Herald*, 27 June 1981.

power in Cambodia.[84] Prime Minister Fraser, after talks with Chinese Premier Zhao Ziyang on 9 August 1982, reaffirmed that Australia would not support the new coalition if it were used merely as a front for a re-emergence of the Khmer Rouge under Pol Pot. Fraser said, 'I put the view very strongly that if international support is wanted for the coalition, it is going to be much easier to obtain if the figure of Pol Pot is not part of it'. He added, 'there is fairly general acceptance that an independent, non-aligned government under the leadership of Prince Sihanouk would be the best final outcome'.[85]

Although this statement by Fraser indicated that Australia was most unlikely to change its policy on recognition in 1982 and would therefore not be willing to support UN recognition for the Cambodian coalition, ASEAN officials renewed efforts to achieve such a policy change in the weeks leading up to the 1982 credentials debate in the UN. In early August 1982, Thailand's Foreign Minister, Air Chief Marshall Siddhi Savetsila, said in an interview that Australia's refusal to recognise the CGDK was a 'strong disappointment' to ASEAN.[86] In early September 1982, Malaysia's Foreign Minister, Tan Sri Ghazali Shafie, made a visit to Canberra to personally put ASEAN's case for the extension of recognition to the Cambodian opposition coalition.[87] In early October, the ASEAN heads of mission in Canberra presented a letter to Street from the ASEAN Standing Committee reiterating ASEAN's request for Australian support at the UN on the recognition question.[88]

On the recognition issue, however, Australia did not accede to the ASEAN request for a change of policy. For the remainder of the period of the Fraser Government, and subsequently under the Hawke Labor Government, Australia abstained in the UN General Assembly vote on the credentials of the CGDK whenever that issue arose.[89] Australia in this period had thus needed to manage a substantial difference of

84   Interview with Mr Street on Radio 3LO Melbourne, Government Information Unit Transcript, 5 August 1982.

85   Tony Walker, 'Pol Pot Will Not Get Our Help, PM Tells China', *The Age*, 10 August 1982.

86   Peter Hastings, 'Canberra Disappoints Thailand', *Sydney Morning Herald*, 10 August 1982.

87   Peter Hastings, 'Australia Remains Cool on Kampuchea Coalition', *Sydney Morning Herald*, 9 September 1982.

88   John Bryant, 'Australian Support Canvassed', *Canberra Times*, 2 October 1982.

89   Ken Berry, *Cambodia from Red to Blue: Australia's Initiative for Peace*, St Leonards, NSW: Allen & Unwin, in association with the Department of International Relations, The Australian National University, 1997, pp. 5–6.

policy with ASEAN while maintaining support for ASEAN's overall approach towards Cambodia. Australia's preparedness to adopt a policy position on Cambodia different to that of ASEAN was notable and can be seen in that sense as a prelude to the approaches that were to be pursued from 1983 by the incoming Labor Government.[90]

Conclusion

The period of the Fraser Government saw ASEAN assume a higher profile in Australian relations with Southeast Asia and in Australian foreign policy overall. Australia's links with ASEAN developed further, and substantial cooperation was achieved in dealing with the regional crisis over refugee outflows from Indochina and over ASEAN's response to the Cambodia conflict. However, greater closeness meant that differences had more significance. In disputes over trade and market access, the Australian Government improved communication with ASEAN but did not substantively alter trade policies. In relation to Cambodia, while the government was supportive of ASEAN's overall position in opposing Vietnam's invasion, it disagreed with ASEAN on the role of the Khmer Rouge. Domestic public opinion forced Australia's withdrawal of recognition from the Khmer Rouge regime, causing discord with ASEAN. The issue of Cambodia continued to be a central element in Australian diplomacy with ASEAN in the next phase of foreign relations under the Labor Government that replaced the Fraser administration from March 1983.

90 Dee and Frost, 'Indochina', p. 191.

3

Regional activism and the end of the Cold War (1983–1996)

The Australian election of 5 March 1983 ushered in a new phase in Australian relations with Southeast Asia and with the Association of Southeast Asian Nations (ASEAN). Australia's domestic priorities shifted towards economic reform, which produced liberalisation of major sectors of the financial system, and ultimately more open trade policies. The Labor Government maintained a strong commitment to the US alliance while seeking deeper engagement with both Southeast and Northeast Asia. The context for ASEAN and for Australian policies was affected by profound changes in the international system at the end of the 1980s, when Cold War tensions and relationships were replaced by a more fluid environment. New challenges arose but avenues opened up for greater regional multilateral cooperation. All these developments had substantial implications for Australia's relations with ASEAN. To explore these issues, this chapter discusses in turn the Bob Hawke and Paul Keating governments' approaches to Asia, Australia's policies and diplomatic initiatives in relation to the Cambodian conflict, the decline in Cold War confrontation and the development of the Asia-Pacific Economic Cooperation (APEC) group and the ASEAN Regional Forum (ARF), and the state of Australia's ASEAN relations in the early 1990s.

The Hawke and Keating governments and Asian relations

When the Hawke Government assumed office, it maintained considerable continuity with the preceding Malcolm Fraser Government in foreign relations. The Labor Government reaffirmed the primacy of the US alliance as a central pillar of foreign policy. There was substantial continuity in key areas of Australia's Asia relations. The Labor Government maintained a strong emphasis on the relationship with Indonesia although there was substantial disquiet within the Australian Labor Party (ALP), and more widely in the Australian community, about East Timor. In Northeast Asia, the Labor governments maintained close relations with Japan and worked to advance linkages with China.[1] By the late 1980s, the increasing significance of the growth of the Chinese and other Northeast Asian economies was emphasised by a report commissioned by the government that called for major changes in Australia's own economic practices to enable a closer and prosperous economic relationship to flourish.[2]

Important areas of policy difference and development that emerged after 1983 were driven by Labor's concerns about the impact of international economic developments and about Australia's economic competitiveness. The Hawke Government (with Keating as Treasurer) inaugurated a series of changes that included the floating of the dollar and the liberalisation of financial markets. Through the 1980s, the government was highly aware of the problems posed for Australia's primary commodity exports in agriculture by protectionist policies in the United States and the European Union (EU). The pursuit of multilateral cooperation was very important to the government, both internationally and regionally. One manifestation of this was the creation of a multilateral grouping to combat protectionist practices,

---

1   For an overview of this period in Australian foreign policy, see Stewart Firth, *Australia in International Politics: An Introduction to Australian Foreign Policy*, 3rd edn, Crows Nest, NSW: Allen & Unwin, 2011, pp. 30–51.

2   Ross Garnaut, *Australia and the Northeast Asian Ascendancy: Report to the Prime Minister and the Minister for Foreign Affairs and Trade*, Canberra: Australian Government Publishing Service, 1989.

the Cairns Group of Agricultural Fair Traders, which campaigned for more favourable treatment for agricultural producers in international trade negotiations.[3] A second major area of attention became the cooperation efforts that led to the APEC grouping (discussed below). In the latter period of the Labor Government, economic reforms were extended to encompass major reductions in tariffs. International challenges drove domestic changes, and that shifting domestic agenda encouraged international activism.

In defence and security, the Hawke Government sponsored a reassessment of Australia's defence priorities to reorient policy towards self-reliance while remaining within the US alliance. From the late 1980s, the government placed special emphasis on the desirability of deeper networks of defence cooperation with neighbouring countries, notably in Southeast Asia.[4]

Australia, ASEAN and the Cambodian conflict

In this overall context, the Labor Government from 1983 sought to emphasise relations with Southeast Asia. Hawke has written that when he came to office, he and Minister for Foreign Affairs Bill Hayden 'agreed that under our Government our involvement with the South-East Asian region should be enhanced. Australia was particularly close to the ASEAN ... countries. And thanks to the intelligent approach of my two immediate predecessors, Whitlam and Fraser, we enjoyed good relations with China.'[5] The government had also come to office with an interest in the conflict over Cambodia and this issue rapidly came to dominate Australia's ASEAN diplomacy and relationships.

---

3   Gareth Evans and Bruce Grant, *Australia's Foreign Relations in the World of the 1990s*, 2nd edn, Carlton, Vic.: Melbourne University Press, 1995, pp. 124–5.
4   Ibid., pp. 104–19.
5   Bob Hawke, *The Hawke Memoirs*, Port Melbourne, Vic.: William Heinemann Australia, 1994, pp. 223–4.

Indochina policies 1983–88: Seeking an independent role

The ALP in Opposition had disagreed with the Fraser Government's policy approach to both Vietnam and Cambodia after 1979.[6] While the ALP leaders criticised Vietnam's invasion of Cambodia and did not advocate recognition of the new regime in Phnom Penh, the People's Republic of Kampuchea (PRK), they had opposed the cancellation of aid to Vietnam by the Fraser Government. In January 1979, Opposition leader Hayden argued that the suspension of aid to Vietnam was neither wise nor constructive and would weaken Australia's influence with the Vietnamese Government.[7]

The ALP welcomed the Fraser Government's withdrawal of diplomatic recognition of the Khmer Rouge Democratic Kampuchea opposition movement in 1981, but continued to advocate revised Australian policies towards Indochina. Labor policy advocated that the Australian Government should support independent and democratic Indochinese regimes, that Australia's aid to Vietnam should be reinstated, and that Australia should discourage all support to the 'Pol Pot forces' and no recognition should be given, bilaterally or multilaterally, to any coalition involving the Pol Pot forces. Australia should provide cultural and developmental assistance to Cambodia and a Labor Government should encourage regional solutions to Indochina's problems with reduced great power involvement.[8]

When the ALP came to office after the elections in March 1983, the new government moved to revise Australia's policies towards Southeast Asia and Indochina. However, the high levels of regional and international sensitivities involved were soon apparent. When the new government suggested that it might fulfil its commitment to restore bilateral aid to Vietnam, ASEAN officials expressed strong

6   This section draws in part from Frank Frost, 'Labor and Cambodia', in David Lee and Christopher Waters, eds, *Evatt to Evans: The Labor Tradition in Australian Foreign Policy*, St Leonards, NSW: Allen & Unwin, in association with the Department of International Relations, The Australian National University, 1997.
7   Susan Woods, 'Govt Denies Peacock Bypassed on Vietnam Decision', *Australian Financial Review*, 25 January 1979.
8   Australian Labor Party, *Platform, Constitution and Rules as Approved by the 35th National Conference*, Canberra: Australian Labor Party, 1982, pp. 83–4.

concern.[9] China's Premier Zhao Ziyang made it clear that China opposed any provision of aid.[10] After consultations with a number of governments including the members of ASEAN, the government indicated in June 1983 that Australia would not make any early move to restore bilateral aid to Vietnam.[11]

However, the Hawke Government decided to try to pursue an initiative in relation to Indochina by exploring dialogue on Cambodia. In his memoirs, Hawke wrote:

> [O]ne of the most important initiatives of my entire prime ministership was our diplomatic effort to help bring about a lasting peace in the tragic, conflict-ridden country of Cambodia ... Both Hayden and I were acutely aware of the obstacles ahead. ASEAN had arisen from the instability in Indo-China and the intrusion of the Soviet Union and China into the affairs of the region; its members remained suspicious of Vietnam and the two communist giants. The antagonism between China and Vietnam stretched back a thousand years. Cambodia itself remained sunk in conflict, with an uneasy alliance of forces arranged against the puppet Hun Sen regime. Our knowledge of and closeness to the regional players had its advantages, but understanding the range of their conflicting interests meant that Australia's diplomacy would have to be deft in the extreme.[12]

Hayden (Minister for Foreign Affairs March 1983 – August 1988) subsequently wrote that he had initial reservations about the proposal:

> The aim was to facilitate a process of dialogue leading to a peaceful settlement of the warring inside and near the borders of Kampuchea.[13] I regarded the proposal with some caution. There were a great number of differences between many of these parties and some had large political interests at stake. Australia strolling into this particular pastry shop and upsetting the wares so carefully if unsteadily arranged, could well be disastrous.[14]

---

9   Peter Samuel, 'Labor's Support for Vietnam Aid Sparks ASEAN Outcry', *The Australian*, 17 March 1983.

10   Wio Joustra, 'Zhao Plans Tough Talk on Our Aid to Vietnam', *The Australian*, 15 April 1983.

11   Mike Steketee, 'Timor, Viet Aid: Hawke Goes Alone', *Sydney Morning Herald*, 6 June 1983.

12   Hawke, *The Hawke Memoirs*, pp. 222–4.

13   'Kampuchea' is the name of the country in the Khmer language. This name was used officially by the Khmer Rouge (who named their regime Democratic Kampuchea) and by the regime which replaced it after Vietnam's invasion in December 1978 (the People's Republic of Kampuchea). That regime renamed the country the State of Cambodia in 1989 and Cambodia has since continued to be used as the country's official name.

14   Bill Hayden, *Hayden: An Autobiography*, Sydney: Angus & Robertson, 1996, p. 380.

Hayden also thought that Hawke was interested in pursuing the Cambodian initiative at least in part because it was a way of deflecting attention within the ALP over the sensitive issue of the status of and situation in East Timor.[15]

Whatever Hayden's reservations, he pursued the government's policies towards Indochina and Southeast Asia. He cautiously developed bilateral relations with Vietnam (which came to include aid donated through multilateral agencies).[16] Hayden also laid the basis for an effort towards dialogue over Cambodia. In a policy statement on Indochina to Parliament on 7 December 1983, Hayden set out a rationale for the government's interests in relation to Cambodia. He argued that there existed a 'new form of stalemate in Indo-China which offers further risks of instability and of great power involvement in the region'.[17] ASEAN had the strength and unity to stand behind Thailand and the Cambodian coalition in their resistance to Vietnam; while on the other hand, Vietnam could take comfort from the fact that the situation on the ground in Cambodia was largely in its favour despite resistance to its occupation, especially in the border areas. The ongoing conflict over Cambodia, Hayden argued, imposed a continuing refugee problem, prevented recovery within Cambodia and involved the ongoing dilemma of growing Soviet influence, particularly because of Vietnam's reliance on Soviet assistance to sustain its military effort.

To address this array of problems, Hayden set out the principles that Australia regarded as necessary in seeking détente and ultimate settlement. Australia would seek to pursue a comprehensive Cambodian solution based on the acceptance by Vietnam of an appropriate accommodation with its neighbours; phased withdrawal of Vietnamese troops from Cambodia matched by an effective arrangement to prevent Khmer Rouge forces going back into Cambodia; an act of self-determination for Cambodia; the creation of conditions for the peaceful return of displaced Cambodians to Cambodia; the acceptance

---

15   Ibid., p. 382.
16   Michelle Grattan, 'PM Resumes Disaster Aid to the Viets', *The Age*, 22 November 1983.
17   Bill Hayden, 'Australia and Indo-China', Ministerial Statement, in *Commonwealth of Australia Parliamentary Debates*, House of Representatives, Official Hansard, No. 134, 7 December 1983, p. 3407.

by all parties that Cambodia should be neutral, independent and non-aligned; and the restoration of normal relations on the part of Vietnam with China, ASEAN and the West.[18]

Hayden explored the concepts he had outlined in a series of discussions with the principal parties involved in the Cambodian conflict, including the ASEAN members, Vietnam, Laos and China. Hayden and the Australian Government encountered considerable resistance from both ASEAN and China in attempting to assert a more independent Australian approach: Hayden acknowledged later that '[a]t the beginning it was all rather rough going'.[19] When Australia withdrew its co-sponsorship of the annual ASEAN resolution on Cambodia in the United Nations (UN) General Assembly in October 1983 (because the government disagreed with some of the wording and did not wish to be seen to be automatically endorsing all ASEAN positions), this was regarded as a breach of solidarity by the ASEAN members.[20] Hayden met with a negative ASEAN response when in July 1984 at the annual ASEAN ministerial meetings he proposed informal talks between ASEAN, Vietnam and Laos and offered Australia as a venue.[21]

By 1985, it was clear that it was difficult for Australia to make much headway in seeking dialogue on Cambodia in the prevailing climate of regional and international confrontation. Hayden found considerable variation in individual attitudes towards the feasibility of negotiations, with Malaysia and Indonesia relatively more sympathetic to Australia's efforts than Thailand or Singapore, but ASEAN as a group had a major stake in Cambodia and was committed to retaining solidarity,

---

18   Ibid., pp. 3404–9.
19   Hayden, *Hayden*, p. 382.
20   Malaysia's Foreign Minister Tan Sri Ghazali Shafie walked out of the UN General Assembly chamber while Hayden was speaking. See Nicholas Rothwell, 'Malaysia Walks Out as Hayden Speaks', *The Australian*, 4 October 1983.
21   Michael Richardson, 'Hayden Rebuffed on Kampuchea Proposal', *The Age*, 14 July 1984. On the first phase of the Labor Government's Cambodian policies, see also Joint Committee on Foreign Affairs and Defence, *Australia and ASEAN: Challenges and Opportunities*, Report, Canberra: Australian Government Publishing Service, 1984, pp. 37–56.

resisting dilution of their stand.[22] Hayden continued to try to insert new ideas into the debate. A series of three seminars on Cambodia were held at Griffith University (Queensland) that brought together representatives of all major contending parties (except the Khmer Rouge). In 1986, Hayden proposed that a tribunal be instituted to try Khmer Rouge figures on charges of genocide as a way of improving the climate for reconciliation. The idea aroused interest but was not adopted.[23]

By 1988, after five years of diplomatic activity, the efforts to promote dialogue over Cambodia had raised Australia's profile as a concerned regional participant but had produced little result. Ken Berry later commented:

> The policies pursued by Bill Hayden did not, at the end of the day, achieve any breakthrough or substantive shift in the position of the major participants in a Cambodian settlement. But they did manage to impart a sense of urgency to the effort to find a solution. Indeed, it was ironic in some ways that Australia's virtual isolation on the question of non-recognition stood it in good stead when putting forward its peace initiative in 1989, since the country was clearly not aligned to any of the major powers or their client Cambodian factions.[24]

Australia's Cambodia initiatives: 1988–91

Towards the end of Hayden's tenure as foreign minister, major changes in the pattern of major power relationships began to exercise strong influences at the regional level in Southeast Asia. A key catalyst internationally was the impact of President Mikhail Gorbachev's policies in the Soviet Union. Gorbachev's speech in Vladivostok in July 1986 introduced a new era of flexibility in foreign relations as the Soviet Union sought to curtail costly foreign involvements. Moves intensified for Sino-Soviet détente. Vietnam was stimulated by internal

---

22 Hayden, *Hayden*, pp. 380–1; Philip O'Brien, 'The Making of Australia's Indochina Policies Under the Labor Government (1983–1986): The Politics of Circumspection?' Australia–Asia Papers No. 39, Nathan, Qld: Centre for the Study of Australian–Asian Relations, Griffith University, September 1987, p. 20. For a concise summary of the individual ASEAN members' approaches to the Cambodia issue, see Ken Berry, *Cambodia from Red to Blue: Australia's Initiative for Peace*, St Leonards, NSW: Allen & Unwin, in association with the Department of International Relations, The Australian National University, 1997, pp. 52–5.

23 O'Brien, 'The Making of Australia's Indochina Policies', p. 21; Berry, *Cambodia from Red to Blue*, pp. 6–7.

24 Berry, *Cambodia from Red to Blue*, p. 7.

economic problems, and by the example of the Soviet Union, to pursue extensive domestic economic reforms from 1986; this process began to create new incentives for ending the drain of the Cambodian conflict and enabling wider foreign relations to be developed.[25]

Perspectives also began to be revised within ASEAN. A series of negotiations among the Cambodian parties was initiated with ASEAN's support at the end of 1987, when Prince Norodom Sihanouk and PRK Premier Hun Sen held discussions. In July 1988, further negotiations occurred when ASEAN's largest member, Indonesia, hosted informal multilateral talks among the Cambodian parties, along with the other ASEAN members and Vietnam and Laos.[26] From 1988, the Thai Government, led by Prime Minister Chatichai Choonhaven, feeling more confident about Thailand's security position after more than a decade of high economic growth and with the Thai Communist Party neutralised, began to pursue more conciliatory policies towards Vietnam and the Cambodian conflict.[27] In this more flexible atmosphere, new opportunities opened for cooperation between Australia and ASEAN over Cambodia.

The pace of negotiations increased from the end of July 1989, with the convening of the Paris International Conference on Cambodia. The conference met for one month and was attended by the four Cambodian factions, the six ASEAN members, the 'Permanent Five' members of the UN Security Council (China, France, the Soviet Union, the United Kingdom and the United States), Vietnam, Laos, Australia, Canada, India, Zimbabwe (representing the Non-Aligned Movement) and a representative of the UN Secretary-General. Indonesia continued its active role in the negotiation effort as co-chair of the conference. The conference developed a general blueprint for peace that involved, essentially, the monitored withdrawal of all Vietnamese forces, a ceasefire, the cessation of external support, the creation of a transitional administration, and the holding of free elections, all under the supervision of an international control mechanism. It also involved measures to guarantee the neutrality of Cambodia and

---

25   MacAlister Brown and Joseph J. Zasloff, *Cambodia Confounds the Peacemakers, 1979–1998*, Ithaca, NY: Cornell University Press, 1998, pp. 34–42.

26   Berry, *Cambodia from Red to Blue*, p. 7.

27   Frank Frost, 'The Cambodia Conflict: The Path Towards Peace', *Contemporary Southeast Asia*, 13(2) 1991.

non-interference in its internal affairs, to deal with the repatriation of refugees and displaced persons, and to provide for reconstruction in Cambodia.[28]

The Paris conference confronted the continuing deep suspicion and hostilities among the Cambodian parties and their main external backers. As a result, at the end of August 1989, the Paris conference was forced to suspend its proceedings without having achieved a comprehensive settlement. Vietnam, facing a decline in economic and military assistance from the Soviet Union and anxious to extricate itself from Cambodia, announced its withdrawal of combat forces from Cambodia, and in September 1989 declared this process completed. However, since the Paris conference had been suspended without agreement, there was no internationally recognised procedure for the monitoring of Vietnam's withdrawal or for confirmation that it had occurred. The stage was thus set for ongoing conflict in Cambodia.[29]

It was at this point, in late 1989, that Australia intensified its efforts to facilitate negotiations. As former Minister for Foreign Affairs Gareth Evans later recalled, he sought to continue and expand the efforts that had been made by Hayden:

> Bill was very actively involved with … trying to create a relationship with Vietnam and to work on Vietnam–ASEAN issues and … that was when Cambodia first started featuring in our policy landscape because Bill took it very seriously as an issue and I really just built on the initial work that he'd done.[30]

Australian policymakers, led by Evans, focused on what they saw as the key stumbling block: the issue of the composition of the transitional administration in Cambodia. The resistance forces of Prince Sihanouk, Son Sann and the Khmer Rouge, together with their international backers, were continuing to demand a place for

---

28 Berry, *Cambodia from Red to Blue*, pp. 14–20.
29 Ibid.
30 Gareth Evans, interview with the author, Canberra, 2 July 2014.

each of the four internal parties, including the Khmer Rouge, in the transitional administration. This was a demand rejected by the PRK Government of Hun Sen and its international backers.[31]

Building on initial suggestions by Prince Sihanouk and US Congressman Stephen Solarz, Australia suggested an enhanced role for the UN in the transitional process (a proposal first announced on 24 November 1989). To sidestep the power-sharing issue that had confounded the Paris conference, and to constrain the role of the Khmer Rouge, Australia proposed that the UN be directly involved in the civil administration of Cambodia during the transitional period. A UN military presence to monitor the ceasefire, cessation of external military assistance, a UN role in organising and conducting elections, and UN involvement in the transitional administrative arrangements would, it was hoped, ensure a neutral political environment conducive to free and fair general elections.[32]

Evans recognised that the Australian proposals involved a more ambitious and complicated role for the UN than any it had attempted before. Nonetheless, the concept of an enhanced UN role in the transitional period of a peace settlement for Cambodia rapidly gained support. Australia devoted extensive diplomatic efforts to advance it. From December 1989, Senator Evans's envoy, Michael Costello, engaged in a major series of consultations. A departmental task force, under the direction of Evans, drew up a detailed set of scenarios and plans for a UN role in Cambodia, and these papers were presented to a meeting of the ASEAN members, the Cambodian parties, Vietnam and Laos in February 1990 (the Jakarta Informal Meeting). These were then published and became known – because of the colour of the cover – as the 'Red Book'.[33]

---

31   Evans provided a detailed account of the origins of Australia's proposals in a speech to the Senate in December 1990; see Gareth Evans, 'Prospects for a Cambodian Peace Settlement', Ministerial Statement, in *Commonwealth of Australia Parliamentary Debates*, Senate, Official Hansard, No. 142, 6 December 1990.
32   Ibid.
33   Australian Department of Foreign Affairs and Trade, *Cambodia: An Australian Peace Proposal*, working papers prepared for the Informal Meeting on Cambodia, Jakarta, 26–28 February 1990, Canberra: Australian Government Publishing Service for the Australian Department of Foreign Affairs and Trade, 1990.

The decline of Cold War confrontation had created a greatly improved climate for detailed discussions on Cambodia. Australia was now able to play the kind of facilitation role that Hawke and Hayden had hoped for from 1983. An important factor in the new climate was that Australia was able to cooperate actively with the ASEAN members in pursuing a settlement. Indonesia, in particular, had taken the initiative in sponsoring the informal talks on Cambodia from 1988, and was co-chairman of the Paris conference. The Australian Government placed special emphasis on operating in close cooperation with Indonesia and with Foreign Minister Ali Alatas. Senator Evans's envoy kept in close contact with Alatas, informing him of every step in Australia's diplomatic efforts.[34] Evans has emphasised the crucial role played by Indonesia and by Alatas in particular:

> Alatas felt that he had to carry ASEAN with him and there was a lot of consultation ... others were significant voices but none were as remotely significant or as consistently engaged as Indonesia and without Indonesia ... and Alatas' personal role I don't think ASEAN would have been anything like a coherent player delivering effective results.[35]

Australia was able to turn its status as a middle-ranking power into an advantage in seeking a settlement. As Berry observed:

> Our coalition-building in this case meant working from the outset with Indonesia and the other ASEANs, all five Permanent Members of the UN Security Council (the P5), Vietnam and the four Cambodia factions themselves. The fact that Australia came to the process without the political and other baggage normally associated with superpower or major power status meant that the various central parties were more prepared to listen and be less suspicious of our proposals.[36]

From early 1990, the concept of a UN transitional authority as part of a comprehensive settlement gained widespread acceptance. The P5 adopted the concept in August 1990, as did the Cambodian parties in November. After further tortuous negotiations, the way was cleared for the development of the Paris Agreements, which were signed on 23 October 1991, and for the deployment of the United Nations Transitional Authority in Cambodia (UNTAC) in February 1992.

34   Michael Costello, 'Cambodia: A Diplomatic Memoir', *Sydney Papers*, 6(3) 1994: 104.
35   Evans, interview with the author, July 2014.
36   Ken Berry, 'UNTAC as a Paradigm: A Flawed Success', *Pacifica Review*, 7(2) 1995: 89.

While UNTAC faced formidable difficulties in many areas, it was able to implement key aspects of the Paris Agreements and organised and conducted elections in May 1993, which led to the inauguration of a new Royal Government of Cambodia.[37]

Australia made a substantial contribution to UNTAC and to supporting the peace process. Australia provided 495 military personnel to support UNTAC's communications capacity and Australian police and civil officials served with UNTAC. In May 1993, when there were concerns about the potential for disruption of the forthcoming elections, Australia contributed an additional 100 military personnel and six Blackhawk helicopters to boost UNTAC's transport capacities.[38] Australians also served in some key roles in UNTAC, including Lieutenant-General John Sanderson in the crucial position of military commander. Lieutenant-General Sanderson's position as head of the diverse multinational UNTAC military component was one of the most prominent roles ever assumed by an Australian in Southeast Asia. Berry has observed that 'the overall successful conclusion of the Cambodia operation can in large measure be attributed to the counsels and calming assessments of the UNTAC military component leadership in Phnom Penh'.[39]

The achievements of the Paris Agreements and of the UN involvement in Cambodia were clearly mixed. Within Cambodia, poverty and dislocation continued and the uneasy governing coalition broke down after the parties and forces led by Hun Sen and by Prince Norodom Ranariddh came into violent conflict in 1997, and Hun Sen and his party emerged as dominant in the country.[40] However, at the regional and international levels, the peace process advocated by Australia and ASEAN produced results. The Paris Agreements enabled both Vietnam and China to decisively withdraw from their active support for the contending Cambodian warring parties. The period after 1991 saw Vietnam and China pursue a substantial (although not trouble-free) redevelopment of relations, Vietnam and the United States normalised relations in July 1995, Vietnam and the ASEAN members transcended

---

37   Ibid.; Brown and Zasloff, *Cambodia Confounds the Peacemakers*, pp. 269–300.
38   Frank Frost, 'The Peace Process in Cambodia: Issues and Prospects', Australia–Asia Paper No. 69, Nathan, Qld: Centre for the Study of Australian–Asian Relations, Griffith University, 1993, pp. 43–7.
39   Berry, *Cambodia from Red to Blue*, p. 328.
40   Brown and Zasloff, *Cambodia Confounds the Peacemakers*, pp. 239–68.

their former animosity to become partners in ASEAN itself (on 28 July 1995), and Cambodia gained a government able to attract international recognition and to pursue a gradually increasing involvement in regional affairs, including ASEAN membership in 1999.[41]

All of these regional and international developments were striking and productive, and it is likely that none could have been achieved without the Paris Agreements. The Cambodian negotiations involved a number of key participants, but ASEAN and Australia played major parts in the process. Australia was able to provide ideas and policymaking resources, and Australian diplomatic communications, including the consultations conducted by Evans and by Costello, were significant contributions. Without the dialogue and communication between Australia and ASEAN, and with Indonesia in particular, the peace process might well not have been developed. The issue of Cambodia was a substantial instance where Australia and ASEAN cooperated on a major issue of security and regional concern and achieved a significant outcome.

Australia, ASEAN and APEC

The decline of Cold War confrontation, which had facilitated efforts towards a Cambodia settlement, also encouraged interest in the formation of new regional groupings to enhance economic and security cooperation. Australia and ASEAN played important roles in the advent of both the APEC process and the ARF. In each case, the establishment of the new groupings in this period involved extensive dialogue and cooperation between Australia and ASEAN. They also involved elements of tension as Australia's interests in pursuing cooperation with a focus encompassing countries both in East Asia and more widely (including the United States) produced some sensitivities with ASEAN over its desire to protect its corporate identity.

As noted in Chapter 2, Australia and ASEAN had clashed over trade and economic relations in the 1970s and early 1980s, but they had by the late 1980s increased bases for common interests in these areas. Both Australia and a number of ASEAN members had moved

---

41   Berry, *Cambodia from Red to Blue*, pp. 311–16; Frost, 'The Peace Process in Cambodia', pp. 48–50.

to liberalise their economies to maximise prospects for growth. They shared concerns about market access for exports to their major trading partners. These concerns fed interest in new avenues to promote trade cooperation. One reflection of this, as has been noted, was Australia's initiative to establish a grouping of agricultural exporters to seek more favourable treatment for these commodities in international trade negotiations. The Cairns Group of Agricultural Fair Traders was established in 1986, and since its membership included four ASEAN member countries (Indonesia, Malaysia, the Philippines and Thailand), it helped to broaden the bases for common interests between Australia and Southeast Asian countries.[42]

Ideas for economic cooperation in the Asia-Pacific region had been promoted by non-governmental groups and by elements in some major economies from the 1960s, including in Japan and Australia. Interest was advanced by the Pacific Basin Economic Council (formed in 1967) and by the Pacific Economic Cooperation Council (PECC) (inaugurated in 1980 in Canberra), which brought together both non-government and official representatives (in a private capacity).[43]

Support for new efforts in cooperation was bolstered in the late 1980s by heightened concern about the emergence of trading blocs that seemed to threaten the interests of regional economies. In Europe, the already protectionist EU was moving towards its Final Unification Act and was developing new connections with Eastern Europe. In North America, the US, Canada and Mexico were pursuing negotiations for a North American Free Trade Agreement. In Australia, there were concerns that the US and Japan might arrive at arrangements to handle their economic relations problems that excluded other Asia-Pacific economies. In Southeast Asia there were added concerns that capital from Western Europe might flow heavily towards the Eastern European states, to the detriment of investment in ASEAN. Singapore's Prime Minister Lee Kuan Yew expressed widespread views

---

42   On the Cairns Group, see Jiro Okamoto, *Australia's Foreign Economic Policy and ASEAN*, Singapore: Institute of Southeast Asian Studies, 2010, pp. 146–9.

43   Donald Crone, 'The Politics of Emerging Pacific Cooperation', *Pacific Affairs*, 65(1) 1992: 70; Amitav Acharya, *The Making of Southeast Asia: International Relations of a Region*, Singapore: ISEAS Publishing, 2012, pp. 224–7.

in the region when he said in July 1989 that 'major trading nations were moving away from the multilateral trading system' towards more restrictive blocs.[44]

There was strong interest in Japan in pursuing regional economic cooperation that could bolster trade in the face of discriminatory regionalism in Europe and North America. In August 1988, a report was issued by a study group sponsored by the Ministry for International Trade and Industry advocating 'new forms of economic cooperation' in the Asia-Pacific region.[45] However, in both Japan and Australia it was considered that it would not be feasible for Japan itself to attempt to take the lead in advocating a new form of cooperation, given ongoing sensitivities in East and Southeast Asia about Japan's regional role. Takashi Terada wrote that 'it would be better for a small non-threatening country like Australia to launch a new regional initiative, without too many specifics about the nature of proposed cooperation'.[46]

Australia under the Hawke Government had developed strong interests in contributing towards economic cooperation in a 'region' that could encompass the economies of Southeast and Northeast Asia and potentially the US. Australia had been frustrated at the slow progress of the Uruguay Round multilateral trade negotiations, particularly in agriculture. With concerns rising in the late 1980s about a possible trade war between the US and the EU, the Hawke Government hoped that an outward-looking Asia-Pacific grouping might counter this trend. The government considered that Australia's financial and manufacturing sectors would benefit from additional international competition and would be better placed to gain advantages from interaction with the East Asian economies.[47] Hawke took the initiative by introducing a proposal for a form of Asia-Pacific economic cooperation in a speech in Seoul on 30 January 1989, calling for 'a more formal intergovernmental vehicle for regional cooperation'.[48] Reviewing earlier initiatives, Hawke said that although

---

44   Crone, 'The Politics of Emerging Pacific Cooperation', p. 73.
45   Rawdon Dalrymple, *Continental Drift: Australia's Search for a Regional Identity*, Aldershot: Ashgate, 2003, p. 85.
46   Quoted in ibid.
47   Hawke, *The Hawke Memoirs*, pp. 232–3.
48   Joseph A. Camilleri, *Regionalism in the New Asia-Pacific Order: The Political Economy of the Asia-Pacific Region, Volume II*, Cheltenham: Edward Elgar, 2003, p. 128.

PECC 'had illuminated large areas of common interest within the region', its informality meant that it could not readily 'address policy issues which are properly the responsibility of Governments'.[49]

The attitudes of ASEAN members would be crucial to the prospects for any new regional forum. Before 1989, ASEAN members had opposed any new cooperative grouping. In July 1984 for example, Indonesia's Foreign Minister Dr Mochtar Kusmaatmaja stated that ASEAN had 'no intention' of considering any new forum, which was 'too difficult' and 'not practical'.[50] Australia therefore needed to place special emphasis on gaining acceptance and support from ASEAN.

After Hawke's Seoul speech, the Australian Government set out to mobilise support from potential participants. Hawke appointed the head of the Department of Foreign Affairs and Trade (DFAT), Richard Woolcott, as his special envoy, and in early 1989 Woolcott visited all the (then) six ASEAN members, New Zealand, Japan and South Korea to canvass support for an inaugural regional meeting. Within the Australian Government there was initial debate about whether the US and Canada should be included, but by May 1989 the government considered that US participation would be highly desirable.[51]

ASEAN's views were critical to the feasibility of the proposal for APEC and, as Amitav Acharya has observed, there were considerable reservations in ASEAN about a possible new grouping:

> ASEAN governments were initially lukewarm to APEC, fearing that it would be dominated by non-Southeast Asian countries such as Japan, Australia and the United States. ASEAN wished to be the model for APEC and was keen to ensure that the new grouping should not on any account reduce the activities or status of ASEAN. ASEAN wished to remain as the core of multilateral processes in the region; other regional institutions should assess the ASEAN experience and proceed from there.[52]

---

49 Robert Hawke, 'Speech by the Prime Minister, State Banquet, Seoul – 30 January 1989'.
50 Quoted in Crone, 'The Politics of Emerging Pacific Cooperation', p. 74.
51 Roderic Pitty, 'Regional Economic Co-operation', in Peter Edwards and David Goldsworthy, eds, *Facing North: A Century of Australian Engagement with Asia, Volume 2: 1970s to 2000*, Carlton, Vic.: Melbourne University Press, 2003, pp. 25–6.
52 Acharya, *The Making of Southeast Asia*, p. 227.

The appointment and role of Woolcott was an important factor in Australia's diplomacy on this issue. Graeme Dobell commented that:

> For Australia, ASEAN held the crucial cards in the creation of APEC. The initial omission of the US from the core membership reflected this concentration on Southeast Asia. A masterstroke in this diplomatic dance was the dispatch in April 1989 of Richard Woolcott, as the prime minister's emissary, to each ASEAN capital.[53]

Woolcott, who had extensive experience in Southeast Asia, went first to Indonesia where in discussions with President Suharto he said that Australia was coming to him for advice on how a new regional body might proceed. President Suharto responded that the APEC concept was an interesting proposal worth discussing. Woolcott then went to Singapore, which was strongly supportive of the idea on condition that it must not harm ASEAN, that it must not take the form of a trade bloc and that its operations should be consistent with the General Agreement on Tariffs and Trade (GATT).[54] The proposal also received support from Thailand and the Philippines. Malaysia's response was cool but the concept had gained momentum. Dobell has written that:

> Malaysian officials later complained at the skilful way Woolcott had played his ASEAN cards, claiming that Suharto's simple expression of willingness to listen had been used to leverage stronger endorsements from the rest of ASEAN. Certainly Woolcott had made full use of the guidance he had received from Suharto and the fact that there was no Indonesian veto. It was shuttle diplomacy of the highest order.[55]

Woolcott reported to the Australian Government that the major concern expressed by the ASEAN members was whether any new regional organisation was in fact required. Some ASEAN members, especially Malaysia, considered that expanding ASEAN's Post-Ministerial Conference (PMC) dialogue process and boosting ASEAN's secretariat could provide a sufficient strengthening of regional arrangements. However, Woolcott felt that ASEAN would not oppose the creation of a new regional group if the agenda were to be confined to economic matters. In a speech in May 1989, Minister for Foreign

---

53   Graeme Dobell, *Australia Finds Home: The Choices and Chances of an Asia Pacific Journey*, Sydney: ABC Books, 2000, p. 36.
54   GATT was a multilateral trade agreement inaugurated in 1948; GATT was replaced by the World Trade Organization in 1995.
55   Dobell, *Australia Finds Home*, pp. 36–7.

Affairs Evans affirmed that ASEAN 'was likely to remain the pre-eminent body in the region' and argued that a broader group would 'enhance the capacity of ASEAN, and of the other participants, to project their economic interests regionally and globally'.[56] ASEAN at its ministerial meeting in July 1989 did not support the Australian proposal directly, but a tentative agreement was made at the PMC to hold an initial exploratory ministerial meeting in Canberra in November.[57] ASEAN economic ministers then expressed support for this proposal in September.[58]

The inaugural APEC ministerial meeting was duly held in Canberra on 6–7 November 1989, chaired by Evans and attended by ministers from all six ASEAN members, Canada, Japan, New Zealand, South Korea and the US. The secretaries-general of ASEAN and of the South Pacific Forum, and the chair of PECC attended as observers. At the meeting it was evident that the ASEAN members continued to have concerns about the implications of a new grouping for the identity and role of ASEAN.[59] The Canberra meeting recognised the central role of ASEAN in regional cooperation, and it was agreed that every second meeting of APEC would be in an ASEAN country. However, ASEAN members were concerned at what they perceived to be the excessive speed of the development of APEC and at its potential to be dominated by wealthier members. They also were not satisfied at the statement of principles for economic cooperation in the Asia-Pacific adopted at the Canberra meeting.[60]

ASEAN accordingly asserted its own position on APEC and how it should evolve. ASEAN held its first joint meeting of foreign and economics ministers in Kuching, Malaysia, in February 1990, and adopted a further list of principles for ASEAN participation in the APEC process. These principles included that ASEAN's identity and cohesion should be preserved and its cooperative relations with

56   Gareth Evans, 'An Idea Whose Time Has Come', *Australian Foreign Affairs Record*, 60(5) 1989: 185.

57   David Goldsworthy, 'Introduction', in Peter Edwards and David Goldsworthy, eds, *Facing North: A Century of Australian Engagement with Asia, Volume 2: 1970s to 2000*, Carlton, Vic.: Melbourne University Press, 2003, p. 26.

58   Sarah Sargent, 'Region Ministers in Favour of Pact', *Australian Financial Review*, 13 September 1989.

59   Paul Grigson, 'ASEAN Bid to Absorb the New Conference', *The Age*, 7 November 1989.

60   John Ravenhill, *APEC and the Construction of Pacific Rim Regionalism*, Cambridge: Cambridge University Press, 2001, pp. 104–5.

dialogue partners and third partners should not be diluted in any enhanced APEC; an enhanced APEC should be based on equality, equity and mutual benefit taking full account of the differences in stages of development and in socio-political systems of members; APEC should not be directed towards the formation of any inward-looking trading bloc; it should provide a consultative forum on economic issues and should not lead to the adoption of any mandatory directives for participants to pursue; and it should proceed gradually and pragmatically, especially in relation to institutionalisation.[61]

In the early phases of APEC's existence and activities, ASEAN members were able to maintain an effective united front and gave ASEAN a central decision-making role in APEC.[62] However, differences in emphasis among major ASEAN members in relation to APEC soon emerged, which were significant both for APEC itself and for Australian policies towards ASEAN and regional cooperation.

APEC made significant progress in its first years of activity. Meetings of senior officials initiated work on areas of economic and technical cooperation, including human resources development. APEC quickly made an important expansion in its coverage of major regional economies. China had not taken part in the initial APEC meeting in Canberra. That meeting had taken place just five months after the crackdown on dissenters in Tiananmen Square in June 1989, which had killed hundreds and was condemned by a number of Western governments, including the US and Australia. In 1991, however, moves were made to involve China in APEC, and at the meeting in November 1991 in Seoul, China joined the grouping, along with Hong Kong and Taiwan (as 'Chinese Taipei'). APEC thus became the one major regional group in which the People's Republic of China participated alongside Taiwan.[63]

APEC began to consider the question of cooperation for trade liberalisation. Australia supported the promotion of discussion on avenues towards liberalisation, and in 1991, Australia also floated the idea of an Eminent Persons' Group (EPG). This ultimately led to the agreement at APEC's ministerial meeting in Bangkok in September

---

61   Ibid.
62   Ibid.
63   Steve Burrell, 'APEC Takes Off as EAEG Nose-Dives', *Australian Financial Review*, 18 November 1991.

1992 of an EPG of 12 representatives (led by Fred Bergsten of the US and including former New South Wales Premier Neville Wran from Australia).[64]

The priority given by Australia to APEC was heightened after Keating replaced Hawke as Australian prime minister in December 1991. Keating proposed that APEC should establish a meeting at leaders' level and raised this with US President George H. W. Bush on New Year's Day 1992. Keating's broader purpose was to turn APEC from a body talking about economic cooperation, to one that could potentially have political authority. Keating later wrote that 'I wanted to use the heads of government meetings to give it more political and institutional weight'.[65] While the formal agenda would be economic, there was value in bringing together key leaders from the major powers including China, Japan and the US, and Keating also considered that there were benefits in having the leaders of China and ASEAN in a multilateral forum. Such a leaders' gathering could help maintain US involvement in the region and would give Australia a place in a potentially significant dialogue.[66]

The first APEC leaders' meeting was held in Seattle in November 1993, hosted by President Bill Clinton. Five out of the then six ASEAN members were represented, but not Malaysia. Prime Minister Mahathir Mohamad continued to be concerned at APEC's potential to challenge ASEAN's identity and role (see below). Mahathir's refusal to attend became the focus of a diplomatic spat between Australia and Malaysia. Keating in discussions with journalists after the gathering said, when the subject of Dr Mahathir was raised '[p]lease don't ask me any more questions about Dr Mahathir. I couldn't care less, frankly, whether he comes here or not'. Keating said that he would be meeting with his Malaysian counterpart in the following year but added that 'APEC is bigger than all of us – Australia, the US and Malaysia and Dr Mahathir and any other recalcitrants.'[67] Mahathir took offence

64   Goldsworthy, 'Introduction', p. 30.
65   Paul Keating, *Engagement: Australia Faces the Asia-Pacific*, Sydney: Pan Macmillan, 2000, p. 84.
66   Ibid., pp. 76–97.
67   Quoted in Dobell, *Australia Finds Home*, p. 40.

at the comments and the dispute added to a sense of discord in the bilateral relationship, which had implications for Australia's overall relationship with ASEAN as a group.[68]

The Seattle meeting received a report from the APEC EPG, which called for enhanced efforts towards trade liberalisation. The leaders called for further action towards liberalisation in the global multilateral trade negotiations process. A significant development at the Seattle meeting was that President Suharto was asked to host the second such leaders' meeting and agreed to do so. In the lead-up to the initial Canberra meeting, Indonesia had been cautious about the prospects for APEC and had been an advocate for the view that ASEAN's Secretariat should be the core around which economic cooperation efforts should be developed. Indonesia at this time had echoed Malaysia's reservations about institutionalising APEC.[69] As John Ravenhill has argued, the invitation to Suharto was significant both for APEC and for ASEAN:

> The decision to invite Suharto to host a follow-up meeting was particularly astute. It appeared to pay tribute to Suharto's role as the elder statesman of ASEAN, and to Indonesia's long-standing claim to be the most important of the ASEAN countries. Moreover, a leaders meeting in Jakarta would pose a vexatious dilemma for Malaysian Prime Minister Mahathir, who had boycotted the Seattle meeting. To fail to participate in a meeting hosted by a fellow ASEAN member would be regarded in the region as a grave insult.[70]

Suharto took up the task of hosting the 1994 APEC meeting. He was encouraged to support efforts towards free trade and investment by Australian and US diplomatic efforts. Suharto may also have considered that advocacy of free trade by APEC would help bolster moves within Indonesia towards domestic liberalisation that would help make Indonesia's economy more competitive. Suharto took an active leadership role within ASEAN on these issues: he forestalled potential objections from other ASEAN members by rejecting efforts by Thailand and the Philippines to hold an informal ASEAN summit before the forthcoming Bogor meeting.[71]

---

68   Harold Crouch, 'Understanding Malaysia', in Anthony Milner and Mary Quilty, eds, *Australia in Asia: Episodes*, Melbourne: Oxford University Press, 1998.

69   Ravenhill, *APEC*, pp. 106–7.

70   Ibid.

71   Ibid.

The second APEC leaders' meeting, in Bogor in November 1994, was a high point for APEC. The leaders agreed on a timetable to achieve free and open trade and investment by 2010 for developed economies and 2020 for developing economies. President Suharto had played a significant role in securing this agreement by withstanding pressures from some ASEAN members for more qualified commitments on the key issues of trade and investment. The existence of differing views within ASEAN, however, continued to be evident.[72]

Malaysia and the East Asian Economic Group proposal

Malaysia's position was particularly significant. Malaysia, as has been noted, had strong reservations about the development of APEC. Dr Mahathir set out his views in comments in 1994:

> When the Asia Pacific Economic Cooperation Forum (APEC) was proposed by Australia, all the ASEAN countries, with the exception of Malaysia, welcomed it. Malaysia's fear was that the inclusion of economic giants like the United States, Canada and Japan would result in the domination of the grouping by these countries ... Fear prevails that ASEAN will disappear within the very much enlarged and more powerful APEC grouping. There may be conflict between ASEAN interest and the broader Pacific interest. APEC is likely to dominate ASEAN and hinder its progress towards greater intra-ASEAN cooperation.[73]

Mahathir's fears about APEC's potential to dominate ASEAN were not realised, primarily because APEC lost cohesion and focus as a vehicle for trade liberalisation in the years after the Asian financial crisis (see Chapter 4). However, Mahathir's reactions to the challenges posed by APEC had some significant impact on debates on regional cooperation in East Asia and the Asia-Pacific. In the period after the initial Canberra meeting, Mahathir had underscored his antipathy towards APEC by proposing an alternative model for cooperation. In December 1990, he advocated the development of an East Asian Economic Group (EAEG) whose participants would be restricted to the ASEAN members and China, Japan and South Korea. Japan was understood to be sceptical about the concept and several ASEAN

---

72   Ibid., pp. 110–11.
73   Quoted in ibid., pp. 109–10.

members (including Indonesia, the Philippines and Thailand) were also understood to be unenthusiastic.[74] At a meeting of ASEAN economics ministers in September 1991, Indonesia, the Philippines and Thailand persuaded Malaysia to reformulate the proposal as an informal arrangement, now termed the East Asia Economic Caucus, that could operate under the aegis of APEC. As countries explicitly excluded from the coverage of the notional grouping, the US and Australia were both opposed to the concept. US Secretary of State James Baker commented frankly that in private he did all he could to 'kill' the proposal.[75] However, while the East Asia Economic Caucus concept did not initially gain substantial support, the idea of a grouping with an explicitly 'East Asian' identity was a significant development with long-term implications.

The diplomatic interaction, including that between Australia and ASEAN, surrounding the emergence of APEC, was thus a complex process. APEC was established successfully and it had participation from all of the six members then in ASEAN. APEC by 1993 involved both economic dialogue and a meeting at leadership level, the first to be established in the Asia-Pacific region. The formation of APEC, however, was also accompanied by the promotion of another model for Asian cooperation, based on a regional conception of East Asia rather than the Asia-Pacific, and with a proposed membership that was exclusively from East Asia. The contest and competition between Asia-Pacific and East Asian modes of cooperation would be an important ongoing issue for Australia in its regional diplomacy.

Regional security and the ARF

The changing international environment in the late 1980s had substantial implications for security policies, both nationally and regionally. New questions arose about the character of security after the demise of the Soviet Union and the end of Cold War confrontation in Europe, and about the role that multilateral cooperation could play

---

74   Alan Boyd, 'Proposal for Asian Trading Bloc Gets Lukewarm Reception', *The Australian*, 8 February 1991; Viberto Selochan, 'New Directions and New Thinking in Australia–Southeast Asia Relations', Australia–Asia Papers No. 62, Nathan, Qld: Centre for the Study of Australian–Asian Relations, Griffith University, March 1992, pp. 42–3.
75   Dobell, *Australia Finds Home*, p. 38.

in enhancing security. Discussions about these issues led to a further major stage in ASEAN–Australia interaction and to the advent of a second new grouping, the ARF.

The decline of Cold War confrontation between the US and the Soviet Union, which had a substantial impact on the character of the Cambodian conflict, also stimulated revised thinking on the requirements for regional security in Southeast Asia and East Asia overall. The changes of policy in the Soviet Union under the Gorbachev regime led to a reduction in tensions with the US, a development that was consolidated in July 1990 by an agreement between the two parties in Irkutsk in which they stated that they no longer regarded each other as adversaries in the Asia-Pacific. The decline in US–Soviet confrontation coincided with the loosening or outright disintegration of a number of alliances, including those between the Soviet Union and Vietnam, the Soviet Union and North Korea, the US and the Philippines, the US and New Zealand, and the US and South Korea.[76]

The regional environment was also influenced by a number of other factors, including the comparative decline in the military presence of the US (with the impending closure of its air and naval bases at Clark Field and Subic Bay in the Philippines) and the economic rise of Japan.[77] China's progress towards market-oriented economic reforms and its greater involvement in the regional and international economy was a further significant development. China from the late 1980s moved to extend its linkages in Southeast Asia through normalising relations with Indonesia and Singapore in 1990 and by expressing interest in establishing formal relations with ASEAN, a move that ASEAN welcomed.[78]

The decline of Cold War antagonisms still left Southeast and East Asia with major security challenges. Some conflicts clearly were outgrowths of Cold War tensions, such as relations between China and Taiwan, and the confrontation on the Korean peninsula. However, a number of conflicts in East Asia could not be attributed solely or even primarily

---

76 Camilleri, *Regionalism*, p. 113.
77 Ibid. On the background to the ARF, see Noel M. Morada, 'The ASEAN Regional Forum: Origins and Evolution', in Jürgen Haacke and Noel M. Morada, eds, *Cooperative Security in the Asia-Pacific: The ASEAN Regional Forum*, London: Routledge, 2010.
78 Ian Storey, *Southeast Asia and the Rise of China: The Search for Security*, London: Routledge, 2011, p. 41.

to Cold War geopolitical bipolarity. There were also ongoing pressures from economic competition and arms acquisitions by regional states. Overall, as Joseph A. Camilleri observed:

> By the late 1980s the idea that new forms of regional as much as global cooperation were needed to contain the structural instabilities generated by the end of the Cold War and economic globalisation was rapidly gaining ground. Relaxation of tensions on the one hand and new uncertainties on the other were combining to create a multilateral window of opportunity.[79]

Australia was keenly interested in the changing regional security environment and in how regional relationships might be affected by it. Canberra's perspectives on regional security had been influenced by its own defence policy reassessment in the second half of the 1980s. Australian policymakers and analysts had sought to reassess the basis for thinking about national security so Australia could seek self-reliance within the context of the US alliance and reduce traditional concerns about vulnerability in relation to its neighbours in Southeast and East Asia. This process was stimulated particularly by the government-commissioned Dibb Report and then the 1987 Defence White Paper.[80] Although the White Paper did little to promote further Australian activities in Southeast Asia, it did have significant implications for Australian regional policies overall. Desmond Ball and Pauline Kerr have argued that:

> [T]he effective implementation of the strategic policy of greater self-reliance/defence of Australia outlined in the White Paper, the greater maturity of Australian policy-makers and the population at large that it reflected, and the national self-confidence that it generated, had effects that went well beyond the defence establishment and laid the ground for greater regional cooperation.[81]

---

79 Camilleri, *Regionalism*, p. 120.
80 Evans and Grant, *Australia's Foreign Relations*, pp. 104–19; Australian Department of Defence, *Review of Australia's Defence Capabilities: Report to the Minister for Defence*, Canberra: Australian Government Publishing Service, 1986 (known as the Dibb Report); Australian Department of Defence, *The Defence of Australia*, Canberra: Australian Government Publishing Service, 1987.
81 Desmond Ball and Pauline Kerr, *Presumptive Engagement: Australia's Asia-Pacific Security Policy in the 1990s*, St Leonards, NSW: Allen & Unwin, in association with the Department of International Relations, The Australian National University, 1996, p. 15.

On 6 December 1989, Evans presented a major statement for the Australian Government on regional security. The statement came just weeks after the fall of the Berlin Wall and one week after the inaugural APEC ministerial conference. The statement provided a 'policy framework' for Australia's relations with Asia and the South Pacific and it was presented as a redefinition of diplomatic means:

> [T]he policy responses or instruments available to protect Australia's security are **multidimensional**. They go well beyond strictly military capabilities, essential though these are. They also embrace traditional diplomacy, politico-military capabilities (in the border-zone between defence and diplomacy), economic and trade relations, and development assistance. And they extend to immigration, education and training, cultural relations, information activities, and a number of other less obvious areas of government activity. The relative importance of this large variety of policy instruments will vary from situation to situation, but none exists in isolation, and all should be regarded as mutually reinforcing contributions to our security.[82]

The statement argued that while Australia had previously seen the relevance of Southeast Asia and the South Pacific to Australian security in largely military terms, there was now an 'opportunity to reinforce our national security by utilising the many dimensions of our external policies in an informed, coordinated and vigorous way to participate in the shaping of the regional environment'.[83] An important element of the statement was its thinking on the importance to Australia of Southeast Asia and of the ASEAN countries. The statement emphasised that 'for reasons of fundamental national security, Australia needs to develop more substantial linkages with its neighbours' in order to become 'an accepted and natural participant in regional affairs … [I]f we can manage to develop a substantial and mutually beneficial range of linkages with the Southeast Asia region, then the motivation and intention to threaten us will be minimal'.[84] Australia would therefore seek to extend its relations with the ASEAN members and (in a further reflection of a major theme in Australia's regional policies since the 1970s) to encourage the participation of Vietnam, Cambodia, Laos and Myanmar in regional affairs. Australia

---

82   Gareth Evans, 'Australia's Regional Security', Ministerial Statement, Canberra: Australian Department of Foreign Affairs and Trade, 1989, p. 2, emphasis in original.

83   Ibid., p. 46.

84   Ibid., p. 44.

would also aim to participate 'actively in the gradual development of a regional security community based on a sense of shared security interests'.[85]

Evans advocated new thinking on regional security issues, but this did not initially find favour with the ASEAN members, or with Japan and the US. Evans, speaking in Australia in March 1990, referred to the process of institutionalised security dialogue in Europe, and said that 'the time may be approaching for a similar process to commence in the Asia region'.[86] He also began to discuss the relevance of the Conference on Security and Cooperation in Europe, a security dialogue that had been established through the Helsinki agreements in 1975 to manage and ameliorate regional tensions in Europe. In July 1990, Evans in a newspaper article wrote that there was a need:

> to be looking ahead to the kind of wholly new or institutional processes that might be capable of evolving in Asia just as in Europe, as a framework for addressing and resolving security problems ... Why should there not be developed a similar institutional framework – a 'CSCA' [Conference on Security and Cooperation in Asia] – for addressing the apparently intractable security issues which exist in Asia?[87]

Evans said 'negative responses' that emphasised the complexity of regional issues in Asia and the diversity of Asian states, should not obstruct 'a process of dialogue, both bilaterally and regionally', in which he said 'Australia is now amply equipped to participate'.[88]

Evans advanced the need for wider security dialogue at the ASEAN PMC held in Jakarta on 27 July 1990. He said that while the region was 'short of institutions for a broad working dialogue about security', Australia's interest was not in establishing a new structure but rather to seek ways of adding further substance to the present framework

---

85   Ibid., p. 44.
86   Gareth Evans, 'Australia and Northeast Asia', Address by the Minister for Foreign Affairs and Trade, Senator Gareth Evans, to the Committee for the Economic Development of Australia (CEDA), Melbourne, 22 March 1990.
87   Quoted in Ball and Kerr, *Presumptive Engagement*, p. 18.
88   Quoted in Roderic Pitty, 'Strategic Engagement', in Peter Edwards and David Goldsworthy, eds, *Facing North: A Century of Australian Engagement with Asia, Volume 2: 1970s to 2000*, Carlton, Vic.: Melbourne University Press, 2003, p. 63.

of sub-regional relationships.[89] The response within ASEAN was cautious. As was the case with the proposals for APEC, there were concerns about the institutional identity of ASEAN. Roderic Pitty has written:

> While there was general agreement at the Jakarta meeting on the need for increased regional consultation and dialogue, there was also concern to avoid creating a proliferation of unnecessary forums in the region. The Philippines and Thailand later asked Australia to sponsor seminars on regional security, and the Philippines Foreign Secretary, Raul Manglapus, commended the Australian sensitivity to ASEAN concerns. Australian officials nevertheless remained aware that other ASEAN states, particularly Malaysia and Indonesia, remained reluctant to support any proposal that might lead to a new institution in which ASEAN might be 'merged into a larger Asia Pacific framework'.[90]

In the next few months, Australia's ideas attracted criticism from both outside and inside Southeast Asia.[91] The US was concerned that further multilateral security dialogue would give legitimacy to Soviet involvement and inhibit long-standing US relationships and interests. The US Deputy Assistant Secretary of State for East Asian and Pacific Affairs, Richard Solomon, said in October 1990 that it 'was difficult to see how a Helsinki type institution would be an appropriate forum for enhancing security or promoting conflict-resolution'. The US position, he said, was based on 'forward deployed forces, overseas bases, and bilateral security arrangements'.[92] US views were reinforced in November 1990 in a private letter by Secretary of State Baker to Evans in which Baker argued that there was no need for change and that traditional bilateral arrangements and agreements were more than adequate to meet regional security needs.[93]

Several ASEAN leaders criticised the relevance of a European-style CSCA. Singapore's Foreign Minister Wong Kan Seng was quoted in an article in October 1990 as saying that 'there has to be common ground before security issues can be discussed' and this was not the case

---

89   Gareth Evans, 'Statement by Senator Gareth Evans, the Minister for Foreign Affairs and Trade, to the 6+6 Session, 23rd ASEAN Post-Ministerial Conference, Jakarta', news release, 27 July 1990.

90   Pitty, 'Strategic Engagement', p. 63.

91   Acharya, *The Making of Southeast Asia*, pp. 232–3.

92   Quoted in Ball and Kerr, *Presumptive Engagement*, p. 20.

93   'Security, in Letter and Spirit', *Australian Financial Review*, 2 May 1991.

in Asia where 'countries are so culturally, ethnically, and politically diverse, that perceptions have to be harmonised'. Indonesia's Foreign Minister Alatas stated that 'we have to be careful not to think that certain things that work in one region ought to be transferred to another'.[94]

The strength of the reactions from ASEAN and the US caused Australia to pull back from some of its advocacy on the regional security issue. In relation to ASEAN perceptions at the time, Dobell observed:

> Evans's effort to promote a new security structure in Asia came at the same time that Australia was throwing itself into an intense round of diplomatic activity to help create a United Nations solution for the Cambodia conflict, and only six months after the first meeting of APEC in Canberra. There were sarcastic remarks from ASEAN bureaucrats about a sense of 'initiative fatigue' over Australia's activism; if there was to be a new regional mechanism, it would be run by ASEAN. Australia and Japan had led the way on economic institution-building with APEC; Australia would not repeat the formula on security.[95]

During an informal meeting with ASEAN representatives in Canberra in April 1991, Australian officials discussed the Australian Government's security policies. Costello (a deputy secretary of DFAT) said that it was 'tremendously useful' that the 1990 ASEAN PMC had 'begun the process of addressing' regional security issues; he hoped that this would continue at the next PMC in 1991 but noted that Australia 'would not be putting new proposals on the table'. The representatives from Singapore and Indonesia both said that the ASEAN PMC was 'the right forum' to explore 'ways of taking Australia's ideas on future regional security arrangements further'.[96]

More positive signs were evident at a regional security seminar held in Manila in June 1991. Woolcott noted at the time that 'it appeared to demonstrate that a consensus is emerging among countries in the region – including Japan and the United States – that there is a need for the development of dialogues, multilateral and otherwise, on regional security issues' based on the ASEAN PMC.[97]

---

94 'ASEAN Wary of Pacific Security Plan', *The Australian*, 8 October 1990.
95 Dobell, *Australia Finds Home*, pp. 186–7.
96 Pitty, 'Strategic Engagement', p. 66.
97 Ibid.

At the next ASEAN PMC (in July 1991) it was in fact a proposal from Japan that was the focus for debate. Japan's Foreign Minister Nakayama Taro proposed the establishment of a mutual reassurance dialogue, in a move that was seen as stemming particularly from Japan's need to try to ameliorate regional sentiments about a plan for Japan to participate in UN peacekeeping operations. The Japanese proposal had been introduced quickly and it was not accepted by either ASEAN or the US.[98]

However, as Acharya has observed, ASEAN had strong motivations to be pro-active on security issues:

> ASEAN could not ignore the growing calls for multilateralism. Lest the outside powers seize the initiative, ASEAN had to come up with an 'indigenous' framework that would enable it to play a central role in developing any multilateral framework for regional security. In this sense, ASEAN was given an opportunity to project its subregional experience in security cooperation onto a larger regional arena and thereby enhance its relevance and role as a regional institution in the post-Cold War era.[99]

At the next major ASEAN meeting, the leaders' summit in January 1992, the ASEAN countries decided formally to add security issues to the PMC. A DFAT ministerial submission at the time described this step as having 'vindicated the efforts Australia has made since December 1989' to encourage formal regional security dialogues. There was a change in the position of the US. Prime Minister Keating had discussed the issue of security dialogue with President Bush on 1 January 1992, when Keating had asked Bush to 'take a more relaxed view of the emerging dialogue' on regional security. By April 1992, it was evident that the US was now fully prepared to accept that security issues would be discussed at the next ASEAN PMC.[100]

A consensus developed on the character of a new forum for security discussions, based on the ASEAN PMC but with a wider membership. This led to the decision by the ASEAN ministerial meeting in Singapore in July 1993 that the first ARF would be convened the next year with the participation of the ASEAN six and the seven ASEAN dialogue

---

98 'ASEAN Opens up on Security', *Canberra Times*, 21 July 1991; Pitty, 'Strategic Engagement', p. 67.
99 Acharya, *The Making of Southeast Asia*, p. 233.
100 Pitty, 'Strategic Engagement', p. 67.

partners – Australia, Canada, the EU, Japan, New Zealand, South Korea and the US – along with China, Russia, Vietnam, Laos and Papua New Guinea.[101]

Australia was keen to promote and advance the new forum. In preparing for the first ARF meeting in Bangkok in July 1994, Australia's main objective was to see the ARF 'firmly established as a regular, inclusive, Asia-Pacific wide security dialogue' that would be a venue for 'substantive discussion of specific security issues' such as tensions on the Korean peninsula.[102] Australia presented a discussion paper in early 1994 on the agenda for the ARF, prepared at the request of Thailand. Indonesia, however, responded that the paper 'provided too comprehensive a range of areas for discussion' in the time available. Australian officials considered that Indonesia was concerned that the ARF might become too institutionalised and that the Indonesian military feared the ARF might act as a watchdog over their activities.[103]

The ARF proceeded to develop in a cautious manner. At the second meeting of the ARF in Brunei in August 1995, it was stated that 'ARF meetings shall be based on prevailing ASEAN norms and practices', with no voting and all decisions 'made by consensus after careful and extensive consultations'. The agenda adopted suggested that the ARF would first focus on confidence-building and then on preventative diplomacy. The task of resolving specific conflicts was postponed, and was regarded as an 'eventual goal' to be addressed only when the reluctance of ASEAN members to consider 'intrusive' mechanisms was overcome.[104]

As with APEC, a significant feature of the development of the ARF was the role of non-governmental and semi-official groups. Research institutes in the ASEAN members were one of the sources of ideas for the process of inauguration and early development of the ARF. These institutes supported some of the activities of the ARF, for example, the meetings of senior officials between the annual formal sessions. In November 1992, the role of non-governmental 'second track' activities was extended with a proposal for the development of the

---

101 'Evans Endorses Defence Forum', *Canberra Times*, 26 July 1993.
102 Pitty, 'Strategic Engagement', p. 69.
103 Ibid.
104 Ibid., p. 70.

Council for Security Cooperation in the Asia Pacific (CSCAP). CSCAP was duly established in Kuala Lumpur in June 1993. It was designed to link-up and focus the research activities of non-governmental bodies devoted to work on security issues in the Asia-Pacific and to be a bridge between the second track and the official dialogues. Australian academic institutions and individuals from the outset played a major role in the CSCAP processes. Ball and Kerr have suggested that CSCAP represented 'a major achievement in the development of multilateralism in the region'.[105]

By 1994, the regional and international discussions about security had resulted in the inauguration of a new dialogue and Australia's interactions with ASEAN had played a substantial role in this process. The new dialogue would be convened by ASEAN and was based on ASEAN's style of consensus decision-making and informality. It included all the major powers with interests in the Asia-Pacific region and it was, in fact, the first regional security dialogue to include all of the major powers, including not only the US and Japan, but also China, India and Russia.[106]

These were important achievements but it would prove difficult to try to advance the ARF beyond the first stage of discussion and promotion of confidence-building. A key issue with the ARF was that while ASEAN's style of consensus-based cooperation was congenial to its major power participants, this style simultaneously limited its potential for activity and influence. Evelyn Goh has observed that:

> The ASEAN style of multilateral institutionalism brought the United States, China, and other major powers to the table because they were reassured that membership in the ARF would be a relatively nondemanding, low-cost, and low-stakes undertaking ... In spite of their rhetorical ascriptions to TAC [Treaty of Amity and Cooperation], the informal character of the ARF assured the United States and China especially that they would not have to be bound by formal agreements; consensual decision-making procedures meant that they could prevent discussion or action on issues against their interest; and the lack of any enforcement mechanism essentially left them with a free hand to pursue unilateral policies when necessary. For instance, Beijing has not felt itself constrained by ARF norms in maritime

---

105 Ball and Kerr, *Presumptive Engagement*, p. 31.
106 Acharya, *The Making of Southeast Asia*, p. 233.

confrontations with the Philippines, Vietnam, and the United States in the South China Sea; and neither China nor the United States adhered to the noncoercive spirit of TAC during the 1996 Taiwan strait crisis.[107]

The limitations of the ARF were to contribute to ongoing interest in avenues for developing further dialogue about regional security, interest that was reflected in the later development of the East Asia Summit after 2005 and Australia's discussion of proposals for an Asia Pacific Community from 2008.

Towards an 'Asia Pacific Community'?

By 1995, Evans considered the advent of both APEC and the ARF could be seen in parallel as dialogues that could provide the basis for longer-term cooperation in the Asia-Pacific. In October 1994, Evans said that the APEC leaders' summit in Bogor and the first meeting of the ARF had put in place 'the key elements of a new regional architecture: two institutional structures, dealing with economic relations and security issues, within the overarching concept of an Asia-Pacific community'.[108] In the previous year, Evans had suggested that there was a sense of 'community' emerging in the Asia-Pacific in which:

> nations that increasingly see and do things the same way – economically, politically and socially – are nations which should find it easier to talk together, to build processes and institutions together and advance common interests or resolve common problems. I believe that the gradual emergence of a sense of community in our own region … is a striking and exciting development, and one we should nourish.[109]

It was also evident, however, that there continued to be contending notions of what was the most appropriate definition of 'region' for the pursuit of cooperation and community-building.[110] In his comments, Evans had referred to the Asia-Pacific as 'our own region', but there was ongoing interest in East Asia in developing cooperation that could be based on a different and more specifically 'Asian' conception of

107 Evelyn Goh, 'Southeast Asia's Evolving Security Relations and Strategies', in Saadia M. Pekkanen, John Ravenhill and Rosemary Foot, eds, *The Oxford Handbook of the International Relations of Asia*, Oxford: Oxford University Press, 2014, p. 475.
108 Quoted in Keith Scott, *Gareth Evans*, St Leonards, NSW: Allen & Unwin, 1999, p. 287.
109 Quoted in ibid., p. 288.
110 See Anthony Milner's discussion of these issues in Anthony Milner, 'Regionalism in Asia', in Juliet Love, ed., *The Far East and Australasia 2014*, 45th edn, Abingdon: Routledge, 2013.

'region'. In the case of the ARF, ASEAN had accepted and assumed leadership of a group that involved both East Asian states and a wider participation including Australia, India and the US as founding members. However, in the realm of economic cooperation, as previously noted, while Australia's favoured vehicle for cooperation was APEC, Dr Mahathir had proposed in 1990 an alternative cooperation model, the EAEG, based on an East Asian identity that would by design restrict its participants to those in East Asia. While the EAEG had not received strong acceptance and had been pursued in a more mild form as a caucus under the aegis of APEC, the idea of 'East Asia-focused' cooperation had strong attractions for many in East Asia. The basis for such a group was reasserted when a number of countries in East Asia moved to establish a dialogue with Europe, as the Asia–Europe Meeting (ASEM), which met for the first time in March 1996. A significant feature of the development of ASEM was that the 'Asian' side comprised countries that Dr Mahathir had envisaged as being the basis for an EAEG; that is, the ASEAN members along with China, Japan and South Korea. In the lead-up to the first ASEM (held in March 1996), Malaysia had made it clear that Australia would not be invited to participate on the Asian side.[111]

Australia's exclusion from the emerging ASEM was discussed widely at the time. One senior Australian analyst, Stephen Fitzgerald, described the exclusion as a matter of the 'utmost gravity', not necessarily because the meeting itself was highly important, but because ASEM was shorthand 'for a closed coalition of East Asian states which began in 1996 and which excluded Australia'.[112] ASEM did not evolve into a gathering of high regional or international importance.[113] Nonetheless, the advent of ASEM had emphasised that the concept of Asia-Pacific as a basis for cooperation and possible community building would be challenged by countries and leaders who considered the conception of East Asia as a more relevant and desirable cooperation focus. The East Asia cooperation model was to be reasserted more strongly after 1997 with the advent of the 'ASEAN Plus Three' grouping of ASEAN along

111 David Goldsworthy, 'Regional Relations', in Peter Edwards and David Goldsworthy, eds, *Facing North: A Century of Australian Engagement with Asia, Volume 2: 1970s to 2000*, Carlton, Vic.: Melbourne University Press, 2003, p. 138.

112 Quoted in Scott, *Gareth Evans*, p. 294.

113 For an assessment of ASEM see Julie Gilson, 'The Asia–Europe Meeting (ASEM)', in Mark Beeson and Richard Stubbs, eds, *Routledge Handbook of Asian Regionalism*, London: Routledge, 2012.

with China, Japan and South Korea. It was evident that Australia would need to continue to contend with multiple and competing models of wider cooperation and that this would be an important context for Australia's relations with ASEAN.

'Partnership' with Southeast Asia and ASEAN

The early 1990s was an important period in ASEAN's evolution. ASEAN had played a substantial role in shaping the development of APEC and it had assumed responsibility for convening a new security dialogue in the ARF. ASEAN at the same time was moving to widen and deepen its own cooperation. As has been noted, the end of the conflict over Cambodia opened the way for ASEAN to embrace the whole of Southeast Asia. A crucial step was taken when Vietnam joined as a full member in July 1995, which both ended the divide between ASEAN and the region's second largest country, and paved the way for the expansion of the Association to include Laos, Myanmar and Cambodia.

The ASEAN members also felt the need to deepen economic cooperation among their own members. It was noted earlier that one of the factors that had led regional states to develop interest in economic cooperation in the Asia-Pacific was progress being made towards greater integration in other regions. The EU was in the process of being established through development of the Maastricht Treaty; the North American Free Trade Agreement was being negotiated (leading to its inauguration in December 1992); and South American states had joined together in MERCOSUR (Southern Common Market). China and India were developing massive domestic markets. In this environment, ASEAN's members saw a need to promote their own integration; as Rodolfo Severino has written, ASEAN members considered that their 'ability to compete for markets and investments would be severely hampered unless they achieved the efficiencies of a large, integrated market'.[114] ASEAN therefore introduced a new phase of economic cooperation by agreeing to develop an ASEAN Free Trade Area,

---

114 Rodolfo C. Severino, *Southeast Asia in Search of an ASEAN Community: Insights from the Former ASEAN Secretary-General*, Singapore: Institute of Southeast Asian Studies, 2006, p. 223.

announced in 1992, with the aspiration of reducing trade barriers within the Association in parallel with the wider efforts being sought through APEC.[115]

Australia welcomed ASEAN's expansion. The rapprochement between ASEAN and Vietnam, which saw Vietnam accede to ASEAN's TAC in 1992 and then gain full membership in 1995, was in line with the interests expressed by successive Australian governments since Gough Whitlam's period. Australia also welcomed ASEAN's acceptance of other Southeast Asian countries into the Association. In the case of Myanmar, Australia hoped that the prospect of ASEAN membership might provide some potential for ASEAN to encourage political liberalisation in the wake of the traumatic period after 1988 when the dominant military had suppressed dissent and refused to accept the results of the 1990 elections, which had been won by the National League for Democracy, led by Aung San Suu Kyi.[116] Australia pursued efforts to encourage change in Myanmar but without evident impact.[117] Evans commented later that:

> [U]p to 97 my strategy was really for ASEAN to use the leverage of membership to actually get some change to not let … [Myanmar] in without there having been fundamental institutional change or at least the realistic promise of it and when that particular bit of leverage was gone … when they nonetheless decided to let them in that was really the end of the road but that was after the end of my period as foreign minister … So that was my strategy during that period; a failed strategy I have to say but it was I think worth pursuing.[118]

ASEAN pressed ahead with plans to incorporate Myanmar and it joined the Association in 1997.[119]

In this phase of change and development in ASEAN in the early 1990s, there was considerable optimism in Australia about the ASEAN relationship. Writing about this period, Nancy Viviani observed:

---

115 Ibid., pp. 222–31.

116 Lindsay Murdoch, 'Australia's Hard Line on Burma Softens', *The Age*, 11 October 1993. On ASEAN's approaches to Myanmar, see Christopher Roberts, *ASEAN's Myanmar Crisis: Challenges to the Pursuit of a Security Community*, Singapore: Institute of Southeast Asian Studies, 2010.

117 Ian McPhedran, 'ASEAN Asked to Press Burma Harder Towards Democracy', *Canberra Times*, 4 May 1994; Cameron Stewart, 'Evans to Urge Tougher ASEAN Stand on Burma', *The Australian*, 25 July 1995.

118 Evans, interview with the author, July 2014.

119 Mark Baker, 'ASEAN Leaders Resist Push to Isolate Burma', *The Age*, 16 December 1995.

> [T]he construction of the ARF, and the Bogor outcome of APEC, showed an expanded ASEAN, now a truly Southeast Asian community, at its most influential. It also showed a special place for Australia – as constructive co-operator with Southeast Asia, and as sometimes in front with the ideas, reaping both the rewards and costs of such policy innovation.[120]

By 1995, Evans argued that relations with ASEAN had moved into a phase of 'partnership and integration' and said that there was greater reciprocity and commitment between the parties. 'Partnership and integration implies a degree of mutual dependency, a degree of reliance upon each other, and a high degree of trust. I would suggest that we are now moving into that phase.'[121]

Alongside this optimism, major bilateral relations with ASEAN members continued to exhibit some variation in cooperation and degree of concord. As has been noted, the political relationship with Malaysia in the early 1990s was affected by issues including Dr Mahathir's reservations about the direction of APEC and his irritation over Keating's use of the term 'recalcitrant' in 1993. Dr Mahathir continued to be unenthusiastic about Australia's credentials for regional involvement (see Chapter 4).[122]

Relations with Indonesia during the Hawke and Keating period underwent considerable change and development. The ongoing potential for misunderstanding and distrust was illustrated in 1986 when a dispute developed over a newspaper article in Australia on the wealth of the Suharto family.[123] There was also ongoing concern in Australia at the situation in East Timor, which was heightened in December 1991 when Indonesian troops attacked mourners at the Santa Cruz cemetery in Dili and between 200 and 500 people were shot or disappeared. There was a strongly critical reaction within Australia

---

120 Nancy Viviani, 'Australia and Southeast Asia', in James Cotton and John Ravenhill, eds, *Seeking Asian Engagement: Australia in World Affairs, 1991–95*, Melbourne: Oxford University Press, 1997, pp. 159–60.

121 Dobell, *Australia Finds Home*, pp. 80–1.

122 Barry Wain, *Malaysian Maverick: Mahathir Mohamad in Turbulent Times*, 2nd edn, Basingstoke: Palgrave Macmillan, 2012, pp. 235–41.

123 David Jenkins, 'After Marcos, Now for the Suharto Billions', *Sydney Morning Herald*, 10 April 1986.

and additional bilateral strains resulted.[124] Alongside these areas of tension, the extensive interactions between Evans and Alatas from the late 1980s on Cambodia, APEC and the ARF, brought an added degree of cooperation and communication to the relationship.

From 1992, Prime Minister Keating gave added emphasis to the importance of Indonesia. A notable point was when the two countries concluded the secretly negotiated Australia–Indonesia Agreement on Maintaining Security in 1995. It committed both parties to consult regularly on matters affecting their common security and 'to develop such cooperation as would benefit their own security and that of the region', to consult each other 'in the case of adverse challenges to either party or to their common security interests and, if appropriate, consider measures which might be taken individually or jointly', and 'to promote … mutually beneficial cooperation in the security field'. The agreement was the first bilateral security arrangement between Australia and any Southeast Asian country and Indonesia's first bilateral security agreement with any country. While the secrecy of the negotiation process was contentious, the agreement itself was endorsed widely in Australia, including by the Opposition.[125] The utility of the agreement, however, depended on the maintenance of cooperative relations and these came under serious strain in the next four years over East Timor (see Chapter 4).

Other developments in bilateral relations bolstered Australia's interactions with ASEAN. While multilateral security dialogue through the ARF proceeded at a cautious pace, there was a rapid expansion of bilateral military contacts. By the mid-1990s, the Australian Defence Forces were involved in more joint exercises with ASEAN member forces than they were with the US, while most of the ASEAN states involved (notably Indonesia, Singapore and Malaysia) were 'more engaged with Australia with respect to cooperative defence activities than with any other country, including their own ASEAN neighbours'.[126]

---

124 Jamie Mackie, 'Australia and Indonesia: Current Problems, Future Prospects', Lowy Institute Paper 19, Sydney: Lowy Institute for International Policy, 2007, p. 58; James Cotton, *East Timor, Australia and Regional Order: Intervention and its Aftermath in Southeast Asia*, London: Routledge, 2004, p. 53.
125 Viviani, 'Australia and Southeast Asia', pp. 159–60; see also Mackie, 'Australia and Indonesia', pp. 55–7.
126 Ball and Kerr, *Presumptive Engagement*, p. 64.

There were also efforts in the early 1990s to consider and explore further developments in Australia's multilateral ASEAN linkages. At the beginning of the 1990s, when Australia was interested in enhancing security relations and dialogue with ASEAN on both a multilateral and bilateral basis, some consideration was given in Canberra to whether Australia should sign ASEAN's TAC. Evans later recalled that 'I wanted to move in that direction … but we didn't succeed in pulling it off'.[127] In January 1991, a draft ministerial submission said that 'accession to the treaty by Australia would have considerable symbolic value'. However, the ASEAN members decided at their January 1992 leaders' summit in Bangkok that other states would not at that stage be invited to accede to the treaty so for Australia this matter lapsed for the next decade.[128]

A further area of potential cooperation was opened for discussion in 1993. In November 1993, Thailand's Deputy Prime Minister Supachai Panitchpakdi suggested that Australia could be invited to join the nascent ASEAN Free Trade Area and even the East Asia Economic Caucus.[129] The Australian Government was interested in the idea of closer economic relations with ASEAN and in 1994 suggested that there could be a linkage between the ASEAN Free Trade Area and the Australia–New Zealand Closer Economic Relations agreement.[130] The idea did not progress beyond the discussion stage, partly because Malaysia was opposed.[131] However, the concept continued to be considered and was later taken up in detail by both sides under John Howard's government after Dr Mahathir's departure from office in Malaysia (see Chapter 4).

At a time when Australia and ASEAN were moving closer, there was even some discussion about Australia's possible membership in the Association. In February 1994, President Fidel Ramos of the Philippines, in an interview with an Australian journalist, spoke about the possibility in the long-term of Australia joining ASEAN, and said,

127 Evans, interview with the author, July 2014.
128 Pitty, 'Strategic Engagement', p. 75.
129 Greg Earl, 'Asian Trade Club Opens Up to Aust', *Australian Financial Review*, 26 November 1993.
130 Peter Cole-Adams, 'PM Looks to Join ASEAN Trade Bloc', *Canberra Times*, 8 April 1994.
131 Greg Earl, 'Malaysian Rebuff Fails to Dent Evans' Confidence', *Australian Financial Review*, 26 July 1994.

'[t]hat kind of thing could be encouraged'.[132] In January 1996 the issue of Australia's institutional relationship with ASEAN was raised again, by Singapore's Prime Minister Goh Chok Tong. At the time of a visit by Keating to Singapore and Malaysia, Goh said in an interview that '[w]e see Australia playing an important role [in ASEAN] and certainly we would like to encourage Australia to do so'. Goh continued:

> If you asked me now is it possible that Australia and New Zealand may one day join ASEAN, I would say that both countries are small enough to be considered as possible members one of these days ... But it depends again on the coinciding of interests, if there is more trade between Australia and New Zealand with ASEAN countries, more investments, more to-ing and fro-ing culturally, people to people, then it is an idea which is thinkable ... to be put into the debate.[133]

Goh soon downplayed these comments. At a subsequent press conference he said that the concept of Australian membership was an 'over the horizon' idea that had not been raised or discussed formally.[134] Keating's visit was followed shortly afterwards by the Australian elections on March 1996 in which a new government led by Howard was elected with a large majority. Prime Minister Goh's comments were, however, an interesting indication that Australia after two decades of cooperation could be considered, albeit in a very speculative manner, as a possible member of ASEAN.

Conclusion

The period of the Hawke and Keating governments from 1983 to 1996 was one of intense interaction between Australia and ASEAN. A key factor in the context for these interactions was the profound changes to the international environment among the major powers from the late 1980s as the patterns of Cold War tensions altered sharply, even if they did not disappear altogether in East Asia. These changes opened the way for a settlement of the Cambodian conflict. In this environment, Australia was able to extend the interest of the Whitlam and Fraser

---

132 Eric Ellis, 'Ramos to Australia: Join Us in ASEAN', *Australian Financial Review*, 23 February 1994.

133 Eric Ellis, 'Goh: Australian Role in ASEAN', *Australian Financial Review*, 16 January 1996.

134 Goh Chok Tong and Paul Keating, 'Joint Press Conference at the Shangri La Hotel, Singapore, 17 January 1996: Transcript'.

governments in encouraging détente between ASEAN and the states of Indochina. The diplomatic cooperation between Australia and ASEAN, and especially with Indonesia, was a highpoint in Australia's post-Second World War foreign relations and contributed both to a Cambodian settlement and to wider cooperation in Southeast Asia.

The decline of Cold War confrontation also stimulated new regional thinking. Australian cooperation with ASEAN played an important role in the creation of APEC and the ARF. In these diplomatic interactions several elements were notable. ASEAN was highly concerned about its identity and institutional distinctiveness and was sensitive about the potential for additional wider groupings to dilute or weaken this. Australia's interest in contributing ideas had to accommodate ASEAN's interests. A key factor in Australia's capacity to pursue cooperation with ASEAN overall continued to be its relations with Indonesia, a relationship that was vital to the Cambodian peace process and to the development of APEC and the ARF. The diplomatic interactions in this period carried cooperation between Australia and ASEAN to a new level and made this multilateral relationship one of the most important in Australia's foreign relations.

4

The Asian financial crisis, multilateral relations and the East Asia Summit (1996–2007)

The Australian elections on 2 March 1996 ushered in a period in which the new John Howard Government emphasised promoting bilateral relationships and appeared for some time to reduce emphasis on multilateral cooperation, including with the Association of Southeast Asian Nations (ASEAN). The diplomatic climate was also influenced greatly by the Asian financial crisis and by the traumatic transition of East Timor from Indonesian rule to independence. By the end of the 1990s, Australia's multilateral relations with ASEAN appeared to have cooled substantially. The latter period of the Howard Government, however, brought a renewal of cooperation with ASEAN after 2001. This chapter discusses these issues by looking in turn at the Howard Government's approach to Asia, the challenges posed to Southeast Asia and ASEAN by the Asian financial crisis, East Timor's transition to independence, the hiatus in Australia–ASEAN relations in the late 1990s, and developments after 2001 that included two major advances: a trade agreement between ASEAN and Australia and New Zealand, and ASEAN's invitation to Australia to accede to the Treaty of Amity and Cooperation (TAC) and to join the new East Asia Summit.

The Howard Government and Asia

The Howard Government came to office committed to what it saw as a pragmatic pursuit of the national interest.[1] In a speech in August 2001, Howard characterised his approach as one of 'positive realism' that involved 'a realistic appreciation of the differences between ... societies and cultures, but positively focused on ... shared interests and on a mutual respect'.[2] Howard emphasised that nations should respect each other's differences: he said in April 2003 that 'good neighbours recognise each other's values and beliefs'.[3]

The Howard Government reaffirmed a strong commitment to Australia's relationship with the US. The relationship deepened further after the terrorist attacks in the US on 11 September 2001. In the immediate aftermath of these attacks, Howard (who was visiting the US at the time) offered Australia's full support to the US and on 14 September 2001 the Australian Government formally invoked the ANZUS (Australia, New Zealand, United States) Treaty for the first time. Australia went on to support and contribute to the US-led military involvements in Afghanistan and in Iraq.[4]

In relations with Asia, the government placed special emphasis on China and Japan. After initial tensions in 1996 over China's confrontation of Taiwan, Australia's China relationship expanded greatly, including through enhanced economic interactions and new areas of regular dialogue.[5] The Howard Government pursued a closer relationship with Japan and inaugurated a new trilateral dialogue with the US and Japan.[6]

1   Stewart Firth, *Australia in International Politics: An Introduction to Australian Foreign Policy*, 3rd edn, Crows Nest, NSW: Allen & Unwin, 2011, p. 53.
2   Quoted in Allan Gyngell and Michael Wesley, *Making Australian Foreign Policy*, 2nd edn, Cambridge: Cambridge University Press, 2007, p. 276.
3   Quoted in ibid., p. 277.
4   Paul Kelly, 'Howard's Decade: An Australian Foreign Policy Reappraisal', Lowy Institute Paper 15, Sydney: Lowy Institute for International Policy, 2006, pp. 47–63.
5   Gyngell and Wesley, *Making Australian Foreign Policy*, p. 313.
6   Rowan Callick, 'Beijing Attacks Curbs on N Korea', *The Australian*, 21 September 2006.

The Howard Government came to office with a commitment to engagement with Southeast Asia and to ASEAN that was asserted by the Minister for Foreign Affairs, Alexander Downer, in some of his early statements in office. On 11 April 1996, Downer said that '[t]here is a national consensus on the importance of Australia's engagement with Asia and there is a strong recognition that no side of Australian politics owns the Asia vision'. Downer declared that the government would base its Asian engagement on three approaches: regional economic dialogue through the Asia-Pacific Economic Cooperation (APEC) grouping, regional security cooperation within the ASEAN Regional Forum (ARF), and strengthening the focus on bilateral relations. On the future of the regional 'architecture', Downer said that APEC and ASEAN were 'central to building the trust' and 'sense of shared interests' that were the basis of the region's security and economic future.[7] In May 1996, Downer re-emphasised the government's commitment to the ARF, which he said 'should continue to develop regional dialogue on issues such as defence planning and acquisition'.[8]

While endorsing the role of regional institutions, the government emphasised the primacy of bilateral relationships. There was also commensurately less emphasis on 'big picture' concepts of multilateral and regional cooperation. The overall approach was affirmed in the government's foreign policy White Paper released in 1997:

> Preparing for the future is not a matter of grand constructs. It is about the hard headed pursuit of the interests which lie at the core of foreign and trade policy: the security of the nation and the jobs and standard of living of the Australian people. In all that it does in the field of foreign and trade policy, the Government will apply the basic test of national interest.[9]

---

7   Don Greenlees, 'Downer Assigns Asia Top Priority', *The Australian*, 12 April 1996.
8   Michael Dwyer, 'Downer Calls for ARF to Arbitrate Regional Disputes', *Australian Financial Review*, 3 May 1996.
9   Australian Department of Foreign Affairs and Trade, *In the National Interest: Australia's Foreign and Trade Policy White Paper*, Canberra: Commonwealth of Australia, 1997, p. iii.

ASEAN, the Asian financial crisis and East Timor's independence: 1996–2001

From mid-1997, ASEAN encountered several issues that challenged it as an institution and that had significant implications for Australia.

ASEAN under challenge: Enlargement issues and the Asian financial crisis

ASEAN from the mid-1990s had been pursuing a policy of incorporating, as members, the other states considered widely to be part of 'Southeast Asia': Cambodia, Laos, Myanmar (Burma) and Vietnam. Vietnam entered the Association in 1995 and Laos and Myanmar followed in 1997. While the government (like the preceding Labor administration) had reservations about internal conditions in Myanmar, Australia supported its membership in ASEAN. In overall terms, Downer considered that there was a strong case for Myanmar's entry: 'it was driven by Dr Mahathir Mohamad and President Suharto who both thought that it made more sense to get Burma into ASEAN than leave it in the Chinese orbit ... I thought that was a pretty damn good argument'.[10]

It had been envisaged that Cambodia would also join in 1997. However, on 5–6 July 1997, this timetable was derailed by the outbreak of conflict between the two parties in the Coalition Government (the National United Front for an Independent, Neutral, Peaceful and Cooperative Cambodia (FUNCINPEC) led by Prince Norodom Ranariddh and the Cambodian People's Party led by Hun Sen). After a period of extensive tensions between the parties, the Cambodian People's Party forces led a coup on 5 July 1997 against its partner in the coalition administration, FUNCINPEC, which resulted in over 40 deaths and hundreds of arrests: Ranariddh and a number of senior figures in his party had left the country a few days earlier. Subsequently there were some executions, particularly by the Cambodian People's Party forces of FUNCINPEC members. These events left Hun Sen as the dominant leader in Cambodia.[11] Australia condemned the violence and expressed concern

---

10   Alexander Downer, interview with the author, Adelaide, 15 April 2014.
11   MacAlister Brown and Joseph J. Zasloff, *Cambodia Confounds the Peacemakers, 1979–1998*, Ithaca, NY: Cornell University Press, 1998, pp. 259–68.

at the overthrow of Ranariddh by military means. The government pursued its approach in association with ASEAN, which Downer saw as 'the first and most important point of influence' in relation to Hun Sen.[12] In response to these events, the ASEAN foreign ministers decided on 10 July to delay Cambodia's entry.[13] The developments in Cambodia were a setback for ASEAN's desired image of a group able to sponsor peaceful cooperation, but the enlargement process continued: Cambodia ultimately was admitted to ASEAN in 1999.

A further set of issues confronted ASEAN members, and other states in East Asia, from mid-1997. In early July 1997, speculative pressure forced a devaluation of the Thai currency and began to inflict major pressure on the Thai economy. By early September, the Malaysian ringgit had fallen to its lowest level of value vis-à-vis the US dollar since 1971, and in a period of six months the Thai stock market had lost 38 per cent of its value, while Malaysia's lost 44 per cent, the Philippines' lost 35 per cent, Indonesia's lost 17 per cent and Japan's lost 4 per cent. By the end of the year, severe damage had been sustained by both the Indonesian and South Korean economies; in 1998, Indonesia's economy declined by about 14 per cent of gross domestic product. A number of ASEAN members experienced a rise in unemployment, which increased pressures on incumbent governments.[14]

The crisis had a substantial political impact in the ASEAN region. Thailand and the Philippines saw governments replaced through elections. The political impact was greatest in Indonesia, where ASEAN's senior statesman President Suharto was forced to resign in May 1998, amid substantial social unrest and political protest. The departure of Suharto was followed by profound changes in Indonesia's political processes, which included the advent of democratic elections and a sharp change in policy towards East Timor in 1999.

---

12   Moreen Dee and Frank Frost, 'Indochina', in Peter Edwards and David Goldsworthy, eds, *Facing North: A Century of Australian Engagement with Asia, Volume 2: 1970s to 2000*, Carlton, Vic.: Melbourne University Press, 2003, p. 212.

13   Mark Baker, 'Hun Sen Defies His Critics', *The Age*, 11 July 1997.

14   Michael Wesley, 'Australia and the Asian Economic Crisis', in James Cotton and John Ravenhill, eds, *The National Interest in a Global Era: Australia in World Affairs 1996–2000*, South Melbourne: Oxford University Press, 2001, pp. 302–3. See also Andrew MacIntyre, T. J. Pempel and John Ravenhill, eds, *Crisis as Catalyst: Asia's Dynamic Political Economy*, Ithaca, NY: Cornell University Press, 2008.

The financial crisis abruptly interrupted the development of the ASEAN economies and had an adverse impact on the image of economic progress and stable development in ASEAN members and in East Asia more widely. Investor confidence declined and funds were withdrawn from many economies.[15] ASEAN's image in this period was also affected adversely by the emergence of major environmental problems arising from annual patterns of burning of large areas of forest and agricultural lands particularly in Indonesia, which produced a 'haze' that caused major health and pollution problems for neighbouring states including Malaysia and Singapore. ASEAN discussed the issue but was not able to pursue cooperation that could alleviate the problem.[16] ASEAN's challenges in this period prompted some internal debate on whether the Association needed to revise its approach to cooperation and modify the doctrine of non-interference in internal affairs to acknowledge the fact that developments within member states could affect the interests of others, as the haze had illustrated. Despite advocacy by Thailand and the Philippines, ASEAN did not adopt a major change in approach, but the debate highlighted the climate of uncertainty in ASEAN that had been triggered by the financial crisis.[17]

Australia, ASEAN and the financial crisis

The impact of the Asian financial crisis was all the more sharp because the setbacks were largely unexpected. In Australia, the Howard Government's foreign policy White Paper (which had been prepared before the onset of the economic crisis and was released in August 1997) had assumed continuing growth in East Asia. The paper said that 'the Government's judgement is that economic growth in industrialising East Asia will continue at relatively high levels over the next fifteen years', and that 'the countries of East Asia will become even more important to Australia as trade and investment partners,

---

15   Wesley, 'Australia and the Asian Economic Crisis', pp. 302–3.

16   Simon S. C. Tay, 'Blowing Smoke: Regional Cooperation, Indonesian Democracy, and the Haze', in Donald K. Emmerson, ed., *Hard Choices: Security, Democracy, and Regionalism in Southeast Asia*, Stanford, CA: Walter H. Shorenstein Asia-Pacific Research Center Books, 2008.

17   Christopher B. Roberts, *ASEAN Regionalism: Cooperation, Values and Institutionalization*, Abingdon: Routledge, 2012, pp. 102–9.

and in security terms'.[18] This was a reasonable long-term projection, but in the short term many regional economies had major problems and the situation was of substantial concern to Australia.

Australia gave significant support to efforts to alleviate the crisis. By February 1998, Downer noted that Australia was contributing over A$4 billion to the packages of assistance being provided by the International Monetary Fund (IMF) to Indonesia, Thailand and South Korea. He observed that apart from Japan, Australia was the only country to be involved in all three packages. Downer had commented earlier (in November 1997) on the positive impact of Australia's assistance when he said that 'by proving we are a partner and a neighbour for the long haul', Australia's image had changed decisively 'from something close to regional mendicant to a regional mate'.[19] Another element in Australia's response was support to Indonesia by making representations to the Bill Clinton administration to encourage the US to support more sympathetic and favourable treatment for Indonesia from the IMF, whose terms of assistance were seen as harsh and demanding.[20]

The Asian financial crisis had a significant influence on the Howard Government's approach to relations with Asia and its appraisal of Australia's role. Australia's economic performance during the period of the crisis brought a sense of increased assurance. Australia's economy continued to grow despite the adverse developments in East Asia. This was striking validation of Australia's extensive economic reform since the 1980s and the value in Australia's wide-ranging international economic linkages.[21]

These perceptions were reflected in statements by the Howard Government that expressed confidence that Australia after the financial crisis was more accepted and influential. Downer said in July 1999 that 'our advice has carried particular weight for two reasons: because it comes from a country that has prospered when others have been

18   Australian Department of Foreign Affairs and Trade, *In the National Interest: Australia's Foreign and Trade Policy White Paper*, Canberra: Commonwealth of Australia, 1997, p. v.
19   Roderic Pitty, 'Regional Economic Co-operation', in Peter Edwards and David Goldsworthy, eds, *Facing North: A Century of Australian Engagement with Asia, Volume 2: 1970s to 2000*, Carlton, Vic.: Melbourne University Press, 2003, p. 42.
20   Paul Kelly, *The March of Patriots: The Struggle for Modern Australia*, Carlton, Vic.: Melbourne University Press, 2009, pp. 460–78.
21   Ibid.

doing it tough, and because we have shown that we are prepared to take our own advice. It has been a case of "do as we say, and do as we do"'. Prime Minister Howard noted in September 1998 that 'Australia is more respected in Asia now than it was five years ago because we've done well and we've been able to help ... Australia is relatively speaking stronger now and has got more influence than it had before'. Downer argued that Australia's image had changed in the wake of the crisis. He argued in July 1998 that '[w]e have ceased being the region's "demandeur", badgering our neighbours for attention and recognition. Australia is now a genuinely close partner and regional friend, a country that can be relied on in good times and bad'.[22]

These responses were understandable in relation to Australia's comparative economic performance and substantial assistance to neighbouring states. However some analysts saw complexity in Australia's response to the financial crisis as conveyed in the messages presented to the domestic audience and to Southeast and East Asia. The assertions of confidence in Australia's own capacities and success could have negative aspects. Anthony Milner commented that:

> Ministers were catering to the needs of what Howard called 'the Australian psyche' when they began to speak of Australia as 'the strong man of Asia' ... In doing so, however, they helped to promote the type of swagger that the government's own White Paper had warned against: the White Paper had insisted that Australians must be prepared to face the fact that their country would become less not more powerful in regional terms over the coming years. It was a swagger that was also likely to be remembered for many years in the region itself.[23]

The policies pursued by the Australian Government in response to the Asian financial crisis had involved bilateral assistance rather than cooperation with ASEAN as a collectivity. But by providing assistance to key member countries, Australia had underscored the importance of relationships with Southeast Asia. The financial crisis, however, also had some significant influences on patterns of regional cooperation with potential implications for Australia.

---

22 Quoted in Wesley, 'Australia and the Asian Economic Crisis', p. 311.
23 Anthony Milner, 'Balancing "Asia" Against Australian Values', in James Cotton and John Ravenhill, eds, *The National Interest in a Global Era: Australia in World Affairs 1996–2000*, South Melbourne: Oxford University Press, 2001, p. 41.

As noted in Chapter 3, debate had been developing about the desirability of cooperation that could be pursued by East Asian states themselves without the participation of countries not considered to be 'Asian'. These views were reflected in Malaysia's proposal in December 1990 for an 'East Asian Economic Group', a concept that had been pursued as a caucus under the aegis of APEC. The impact of the financial crisis led to renewed interest in 'East Asian-focused' cooperation that could help forestall any future crisis and add greater 'weight' for Asia in dealing with international financial institutions such as the IMF. These views helped create support for a meeting of the ASEAN members along with Japan, China and South Korea in Kuala Lumpur in December 1997 that led to the inauguration of the 'ASEAN Plus Three' forum.[24] Australia had been able to participate as a founding member in the security grouping that ASEAN had sponsored, the ARF, but Australia was not a member of this new group.

The advent of ASEAN Plus Three clearly challenged Australia's view of its Asian role and how best to approach emerging patterns of cooperation involving ASEAN and Northeast Asia. The Howard Government ultimately adopted a cautiously positive approach to the new group.[25] The government's second foreign policy White Paper, released in 2003, stated:

> While the process still has a long way to go before its full significance can be determined, it is reasonable to assume that there will be a benefit to the region and to partners such as Australia in a process which fosters dialogue and co-operation among the countries of East Asia and thereby contributes to stability and harmony … Australia would be pleased to be involved in the ASEAN+3 process. We have registered our interest in joining the grouping if invited at some later stage.[26]

---

24   Richard Stubbs, 'ASEAN Plus Three: Emerging East Asian Regionalism?' *Asian Survey*, 42(3) 2002: 441–8.
25   The issue of how Australia should approach ASEAN Plus Three was discussed by Downer and the members of his foreign affairs council of academic and private sector advisors. Milner considers that the council's views were an important influence on the government's thinking on the issue; Anthony Milner, personal communication, 30 November 2014.
26   Australian Department of Foreign Affairs and Trade, *Advancing the National Interest: Australia's Foreign and Trade Policy White Paper*, Canberra: Commonwealth of Australia, 2003, pp. 84–5.

Although Australia did not gain entry to the ASEAN Plus Three grouping, it was later able to participate in a dialogue that grew out of this grouping, the East Asia Summit (see below).

East Timor's independence

A further significant issue for Australia and Southeast Asia in this period was the process of conflict and change that led to independence for the territory of East Timor.[27] This process can be seen partly as another major outcome of the Asian financial crisis, which had led to the resignation of President Suharto and the potential for new policy avenues for Indonesia and for East Timor.

The status of East Timor had been a focus of strain and tension in Australia–Indonesia relations since 1975. Australia after 1979 under successive governments had maintained *de jure* recognition of Indonesia's incorporation of the territory. When the Howard Government came to office there was no sign that Australian policymakers expected any change to the territory's status: Downer commented in April 1996 in relation to the condition of human rights in East Timor, that the issue was a 'pebble in the shoe' of the Australia–Indonesia relationship and that little would be achieved by making an 'enormous amount of noise'.[28]

In the years after 1975, however, it was clear that Indonesia's incorporation of East Timor had not been accepted by the great majority of the East Timorese people and ongoing conflict in the territory, which had involved the loss of as many as 200,000 lives, had been highlighted again by the Santa Cruz massacre in November 1991 (in which between 200 and 500 people were shot or disappeared).[29] The end of the Suharto regime opened the way for revision of attitudes towards the territory in Australia and the Howard Government altered Australian policies. Howard sent a letter in December 1998 to President B. J. Habibie (Suharto's successor), proposing that Indonesia review its position and consider a transition to autonomy for the territory. When President Habibie announced in January 1999 a change of

---

27   For a comprehensive analysis, see James Cotton, *East Timor, Australia and Regional Order: Intervention and its Aftermath in Southeast Asia*, London: Routledge, 2004.
28   Greenlees, 'Downer Assigns Asia Top Priority'.
29   Cotton, *East Timor*, p. 53.

policy that would review the status of the territory, a process was initiated that led to a ballot on 30 August 1999 on a proposal for a revised status of 'special autonomy' for East Timor within Indonesia.[30] The voters decided by a majority of 78.5 per cent to reject the proposed special autonomy and to separate from Indonesia.[31] The lead-up to the ballot was accompanied by substantial violence, particularly by pro-Indonesian militias, and further serious violence occurred after the ballot. In this circumstance, Australia took a leading role in seeking to facilitate an intervention authorised by the United Nations (UN) and accepted by the government of Indonesia.[32]

In the years after 1975, ASEAN members had not criticised Indonesia's policies in East Timor because of ongoing sensitivities in the region in relation to the principle of non-interference in internal affairs and the members' reluctance to criticise Indonesia, given its central role in ASEAN.[33] In the period up to the 30 August ballot, neither ASEAN nor the ARF – which operated on the basis of consensus in discussion and decision-making – played any major role in deliberating on or attempting to influence the process of change in East Timor.[34] In relation to regional groupings, it was a summit of APEC (in Auckland in September 1999) where a number of bilateral discussions were held on the sidelines of the summit meetings, with Australia playing a leading role, which helped develop a multilateral response to the crisis. James Cotton has observed that '[w]hen confronted by the post-ballot bloodshed and the Indonesian Government's clear inability, or disinclination, to discharge its obligations to the United Nations and to the East Timorese to maintain order, ASEAN as an organisation could find no mechanism through which to influence developments'.[35]

---

30 Ibid., pp. 49–67.
31 The ballot presented two options to voters: 'Do you accept the proposed special autonomy within the unitary state of the Republic of Indonesia?' and 'Do you reject the proposed special autonomy for East Timor, leading to East Timor's separation from Indonesia?' See 'Question of East Timor: Report of the Secretary-General', New York, United Nations, 5 May 1999, in Australian Department of Foreign Affairs and Trade, *East Timor in Transition 1998–2000: An Australian Policy Challenge*, Canberra: Australian Department of Foreign Affairs and Trade, 2001, p. 206.
32 Cotton, *East Timor*.
33 Alan Dupont, 'ASEAN's Response to the East Timor Crisis', *Australian Journal of International Affairs*, 54(2) 2000.
34 Amitav Acharya, *Constructing a Security Community in Southeast Asia: ASEAN and the Problem of Regional Order*, 3rd edn, Abingdon: Routledge, 2014, pp. 152–3.
35 Cotton, *East Timor*, pp. 82–3.

Subsequently, four ASEAN members (Thailand, the Philippines, Malaysia and Singapore) took part on an individual basis in INTERFET (International Force for East Timor), which entered East Timor to promote stabilisation, with Thailand providing the deputy commander for the force. The participation of the four ASEAN members was important to the success of INTERFET; of the total force of 9,900 deployed in late September 1999, about 2,500 were from the four ASEAN members, with Australia providing 5,500 personnel. Alan Dupont has observed that '[w]ithout ASEAN participation Australia would have been dangerously isolated regionally and even more stretched militarily on the ground in East Timor'.[36]

Australia played a very substantial role in INTERFET and provided the commander, Major-General Peter Cosgrove, who became the second Australian military leader in a decade to lead a multinational force to promote security and stabilisation in a UN-authorised operation in Southeast Asia. The Australian-led intervention succeeded in stabilising conditions and helped initiate a process of UN-sponsored assistance that led to East Timor gaining formal independence in May 2002. In the period leading up to the intervention and in the aftermath, Australia's relations with Indonesia experienced severe strain. Indonesia abrogated the Australia–Indonesia Agreement on Maintaining Security that had been negotiated by Paul Keating's government in December 1995.[37] In the longer term, however, the process of independence for East Timor gradually removed an issue that had been a major obstacle and cause of tension in the Australia–Indonesia relationship since the 1970s and this assisted in improving the climate for Australia's ASEAN relations.

Hiatus in ASEAN relations

At the end of the 1990s there were indications of a sense of hiatus in Australia's engagement with ASEAN. Australia had played a substantial role in contributing to efforts to alleviate the effects of the Asian financial crisis but Australia's multilateral relationships with Southeast Asia experienced some setbacks. Several factors contributed to this. Australia's image had been compromised by the

---

36   Dupont, 'ASEAN's Response', p. 166.
37   Jamie Mackie, 'Australia and Indonesia: Current Problems, Future Prospects', Lowy Institute Paper 19, Sydney: Lowy Institute for International Policy, 2007, pp. 59–62.

controversy in Australia over the policies and approaches of Pauline Hanson, a controversial parliamentary candidate who had lost Liberal Party endorsement but had won a seat in Federal Parliament as an independent in the March 1996 elections: she went on to form the One Nation Party. In her inaugural speech in Federal Parliament in September 1996, Hanson had expressed concern at the level of Asian immigration to Australia and her popularity after 1996 was seen as harking back to earlier phases of Australian reservations about engagement with Asia. Although her party held only one seat in the national parliament, extensive media coverage in Australia and Asia gave the impression she represented a major new political force. Prime Minister Howard was perceived as having been slow to react to the rise of Hanson and his response drew some criticism both in Australia and in Southeast Asia.[38]

Further controversy was aroused by comments associated with Howard during the early phase of Australia's involvement in East Timor after the 30 August 1999 ballot. In an article in September 1999 in *The Bulletin* magazine in which he was interviewed by the journalist Fred Brenchley, Howard commented in positive terms about his government's approach to Asian relations.[39] He argued that the former Labor Government's approach towards Asia made Australia look as though 'we were knocking on their door saying "please let us in": instead we were always somebody they would want to have in because of our particular strengths'. In the East Timor intervention, Howard suggested, Australia was playing an 'influential, constructive and decisive role in the affairs of the region'. In the same article, however, Brenchley introduced the term 'deputy' to refer to Australia's position vis-à-vis the United States in its approach to regional involvements.[40] Although Howard himself had not used the word 'deputy' and soon after disavowed it, the notion of Australia as a 'deputy sheriff' to the US gained considerable currency in Southeast Asia and attracted critical comments.[41] Thailand's Deputy Foreign Minister Sukhumbhand Paribatra compared Howard's reported comments unfavourably

---

38 Kelly, *The March of Patriots*, pp. 363–76.
39 Fred Brenchley, 'The Howard Defence Doctrine', *The Bulletin*, 28 September 1999.
40 Ibid.
41 More than a decade later, a study found that the term 'deputy sheriff' was widely cited by analysts and officials in ASEAN members in relation to Australia–US relations; see Anthony Milner and Sally Percival Wood, eds, 'Our Place in the Asian Century: Southeast Asia as "The Third Way"', Melbourne: Asialink, University of Melbourne, 2012, p. 29.

with President Theodore Roosevelt's recommendation to 'talk softly and carry a big stick'. Dr Mahathir labelled Howard's comment as 'unmitigated arrogance. When Australians claim to be Asian, they see only themselves lording it over [Asia].' Malaysia's Foreign Minister Syed Hamid denied that Australia had a leadership role: 'We feel that regional affairs should be handled by the countries of the region. We do not need a supervisor or police inspector or anything of the sort to oversee our activities.'[42]

Comments and reactions by the government also seemed to reflect reservations about the potential for regional institutions and for Australian involvement in them. In a speech in Beijing in April 2000, Downer appeared to place limits on the potential for Australia's regional institutional ties. He suggested that Australia could not expect to take part in the 'cultural' and 'emotional' dimensions of East Asian regionalism and that its role would appropriately be in functional realms:

> If we describe regionalism on the basis of what you might broadly describe as an emotional community of interests, then Australia doesn't have those types of emotional association with the region, and ethnic and cultural associations very obviously ... For us, regionalism is always going to be practical regionalism looking at ways that we can work with our region to secure our own economic and security objectives.[43]

In July 2001, Downer expressed some frustration at the Asian (and ASEAN) way of diplomacy in a speech in Singapore when he said, 'ASEAN has a culture of working around problems rather than confronting them. The limits of this approach have been exposed by the financial crisis, and by the way in which expansion has increased ASEAN's political and economic diversity'.[44]

These comments were perceived at the time as indicating that the government was stepping back from the challenges of institutional engagement in Asia.[45] Milner observed about this period in Australian

42   Quoted in Wesley, 'Australia and the Asian Economic Crisis', p. 316.
43   Paul Kelly, 'One Club We Won't Be Joining', *The Australian*, 26 April 2000.
44   Alexander Downer, 'What Australia Wishes for ASEAN', Speech to the Singapore Institute for International Affairs, Singapore, 23 July 2001.
45   Greg Sheridan, 'Inept Downer a Regional Flop', *The Australian*, 28 April 2000.

foreign relations that many of those Australians who had been deeply committed to developing Asian engagement, including members of the Coalition Government, were anxious:

> They worried about the impact on the region of Australian talk about being the 'strong man' of Asia, and of the widely publicised suggestion that its special security role was that of a US 'Deputy'. They were concerned also that Australians, in gaining a new confidence in their country and its values, were conveying an element of complacency and even belligerence in handling regional sensitivities.[46]

Against this background, it was notable that Australia's long-standing efforts to increase dialogue and cooperation with ASEAN met some setbacks after 2000, on economic and political levels.

From 1993 Australia had sought an association between the Australia–New Zealand Closer Economic Relations (CER) and the ASEAN Free Trade Agreement (AFTA). In October 1999, ASEAN and Australian and New Zealand ministers decided to establish a task force to explore a free trade linkage. ASEAN was willing to consider the proposal although it was known that Malaysia, Indonesia and the Philippines were not as keen on the concept as were Singapore, Thailand and Brunei, and that the Indochina countries were at best non-committal.[47]

At a meeting of ASEAN and the Australian and New Zealand ministers in Chiang Mai in Thailand in early October 2000, the task force recommended the establishment of a free trade area between AFTA and CER as desirable and feasible. However, the Chiang Mai meeting decided against pursuing any direct linkage between the two trade arrangements. Instead, the ministers decided to deflect the proposal by asking senior officials to study the scope for a 'closer economic partnership' to pursue trade facilitation and capacity-building. At a time when economic recovery was still not assured, some ASEAN members were reluctant to support further trade barrier cuts. However, it was significant that the countries opposing the linkage included not only Malaysia but also Indonesia, which in the early 1990s had been a key partner with Australia in pursuing regional trade liberalisation through APEC.[48]

---

46   Milner, 'Balancing "Asia"', p. 46.
47   Pitty, 'Regional Economic Co-operation', pp. 43–4.
48   Ibid.

The rebuff for Australia highlighted the close inter-relationship between political and economic issues in ASEAN's cooperation and external relations. The importance of political factors in any such negotiations was stated clearly by Malaysia's Trade Minister Rafidah Aziz in a notable comment during the Chiang Mai meetings. Rafidah said that the free trade proposal 'had to be looked at in its totality … It has to be a political decision and then we have to have the right environment. It's not simply an economic thing, its political.'[49]

Australia had a further setback in 2002 when it sought to gain dialogue status for Australia's head of government at ASEAN's leadership summit meetings (now held annually). At the summit in Phnom Penh in November 2002, Australia's bid was supported by Brunei, Singapore and Cambodia, was opposed by Malaysia, and received only lukewarm support from Indonesia and Thailand.[50] At the 2003 Bali meetings it was reported that Australia did not renew its efforts to gain representation and that the issue of Australian representation had been dropped from the agenda for discussion and had been shelved indefinitely.[51] It thus seemed at this point as if Australia had little prospect of extending its interactions with ASEAN at the leadership level.

Renewal of progress: 2001–04

While Australia's multilateral ASEAN relations had appeared to be at a low point at the beginning of the decade, several factors in the international and regional environment emerged after 2001 and contributed to a new and more positive context for the relationship. The key developments were the global and regional impact of the terrorist attacks in the US on 11 September 2001 and in Bali on 12 October 2002, regional responses to China's increasing role and profile, and leadership changes in two key members of ASEAN, Malaysia and Indonesia, which had significant implications for both bilateral relations and Australia's relations with ASEAN overall.

---

49   Tim Dodd, 'ASEAN Stifles New Merger Deal', *Weekend Australian Financial Review*, 7–8 October 2000.
50   Mark Baker, 'Beyond the Pale', *Sydney Morning Herald*, 9 November 2002.
51   Mark Baker, 'Australia Drops Bid to Join Summit', *The Age*, 7 October 2003.

The political context was clearly affected by the terrorist attacks in the US on 11 September 2001 (including the destruction of the World Trade Center in New York and the attack on the Pentagon in Washington) and the increased international and regional concerns about terrorism that followed. From late 2001, attention focused intensely on the threats perceived to be posed to the countries in the ASEAN region by terrorist movements of which Jemaah Islamiyah was the most prominent. Attention was heightened after the bombings in Bali in October 2002 (in which 88 Australians were among the 202 persons killed), at the Marriott Hotel in Jakarta in August 2003 and outside the Australian Embassy in Jakarta in September 2004.[52]

Australia after 2001 expanded cooperation on counter-terrorism, signing bilateral agreements with a number of ASEAN members and a multilateral declaration with ASEAN itself. The Australian Federal Police (AFP) developed close contacts with their regional counterparts. One reflection of this was an invitation to AFP Commissioner Mick Keelty to attend a meeting of ASEAN police chiefs as an observer in August 2004.[53]

While security cooperation developed extensively, the issue of terrorism in Southeast Asia caused some tensions between Australia and ASEAN members. There was concern in Indonesia and Malaysia at raids by Australian security authorities within Australia against suspected supporters of Jemaah Islamiyah: Malaysia's Prime Minister Mahathir accused Australia in November 2002 of being 'unsafe for Muslims'.[54] In December 2002, controversy arose when Howard was asked by a journalist whether he would consider launching 'pre-emptive' strikes against terrorist bases overseas. Howard responded that '[i]t stands to reason that if you believe somebody was going to launch an attack on your country, either of a conventional kind or of a terrorist kind, and you had the capacity to stop it, and there was no alternative other than to use that capacity, then of course you would have to use it'.[55]

---

52   Michael Wesley, 'Rebuilding Engagement: Australia and South-East Asia', in James Cotton and John Ravenhill, eds, *Trading on Alliance Security: Australia in World Affairs 2001–2005*, South Melbourne: Oxford University Press, 2007, pp. 61–5.
53   'Building Trust with ASEAN', *Daily Telegraph*, 14 August 2004.
54   Greg Sheridan, 'ASEAN Thumbs Down Caps Our Bad Week in Asia', *The Australian*, 7 November 2002.
55   Steve Lewis, 'Howard Runs the Gauntlet of Asia', *The Australian*, 2 December 2002.

Howard's comments on 'pre-emptive strikes' had been made in the context of discussion in the US about pre-emption as a tool in foreign and security policy (including in the George W. Bush administration's National Security Strategy in September 2002) and at a time when there was widespread debate in the US about a possible strike against the Saddam Hussein regime in Iraq. They aroused regional sensitivities about interference in internal affairs and were criticised in several ASEAN member countries. Mahathir said that any pre-emptive strikes against Malaysian targets would be considered 'an act of war'. Malaysia and the Philippines threatened to suspend bilateral counter-terrorism cooperation with Australia and there were also critical editorials in the media in Singapore, Thailand, Indonesia, Malaysia and the Philippines.[56]

Despite these arguments, Australia pursued extensive cooperation with ASEAN members on counter-terrorism after 2001. Most of the cooperation on terrorism in Southeast Asia was bilateral. However, this increased contact extended the sense of mutual interest between Australia and many ASEAN members, as ASEAN's Secretary-General Ong Keng Yong emphasised in comments during a visit to Australia in April 2004. Ong noted that:

> We have to talk about what are the substantial issues for us, and there are many shared challenges. One example is terrorism. Australia is a peaceful and stable country. It has a great influence in counter-terrorism initiatives and, in this area at least, we are working together and through that we can socialise more and be more comfortable together.[57]

A second key development in this period was ASEAN's perceptions of the rising economic and strategic presence of China in Southeast Asia. China had been involved increasingly in ASEAN-sponsored regional cooperation since the mid-1990s, particularly in the ARF. Its economy continued to perform strongly through the period of the Asian financial crisis. In the wake of the crisis, China was participating in the ASEAN Plus Three process and it expanded interactions with ASEAN by the development of a China–ASEAN

---

56   Wesley, 'Rebuilding Engagement', pp. 58–9.
57   Tony Parkinson, 'ASEAN Ready to Strengthen Australian Ties', *The Age*, 14 April 2004.

124

Free Trade Agreement.[58] While welcoming many aspects of China's involvement, ASEAN members were also keenly aware that they were competing with it for access to foreign direct investment. This perceived competition was a stimulus for ASEAN to move to deepen its own cooperation through development of an 'ASEAN community', agreed at the Bali meetings in 2003 (see below).[59] ASEAN members were also sensitive to China's increasing strategic weight in Southeast Asia, which had been reflected in its growing emphasis on asserting its claims in the South China Sea (see Chapter 5).[60]

ASEAN members wanted to avoid an over-dependence on the Chinese market and maintain a diversity of international partnerships. ASEAN concluded an Economic Partnership Agreement with Japan in 2002. ASEAN also moved to increase interest in associations with Australia and New Zealand. As has been noted, ASEAN had reasserted interest in considering an economic linkage with Australia and New Zealand in 2002 and this was affirmed the following year. ASEAN also expressed interest in enhancing political dialogue with Australia. ASEAN's Secretary-General Ong commented that '[w]e cannot just be focused on China or Japan or India. Australia is our neighbour and it's been around South-east Asia for so long and its logical for us to try to find ways to strengthen the political relationship through more formal exchange'.[61]

A third key development in Australia's regional relations after 2001 was leadership transitions in Malaysia and Indonesia. In Malaysia, Mahathir had been a critic of Australia's policies and had advocated a mode of regional cooperation with an explicit focus on East Asia, which would not include Australia. Malaysia had been a leading force in blocking consideration of a formal trade agreement with Australia in October 2000.[62] Prime Minister Mahathir retired in November 2003 and his successor, Abdullah Badawi, adopted a more favourable attitude towards Australia. During a visit by Minister for

---

58   Ian Storey, *Southeast Asia and the Rise of China: The Search for Security*, London: Routledge, 2011, pp. 64–98.
59   Roberts, *ASEAN Regionalism*, pp. 88–101; Etel Solingen, 'ASEAN Cooperation: The Legacy of the Economic Crisis', *International Relations of the Asia-Pacific*, 5(1) 2005: 20.
60   Michael Wesley, *The Howard Paradox: Australian Diplomacy in Asia, 1996–2006*, Sydney: ABC Books, 2007, pp. 91–8.
61   Parkinson, 'ASEAN Ready'.
62   John Funston, 'The Legacy of Dr Mahathir', *Australian Financial Review*, 30 July 2004.

Foreign Affairs Downer to Kuala Lumpur in April 2004, the two sides announced a new annual dialogue between their foreign ministries, annual consultations between senior officials on regional security issues and plans for a state visit by Prime Minister Badawi to Australia (which would be the first by a Malaysian prime minister since Dr Mahathir visited in 1984). It was made clear that Malaysia would now not block closer economic associations between Australia and ASEAN.[63]

Relations with Indonesia had been tense in the aftermath of the East Timor intervention and discord continued during the period of the presidency of Megawati Sukarnoputri (July 2001 – October 2004). However, new areas for dialogue and cooperation were developed, particularly after the Bali bombings in October 2002. Extensive cooperation developed in counter-terrorism activities, with AFP Commissioner Keelty and his counterpart General Da'i Bachtiar playing important roles. A component of AFP personnel was based in Jakarta and worked well with their Indonesian partners; dialogue between intelligence agencies was extensive.[64] Counter-terror cooperation was a focus for increased numbers of ministerial visits; it was reported in December 2004 that there had been 42 such visits in the past two years, including nine by Downer.[65]

Australia sought to extend its cooperation with Indonesia through new multilateral dialogue. Australia and Indonesia co-hosted four workshops on counter-terrorism and illegal immigration in Bali between February 2002 and February 2004. The workshops were designed to pursue broader dialogue and cooperation on issues that had been the focus of discord in Australia's regional relations. Tensions had developed over aspects of counter-terrorism policies (as noted above).

---

63   Mark Baker, 'Malaysia's New PM Leaves Mahathir's Acrimonious Legacy at the 19th Hole', *The Age*, 12 June 2004.
64   Patrick Walters, 'Framework for Close Ties First Imperative', *The Australian*, 12 November 2004.
65   Andrew Burrell, 'Downer Enjoys A Warmer North', *Australian Financial Review*, 8 December 2004.

There had also been considerable disagreement over approaches towards illegal migration. From 1998, Australia had faced an increasing flow of asylum-seekers, who had come from countries outside Southeast Asia and transited through states in that region (particularly Malaysia and Indonesia) before travelling by boat to seek entry to Australia. Many boat journeys were organised by people-smugglers and the unauthorised arrivals were unpopular in Australia. The asylum-seeker issue was a focus of tension in key bilateral relationships, especially with Indonesia.[66] The issue was highlighted further when Australia came into dispute with Indonesia in August 2001 over the issue of the *MV Tampa*, which Australian authorities had prevented from entering Australian waters while carrying asylum-seekers and which the government had tried to divert to Indonesia, the country through which the asylum-seekers had transited.[67]

The Bali workshops sought to recast the issues of illegal migration and terrorism as 'common management problems rather than the sites of rival responsibilities and prerogatives' and helped defuse these issues as irritants in bilateral relations.[68] The first Bali workshop (on people smuggling, trafficking in persons and related transnational crime) involved 38 countries, including all the ASEAN members. Michael Wesley has argued that the 'Bali process' of discussion achieved considerable success in this period in building increased cooperation in the areas addressed: 'Australian officials realised from their experiences in gaining regional support for APEC and the ASEAN Regional Forum over a decade earlier, that a proposal strongly supported by significant regional countries would carry more weight than a proposal made by Canberra alone.'[69] It was clear that Australia–Indonesia cooperation was integral to the development of the Bali process. In another multilateral collaboration, Australia and Indonesia in December 2004 co-hosted the first of what became a series of inter-faith dialogues in Jakarta to build understanding between Muslims and non-Muslims.[70]

---

66 Kelly, *The March of Patriots*, pp. 541–5.
67 For a detailed account of the issues in relation to the *MV Tampa*, see ibid., pp. 541–65.
68 Wesley, 'Rebuilding Engagement', p. 61. See also Wesley, *The Howard Paradox*, pp. 174–212.
69 Wesley, *The Howard Paradox*, p. 193.
70 Ibid.

The election of former general Susilo Bambang Yudhoyono as president in September 2004 brought to office a leader familiar with Australia (he had a son studying at university in Perth). Howard made a special visit to attend Yudhoyono's inauguration, and was well received at the inauguration. He described his meeting with the president as 'a wonderful opportunity to reaffirm the importance of the relationship'.[71] Plans for further senior-level dialogue were developed and the potential for a new security agreement between the parties was foreshadowed.

An unexpected and major additional basis for cooperation emerged after the tsunami that struck Indonesia and other countries in South and Southeast Asia on 26 December 2004, causing widespread destruction and the loss of over 200,000 lives. The Australian Government subsequently announced a A$1 billion aid package for Indonesia and the Australian public also contributed substantially. As well as extensive bilateral cooperation, Howard took part in a special ASEAN leaders' meeting in Jakarta on 6 January 2005 attended by 23 countries to help co-ordinate relief.[72] Following a visit to Australia by President Yudhoyono in March 2005, consideration was given to developing a formal security treaty and in November 2006 the Agreement between the Republic of Indonesia and Australia on the Framework for Security Cooperation (known widely as the Lombok Treaty) was unveiled, and was ultimately brought into effect in 2008.[73] All these developments contributed greatly to bilateral relations and to Australia's position in the ASEAN region overall.

A fourth development in this period that aided Australia's position in relation to ASEAN was an increased awareness of the depth and breadth of Australia's interactions with Southeast Asia. A report issued by the Institute of Southeast Asian Studies (ISEAS) in 2004 observed that:

---

71   Andrew Burrell, 'PM Hails Stronger Ties with Jakarta', *Australian Financial Review*, 21 October 2004.
72   Patrick Walters and Roy Ecclestone, 'PM to Fly to Jakarta Summit', *Weekend Australian*, 1 January 2005; John Howard, 'Statement at the Special ASEAN Leaders' Meeting on the Aftermath of the Tsunami, Jakarta Convention Centre, Indonesia', Transcript, 6 January 2005.
73   Ian McPhedran, 'Underlying Fears as Australia Strengthens Ties with Indonesia', *Adelaide Advertiser*, 18 November 2006.

[I]n recent years much of the real substance in the relationship between ANZ [Australia and New Zealand] and Southeast Asia has developed without the direct assistance or guidance of governments as private business, education and travel have mushroomed. From being largely government-fostered in the 1970s, the links between ANZ-Southeast Asia have become more broadly based and oriented towards closer contacts between people from the two areas.[74]

The ISEAS report noted, for example, that in 2003 over 625,000 Southeast Asians visited Australia, more than three times the numbers a decade earlier; in the same year, 722,000 Australians visited Southeast Asia, close to double the numbers in the early 1990s. Since 1991, over 186,000 Southeast Asians had settled in Australia and in 2003 nearly 76,000 Southeast Asians were studying in educational institutions in Australia (secondary and tertiary), up from 12,690 in 1990.[75]

Looking back at this period, Downer considered that Australia's standing in ASEAN had increased substantially in the wake of the Asian financial crisis:

Their slightly patronising attitude towards Australia changed, and I've not seen it re-emerge ... They learnt something between 1998 and 2004, in those six years ... they learnt something new about Australia they hadn't known before; that is how big the Australian economy was and how capable Australia is ... What Australia demonstrated between 1998 and the end of 2004–early 2005 was capability, it could do things. It was solid through the Asian economic crisis and it won a degree of respect for its solidity and stability. And then there was East Timor when they suddenly could see Australia could act decisively to make things happen ... [T]he response to the tsunami by Australia was massively beyond their expectations.[76]

---

74   Michael Richardson, 'Shared Perceptions', in Michael Richardson and Chin Kin Wah, *Australia–New Zealand & Southeast Asia Relations: An Agenda for Closer Cooperation*, Singapore: ISEAS Publications, 2004, pp. 35–6.

75   Ibid., p. 38.

76   Downer, interview with the author, April 2014.

The Vientiane Commemorative Summit: November 2004

Opportunities now opened up for further multilateral linkages between ASEAN and Australia. ASEAN had been taking steps to deepen its own cooperation and these had implications for its major dialogue partners, including Australia. In the wake of the Asian financial crisis, ASEAN members had realised that if the Association was to retain credibility and momentum, it needed to deepen its economic and political cooperation. For example, ASEAN members were competing with China for foreign direct investment, but they were doing so as 10 separate economies with many different sets of rules in economic activity.

In October 2003, at a leaders' summit in Bali (referred to as the 'second Bali conference', or 'Bali II', after the one held in 1976), ASEAN committed itself to developing an 'ASEAN Community'. The members endorsed the 'Declaration of ASEAN Concord II', which stated that '[f]or the sustainability of our region's economic development we affirmed the need for a secure political environment based on a strong foundation of mutual interests generated by economic cooperation'. To pursue ASEAN's goals, the members declared '[a]n ASEAN Community shall be established comprising three pillars, namely political and security cooperation, economic cooperation, and socio-cultural cooperation that are closely intertwined and mutually reinforcing for the purpose of ensuring durable peace, stability and shared prosperity in the region'.[77]

The ASEAN Bali Concord II declaration also reaffirmed ASEAN's commitment to foster ASEAN competitiveness and a favourable investment environment, to enhance 'economic linkages with the world economy', and advance adherence to TAC as a functioning and effective code of conduct for the region.[78] The target date set for achieving an ASEAN Community was the year 2020, but this was later brought forward to 2015.

---

77   ASEAN, 'Declaration of ASEAN Concord II (Bali Concord II)', Bali, 7 October 2003.
78   Solingen, 'ASEAN Cooperation', p. 20.

Progress had been made by 2004 on a free trade deal between ASEAN and Australia and New Zealand. A meeting between ASEAN trade ministers and their Australian and New Zealand counterparts held in Brunei on 14 September 2002 declared support for expanding trade and investment and fostering closer economic integration. In August 2004, ASEAN economics ministers agreed with their Australian and New Zealand counterparts to begin negotiations on a free trade agreement in early 2005 with completion to be reached within two years.[79]

In this positive atmosphere, Australia and New Zealand were invited to attend a special summit meeting with the ASEAN members to commemorate 30 years of the multilateral relationship; the ASEAN–Australia and New Zealand Commemorative Summit was held in Vientiane, Laos, on 30 November 2004. The meeting reviewed the wide areas of cooperation being pursued and the ASEAN members expressed their appreciation of Australia and New Zealand's ongoing assistance to economic and social progress in ASEAN and to the bridging of the development gaps among ASEAN member states. The ASEAN leaders also invited both Australia and New Zealand to extend their association with ASEAN. The meeting endorsed the proposal by economics ministers of the 12 countries and agreed to deepen economic relations through negotiations for an ASEAN–Australia–New Zealand Free Trade Agreement. The chairman's statement for the meeting reaffirmed the importance of the ASEAN TAC in building peace and stability in the region and strengthening ASEAN's relations with its dialogue partners. The statement added:

> In this connection, the ASEAN Leaders encourage Australia and New Zealand to positively consider acceding to the Treaty in the near future in the spirit of the strong trust and friendship between ASEAN and Australia and New Zealand, and their common desire to contribute to regional peace and stability.[80]

The ASEAN leaders at the Vientiane summit took another decision of major relevance to Australia. The leaders discussed the convening of a new dialogue, the East Asia Summit, and 'agreed to hold the first EAS

---

79   Chin Kin Wah, 'Background to an Evolving ASEAN–ANZ Relationship', in Michael Richardson and Chin Kin Wah, *Australia–New Zealand & Southeast Asia Relations: An Agenda for Closer Cooperation*, Singapore: ISEAS Publications, 2004, pp. 22–3.
80   ASEAN, 'Chairman's Statement of the ASEAN–Australia and New Zealand Commemorative Summit', Vientiane, 30 November 2004'.

[East Asia Summit] in Malaysia in 2005, and in this connection tasked our foreign ministers to work out the details concerning its modality and participation'.[81]

The way was now open for a significant advance in Australia's ASEAN association. In addition to the negotiations for an economic agreement, the East Asia Summit would bring together ASEAN and key dialogue partners. This was clearly of major interest to Australia, but the issue of the new summit became inter-linked with the question of ASEAN's TAC and of whether Australia would accede to the treaty. This became a significant area of debate.

The TAC issue and the East Asia Summit

The more favourable climate for Australian relations with ASEAN by 2004 saw increased attention on whether and how Australia might be able to be more closely associated with ASEAN as an institution. In this context, TAC gained greater attention. The original five ASEAN members had unveiled TAC at the Bali summit in February 1976 (see Chapter 2) and it had been a central declaratory statement of principles of ASEAN cooperation.

TAC was originally an agreement for ASEAN members and for other potentially interested countries in Southeast Asia. However, the treaty was amended in 1987 and again in 1998 to enable states beyond those considered to be 'Southeast Asian' to sign. Accession to TAC was seen by ASEAN as a central requirement for potential new members of the Association.[82] Accession also became a way for non-ASEAN members to indicate formally their support for the Association and for its goals and policies. China in 2003 became the first non-potential member to sign TAC and other states followed suit including India, Japan and South Korea. By 2004, accession to TAC was therefore 'on the agenda' for countries seeking to advance interactions with ASEAN.[83]

---

81   ASEAN, 'Chairman's Statement of the 10th ASEAN Summit', Vientiane, 29 November 2004.
82   Papua New Guinea became the first non-ASEAN member to accede to TAC in 1989.
83   Rodolfo C. Severino, *Southeast Asia in Search of an ASEAN Community: Insights from the Former ASEAN Secretary-General*, Singapore: Institute of Southeast Asian Studies, 2006, pp. 167–8.

Hawke's government had considered the possibility of Australian accession to the treaty in 1991 but, as noted in Chapter 3, ASEAN at that stage had not wanted other non-regional states to accede to the treaty and the issue had not been pursued further. The issue gained attention in the lead-up to the Vientiane summit when it was reported that a number of ASEAN members now considered that Australia should sign the treaty. Thai, Filipino and Indonesian officials urged Australia to sign and a foreign affairs adviser to President Gloria Macapagal-Arroyo stated that '[w]e think Australia should sign the [treaty] and that is something all the ASEAN leaders will talk about'.[84]

The Howard Government's initial attitude towards the treaty was negative. Downer, speaking in Parliament on 29 November 2004 just before leaving Australia for the Vientiane summit, invoked memories of an earlier era of regional cooperation (the 1955 Bandung Conference of Asian and African nations that had been viewed with disfavour by Robert Menzies' government) when he said that:

> One of the components of the Bandung Declaration was that governments that signed up to the Treaty of Amity and Cooperation would abstain from the use of arrangements of collective defence to serve the particular interests of any of the big powers. Bearing that in mind, successive Australian governments … have interpreted that particular principle as one that would be inconsistent with the ANZUS alliance.[85]

Downer noted that the preceding Labor Government had not moved to accede to the treaty during its 13 years in office.[86]

Prime Minister Howard, in comments at a press conference in Vientiane on 30 November 2004, described the treaty as 'an agreement which has its origins, has particular origins at a time when Australia was not part of ASEAN and we just don't, for those reasons, think it's, at this stage, appropriate to sign it'.[87] Howard maintained his reservations

84   Tim Colebatch, 'Australia May Be Alone On Treaty', *The Age*, 30 November 2004.
85   Aleander Downer, 'Association of Southeast Asian Nations', Question, in *Commonwealth of Australia Parliamentary Debates*, House of Representatives, Official Hansard, No. 2, 29 November 2004, p. 32.
86   Ibid.
87   Tom Allard, 'Economic Powerhouse Attracts Howard's Eye', *Sydney Morning Herald*, 1 December 2004.

into the early part of 2005. At a joint press conference on 7 April 2005 with the visiting Malaysian Prime Minister Badawi, Howard referred to the treaty as 'of a mindset that we've all moved on from'.[88]

TAC, however, was a significant issue for Australia in its approaches to ASEAN in 2005. At the 2004 Vientiane summit, Badawi suggested that Australia might be invited to the next ASEAN summit, to be held in Kuala Lumpur. This comment was made in the context of ASEAN's decision in Vientiane to establish a new dialogue, the East Asia Summit. The importance of TAC was affirmed when ASEAN foreign ministers met in Cebu in April 2005 and clarified the criteria that would qualify countries to be considered as members of the East Asia Summit. Prospective East Asia Summit members, the ministers stated, must have 'substantive relations with ASEAN, they must be a full dialogue partner, and they must accede to the TAC'.[89] Australia met the first two criteria, but it would have to accede to the treaty to qualify fully for membership.

The announcement by ASEAN's foreign ministers in Cebu necessitated a decision by Australia on TAC and stimulated a process of internal review in which Downer played a major part. On 12 April 2005, just a few days after Howard's negative comments, Downer made the following statement:

> [W]e've got some problems with the treaty. I mean the thing is in this country we do interpret treaties and other legal documents very literally. I mean we take the words to mean what they say and so, you know, that is obviously a problem for us in terms of some of the language of the treaty. But I don't want to go into it in any more detail except to say two things. One, I'm very optimistic that Australia will be part of the East Asia Summit process and I think that is very good news for Australia in terms of its participation in regional architecture. In terms of the Treaty of Amity and Co-operation well, I've had discussions during President Yudhoyono and Abdullah Badawi's visits about this issue with my counter-parts and further discussions last night with the Indonesian foreign minister. I think we can work our way through this issue.[90]

---

88   Quoted in James Cotton, 'Asian Regionalism and the Australian Policy Response in the Howard Era', *Journal of Australian Studies*, 32(1) 2008: 124.

89   'ASEAN: Sign the Pact or Stay Away', *The Australian*, 12 April 2005.

90   Alexander Downer, media interview, 12 April 2005, quoted in Cotton, 'Asian Regionalism', p. 124.

In late June 2005, Downer made it clear that the government realised that there was a direct linkage between signing TAC and being able to join the nascent East Asia Summit:

> If we can satisfy ourselves about various concerns we have then we would be prepared to sign it [TAC], particularly as signing it will ensure that Australia can participate in the East Asia Summit process and we see the East Asia Summit as the birth of a growing East Asian community, so it makes good sense for the region, for Australia to be involved. And if the price is signing the Treaty of Amity and Cooperation, we'll do that, if we can sign it without it in any way interfering with treaties and other arrangements we have with countries outside of the ASEAN region.[91]

Downer acknowledged later that 'I did have to persuade John Howard that I had to sign this thing ... I told him not to worry about it; let me sign it and suck it up'.[92]

The government had a deadline for its decision. In late July 2005, ASEAN was due to hold its annual ministerial consultations and would be preparing to launch the East Asia Summit. At the ASEAN ministerial meetings, a joint ASEAN–Australia statement on 28 July 2005 announced that Australia would sign the treaty.[93] The basis on which the government had acceded to the treaty was clarified by a subsequent submission to the Australian Parliament by the Department of Foreign Affairs and Trade (DFAT). Under provisions introduced by the Howard Government, a parliamentary committee – the Joint Standing Committee on Treaties (JSCOT) – had been inaugurated to scrutinise all new treaty commitments.[94] The DFAT submission included the text of the letter that Downer had sent on 13 July 2005 to Lao Foreign Minister Somsavat Lengsavad (whose country was the chair of ASEAN for 2005) on Australia's approach to the treaty. Downer's letter noted that accession to TAC by Australia would not be 'inconsistent with Australia's treaty commitments, including on security matters', particularly ANZUS and the Five Power Defence Arrangements. Accession would not place any limitation on Australia's

---

91   'Australia to Sign ASEAN Treaty', *The World Today*, ABC Radio, 22 July 2005.
92   Downer, interview with the author, April 2014.
93   Cotton, 'Asian Regionalism', p. 124.
94   Ibid., p. 125.

rights and obligations as a member of the UN, and it would not have any bearing on Australia's relations with countries outside the ASEAN group.[95]

Downer's letter affirmed that the dispute resolution mechanism set out in TAC would only come into operation with Australia's explicit approval.[96] The government's submission to JSCOT made clear that in accepting the treaty's provision for the 'renunciation of the threat or use of force', Australia also retained its rights under the United Nations Charter (in Article 51) that recognises the right of states to engage in self-help to maintain their collective defence.[97] Australia was thus explicitly retaining its right to take independent actions in foreign and security policy, alongside its accession to the treaty.

Since discussions about TAC had included the issue of Australia's commitment to the ANZUS alliance, the government evidently considered it appropriate to discuss its decision to accede to the treaty with the US. Howard raised the issue of the treaty and the advent of the new East Asia Summit with Bush in a visit to Washington in late July 2005 (which was after Australia had acceded to the treaty). It was reported that President Bush said that he would be glad for Australia to join the East Asia Summit and to sign TAC. A US official said after the meetings that the Bush administration considered that it was in the interests of the US for Australia, Japan and other allies to join the new Summit to 'counter' the presence of China.[98]

The process by which Australia signed TAC and set out its explicit conditions in so doing had relevance for the US approach towards the treaty. A paper prepared by the United States Congressional Research Service in May 2009 cited the example of Australia in pursuing accession as having relevance for the US as it now moved towards

---

95   Ibid.

96   Under TAC, a High Council comprising of ministers (presumably foreign ministers) can be convened to 'take cognizance of disputes or situations likely to disturb regional peace and harmony', and in case the parties to a dispute are unable to settle it through negotiations, make recommendations on 'appropriate means of settlement'. Resort to the High Council and any action taken by it needs the consent of all parties to the dispute. The Council has never been convened by ASEAN. See Severino, *Southeast Asia*, pp. 11–12.

97   Cotton, 'Asian Regionalism', p. 125.

98   Peter Hartcher and Cynthia Banham, 'Bush Gives Howard the Nod for Summit', *Sydney Morning Herald*, 21 July 2005.

acceding itself. The paper included the text of Downer's 13 July 2005 letter to the Lao foreign minister and the Lao minister's letter of reply (the US went on to accede to TAC in July 2009, see Chapter 5).[99]

With TAC signed, Australia could look forward to joining the new East Asia Summit. The process through which the East Asia Summit was established, however, illustrated again the difficulties and obstacles posed by the sensitivities and competitive tensions among the major powers, particularly China and Japan, to efforts at multilateral cooperation in East Asia.

Joining the East Asia Summit

The proposal for an East Asia Summit grew out of suggestions made by President Kim Dae-jung of South Korea at the second meeting of the ASEAN Plus Three grouping, in Vietnam in November 1998, that an East Asia Vision Group should explore the prospects for the formation of an East Asian community. The vision group comprised 26 civilian experts and was tasked to research and recommend concrete measures that ASEAN Plus Three could take to increase East Asian regional cooperation. In 2001 the group released its findings and among the conclusions was a proposal for an East Asia Summit. Based on its assessments of regional developments, the group envisaged that East Asian nations would move towards the development of an East Asian community. Such a community, the group suggested, would benefit the states in the region and could be achieved by building on the existing cooperation processes. The East Asia Summit would be a useful way of building community and pre-empting or resolving future regional challenges that might arise.[100]

ASEAN and its partners in the ASEAN Plus Three group did not move immediately to develop an East Asia Summit. At their 2002 summit in Phnom Penh, the ASEAN Plus Three leaders had 'expressed their willingness to explore the phased evolution' of the ASEAN Plus

---

99 Mark E. Manyin, Michael John Garcia and Wayne M. Morrison, 'US Accession to ASEAN's Treaty of Amity and Cooperation (TAC)', CRS Report For Congress, Washington, DC: Congressional Research Service, 5 May 2009, pp. 19–22.
100 Ralf Emmers, Joseph Chinyong Liow and See Seng Tan, *The East Asia Summit and the Regional Security Architecture*, Maryland Series in Contemporary Asian Studies, No. 3, Baltimore, MD: School of Law, University of Maryland, 2010, pp. 22–3.

Three summit into an East Asia Summit.[101] However, at ASEAN's annual summit in December 2004 in Vientiane, Malaysian Prime Minister Badawi (as the host of the next ASEAN summit, to be held in Kuala Lumpur in 2005) announced that an East Asia Summit would be convened during those meetings. The intended participants were not specified at the Vientiane summit. This set the scene for some competitive diplomacy about exactly who the participants should be.[102]

The initial reactions to the proposal for an East Asia Summit had been cautiously favourable and it was notable that the kind of summit suggested would be based on a membership exclusively from East Asia itself. However, the sensitivities involved in efforts to pursue regional cooperation soon became evident, particularly because of the competing interests of China and Japan.[103] As Mohan Malik suggested:

> The EAS began with a backdrop of intense diplomatic maneuvering and shadow boxing, and ended with the power game being played out in the open. China and Japan were locked in a bitter struggle for supremacy, with Beijing attempting to gain the leadership position in the planned EAC (i.e. East Asian Community), and Tokyo trying to rein in its rival with the help of other 'China wary' nations in the Asia-Pacific.[104]

China was initially enthusiastic about the East Asia Summit proposal and argued that it should most appropriately be based on the 13 member countries of ASEAN Plus Three. In China's view, ASEAN Plus Three could become the East Asia Summit, with the chair rotating among the 13 members.[105] In the case of Malaysia, initiatives such as ASEAN Plus Three and the East Asia Summit were seen as extensions of proposals by Prime Minister Mahathir for the creation of an exclusively East Asian grouping, proposals that had been supported by China.[106]

---

101 Severino, *Southeast Asia*, p. 270.
102 Ibid., pp. 270–1.
103 Michael Yahuda, *Sino-Japanese Relations after the Cold War: Two Tigers Sharing a Mountain*, Abingdon: Routledge, 2014, pp. 82–98.
104 Mohan Malik, 'China and the East Asian Summit: More Discord than Accord', Honolulu: Asia-Pacific Center for Security Studies, February 2006.
105 Chien-Peng Chung, 'China and Japan in "ASEAN Plus" Multilateral Arrangements: Raining on the Other Guy's Parade', *Asian Survey*, 53(5) 2013: 812–15.
106 Emmers, Liow and Tan, *The East Asia Summit*, p. 23.

However other states were reserved about the prospect of a summit based solely on ASEAN Plus Three membership, since this would be likely to be open to a high level of influence from China. In ASEAN, this view was held strongly by Indonesia: President Yudhoyono in February 2005 expressed support for the inclusion of India, Australia and New Zealand.[107] Indonesia's view was supported by countries including Singapore and Vietnam. Japan, with the backing of these members of ASEAN, argued that other relevant countries, in particular India and Australia, should be invited to join the new forum. China continued to argue against this proposal into the early months of 2005, but most ASEAN members came to support the Japanese position. It was ultimately resolved at the ASEAN meeting in Cebu in April 2005 that India, Australia and New Zealand would be invited as inaugural members of the Summit.[108]

After the issue of participation in the first East Asia Summit was agreed, dispute continued about the character and possible role of the Summit.[109] China argued that the ASEAN Plus Three membership should be considered to be a 'core' group in subsequent efforts to develop an ultimate East Asia community and was reported to have gained some support for this approach from Malaysia, Thailand, Myanmar and South Korea. However, China's notion of a 'two tiered' East Asia Summit, with the ASEAN Plus Three grouping as the centre for concerted cooperation efforts, was resisted by Japan, India and Australia, with support from Indonesia and Singapore.[110]

Tensions between China and Japan were evident during the lead-up to the first meeting of the Summit in Kuala Lumpur. Disharmony between the two countries had been increased by the visit to the Yasakuni shrine in Tokyo by Prime Minister Koizumi Junichiro.[111] The lack of accord between the two largest East Asian nations was

---

107 Severino, *Southeast Asia*, p. 271.
108 Malik, 'China and the East Asian Summit', pp. 2–4.
109 'Japan, China Clash Over E. Asia Summit', *Yomiuri Shimbun*, 25 November 2005.
110 Richard McGregor and Anna Fifield, 'Divisions Undermine East Asia Summit', *Financial Times* (London), 1 December 2005.
111 The Yasakuni shrine has been a source of discord in Japan's relations with its neighbours, especially China and South Korea. The shrine is a memorial to Japan's war dead but it includes among those remembered 14 figures determined by the Allies after the Second World War to have been 'Class A' war criminals. Visits to the shrine by Japanese political figures, especially the prime minister, have aroused concern and protest by neighbouring states on several occasions, particularly from China; see Yahuda, *Sino-Japanese Relations*, pp. 44–52.

highlighted by the refusal of Premier Wen Jiabao to hold a bilateral meeting with his counterpart Prime Minister Koizumi during their visits to Kuala Lumpur for the ASEAN meetings and the first East Asia Summit.[112] The new East Asia Summit had been inaugurated but the discord on public display between China and Japan emphasised that the prospects for the Summit were, from the start, uncertain.

Australia and the first East Asia Summit: December 2005

At the first East Asia Summit on 14 December 2005 the emphasis was on developing communication among the members. The 'Kuala Lumpur Declaration on the East Asia Summit' affirmed that the East Asia Summit was intended to be an 'open, inclusive, transparent and outward-looking forum in which we strive to strengthen global norms and universally recognised values with ASEAN as the driving force working in partnership with other participants of the East Asia Summit'. The Summit would be 'convened regularly', would be hosted and chaired by an ASEAN member and would be held 'back-to-back with the annual ASEAN Summit'.[113]

Initial reactions to the Summit were cautious. Some observers argued that the East Asia Summit was an important further step toward dialogue in a region that had strong motivations for cooperation, but which would not necessarily follow the type of institution-building models pursued by other regions (particularly Europe).[114] Other analysts emphasised the wide differences in character and policy among the members and the very cautious nature of the first meeting. Malik commented that '[i]n the absence of a thaw in Sino-Japanese or Sino-Indian relations or great power cooperation, the EAS is unlikely to take off because multilateralism is a multi-player game ... At best, the EAS will be a talk shop like the APEC or the ARF where leaders meet, declarations are made, but little community building is achieved.'[115]

---

112 McGregor and Fifield, 'Divisions Undermine East Asia Summit'.

113 ASEAN, 'Kuala Lumpur Declaration on the East Asia Summit', Kuala Lumpur, 14 December 2005.

114 Barry Desker, 'Why the East Asian Summit Matters', *PacNet*, No. 55B, Pacific Forum/CSIS, Hawaii, 19 December 2005.

115 Mohan Malik, 'The East Asia Summit: More Discord than Accord', *YaleGlobal Online*, 20 December 2005.

The Australian Government's approach was positive but also cautious. In a speech on 1 December 2005 just before the Summit, Downer suggested that the character and direction of the East Asia Summit might take some time to become apparent but welcomed the fact that Australia would be an inaugural participant. Downer expected the Summit to develop alongside other institutions and in a pluralist regional environment:

> This is just the first meeting and nothing is set in stone. And if there is to be an emergence of an East Asian community, it will not, in my view, be built around one institution or meeting. An East Asian community will emerge for practical reasons, not for ideological reasons. APEC, the ASEAN Regional Forum, ASEAN plus three, and the East Asia Summit will all contribute to an open but increasingly integrated region …

> The East Asia Summit is only in its very first iteration and will take some time to bed down. But we can say now that we have a regional architecture that serves Australia's interests well. It is open and inclusive. It addresses security and economic issues in a practical way. And Australia has a very strong voice in how it develops.[116]

Prime Minister Howard, in Kuala Lumpur on 14 December 2005, just before the Summit, stated that 'although the meeting is a short one, it's a very important one not only for its symbolism but also for its substance because it will bring together for the first time, 16 countries of the East Asian region. We will have an opportunity to talk necessarily in general terms about the major issues confronting the region.' Howard emphasised that the Australian Government continued to see APEC as the single most important avenue for regional dialogue: he commented that APEC is 'the premier body' that has the 'great advantage … that it does bring the United States to this region … I've got APEC and now I've got this, they're all important and they all have a role to play'.[117]

Gaining entry to the East Asia Summit was a high point for the Howard Government in foreign policy and for Australia's multilateral engagements with ASEAN and East Asia. It meant that Australia had been able to participate in all the ASEAN-sponsored groupings in

116 Alexander Downer, 'Australia's Engagement with Asia', Speech to the Asialink Chairman's Dinner, Melbourne, 1 December 2005.
117 John Howard, 'Doorstop Interview, Regent Hotel, Kuala Lumpur', Transcript, 14 December 2005.

which it was eligible to be a member. Australia had now entered a regional cooperation institution that included the three major East and South Asian powers (China, Japan and India), but not the US.[118] Paul Kelly observed in August 2005 that 'the irony is stunning: the most pro-US government in Australia's history has taken Australia into an East Asia structure that excludes the US. It is exactly what Paul Keating, with Clinton, fought to avoid throughout his prime ministership.'[119] Six years later, however, the East Asia Summit was expanded to include the US and Russia, as ASEAN continued to seek to broaden and balance its dialogue forum to include all the major powers.

Conclusion

Australia's ASEAN relations encountered some strains and pressures after 1996. Australia provided substantial support to two key ASEAN members, Indonesia and Thailand, during the Asian financial crisis after mid-1997, but for several years Australia seemed to downplay multilateral engagements. The crisis over East Timor in 1999 and the Australian-led intervention helped resolve the instability in the territory but it caused strains with Indonesia. At the beginning of the new decade, Australia's ASEAN relations seemed to be in a period of some hiatus and its efforts to advance economic relations (through the AFTA–CER linkage proposal) and to enhance its dialogues with ASEAN did not succeed.

However, after 2001 the climate for relations was transformed. The challenge of terrorist threats internationally and in Southeast Asia produced substantial cooperation with ASEAN members, China's rising profile encouraged a re-evaluation in ASEAN of Australia's relevance as a regional partner, leadership changes in Malaysia and Indonesia facilitated multilateral interactions and Australia's profile as a valuable economic partner was enhanced in the wake of the financial crisis. Important steps were possible, with agreements reached to pursue in earnest the AFTA–CER negotiations and then through ASEAN's decision to invite Australia to take part in the new East Asia Summit. After hesitation about signing TAC, Australia took that step

---

118 Paul Kelly, 'The Day Foreign Policy Won Asia', *Weekend Australian*, 6 August 2005.
119 Ibid.

and became an inaugural member of the East Asia Summit. Australia therefore now had the potential to advance cooperation in both economic and security dialogue with ASEAN and its key dialogue partners.

5

From the 'Asia Pacific Community' to the fortieth anniversary summit and beyond (2007–2015)

The years after 2007 saw considerable policy continuity in Australia's Association of Southeast Asian Nations (ASEAN) relations. Australia concluded a multilateral free trade agreement with ASEAN and New Zealand and joined new ASEAN-sponsored ministerial-level dialogues in economic cooperation and defence and security, the Regional Comprehensive Economic Partnership (RCEP) negotiations and the ASEAN Defence Ministers' Meeting (ADMM) Plus Eight. ASEAN in this period was moving to consolidate its own cooperation through the development of a new Charter as it pursued the commitments it had made in 2003 to develop an 'ASEAN Community'. Australia strengthened its institutional linkages with ASEAN and appointed an ambassador to the Association in 2008. Australia, however, also encountered substantial discord with ASEAN over a proposal for a wider regional 'Asia Pacific Community'. A key theme recurred – the challenges for Australia in relating to ASEAN as an institution. To explore these issues, this chapter discusses in turn the Kevin Rudd Government's ASEAN policies with particular reference to the Asia Pacific Community proposal and regional responses; the Julia Gillard Government's approach to ASEAN including regional economic and security cooperation, increasing tensions in relation to the South China

Sea and developments in Myanmar; and Tony Abbott's government, the 2014 Commemorative Summit and the continuing challenge of major power competition in Southeast Asia.

The Rudd Government, Southeast Asia and ASEAN

From December 2007 to September 2013, Australian policies towards Southeast Asia and ASEAN were directed by Labor governments led first by Rudd and then by Gillard (from June 2010), with Rudd making a brief return to office as prime minister (June to September 2013). Rudd as Opposition spokesperson on foreign affairs and then as leader of the Australian Labor Party from December 2006 had advanced a foreign policy for Labor based on 'three pillars' – commitment to the US alliance, emphasis on engagement with the Asia-Pacific, and support for the United Nations (UN) and multilateral cooperation.[1] This was effectively a restatement of long-standing Labor Party emphases in Australian foreign policy, rather than a new departure. Rudd was also highly critical of some of the John Howard Government's foreign policies, especially its support for the US-led invasion of Iraq in 2003.[2] In office after the elections of 24 November 2007, the Rudd Government placed special emphasis on Australia's major power relations. Rudd reaffirmed the primacy of the alliance with the US as 'our key strategic partnership and the central pillar of Australian national security policy'.[3] The evolution of the US role in the Asia-Pacific and in particular its relationship with China was crucial; Rudd said in April 2008 of the US and China that '[f]or Australia, the single core question of whether ours will be a Pacific century rests on the long-term management of this most critical relationship'.[4]

---

1   See Kevin Rudd, 'Smart Power', *The Diplomat*, February–March 2007.

2   See Allan Gyngell, 'Emerging Challenges for Australian Foreign Policy', *Australian Journal of International Affairs*, 68(4) 2014.

3   Kevin Rudd, 'National Security', Ministerial Statement, in *Commonwealth of Australia Parliamentary Debates*, House of Representatives, Official Hansard, No. 18, 4 December 2008, p. 12552.

4   Quoted in Allan Gyngell, 'Ambition: The Emerging Foreign Policy of the Rudd Government', *Analysis*, Sydney: Lowy Institute for International Policy, December 2008, p. 5. On the Rudd Government's approach towards the US and China, see Alan Bloomfield, 'To Balance or to Bandwagon? Adjusting to China's Rise during Australia's Rudd–Gillard Era', *Pacific Review*, published online, 16 March 2015.

A key element in the Rudd Government's approach to regional security challenges was its proposal for an 'Asia Pacific Community' (see below).[5] In the multilateral arena, the government sought a seat on the UN Security Council (ultimately secured for the 2014–2015 term), gave special emphasis to the development of the G20 (Group of Twenty) grouping, and made substantial efforts through the G20 to coordinate approaches to the global financial crisis from late 2008 (the dominant concern for the government in 2008 and 2009).[6] Australia sought to contain the dangers from nuclear weapons by supporting the International Commission on Nuclear Non-proliferation and Disarmament.[7] In 2010, Australia also finally gained membership in the Asia–Europe Meeting (ASEM) process, as a part of the 'Asian' side of the dialogue. This brought to realisation for Australia a group membership – with an 'Asian chair' – that Australia had sought since Paul Keating's government in the early 1990s, although by the time Australia joined the success was primarily symbolic since ASEM had not attained a profile among the first rank of Asian and Asia-Pacific regional forums.[8]

With ASEAN, there were substantial areas of policy continuity in the Rudd Government's approach. ASEAN itself had been moving to enhance its corporate character by adopting a new Charter. The Charter reaffirmed the key bases for ASEAN's cooperation, made some revisions to the Association's institutional structure and gave it a formal legal identity for the first time.[9] A significant outcome of the Charter was an increased declaratory focus for ASEAN on human rights. In line with Article 14 of the Charter, the ASEAN Intergovernmental Commission on Human Rights was inaugurated in 2009. The commission followed long-standing ASEAN practices by

---

5   Facing ASEAN opposition, this proposed 'large C' community became a discussion about a 'small c' community.

6   Gyngell, 'Ambition', p. 12.

7   Ramesh Thakur, 'Nuclear-Free Dream For Real', *Canberra Times*, 8 April 2010; Graeme Dobell, 'Australia–East Asia/US Relations: Australia Adjusts to New Realities', *Comparative Connections: A Quarterly E-Journal on East Asian Bilateral Relations*, 11(3) 2009.

8   Sebastian Bersick, 'Europe's Role in Asia: Distant but Involved', in David Shambaugh and Michael Yahuda, eds, *International Relations of Asia*, 2nd edn, New York: Rowman & Littlefield, 2014, pp. 131–2; Melissa Conley Tyler and Eric Lerais, 'Australia and ASEM: The First Two Years', Working Paper 2013/1, Caulfield East, Vic.: Monash University European and EU Centre, May 2013.

9   Mely Caballero-Anthony, 'The ASEAN Charter: An Opportunity Missed or One that *Cannot be Missed*', *Southeast Asian Affairs 2008*, Singapore: Institute of Southeast Asian Studies, 2008.

not including procedures for compliance or enforcement. ASEAN also issued a Human Rights Declaration in 2012. These developments were viewed as a cautious extension of ASEAN's ambitions for regional dialogue.[10]

After the inauguration of the Charter, ASEAN was keen for dialogue partners to raise the profile of their institutional links with the Association. On 13 June 2008, Rudd visited the ASEAN Secretariat in Jakarta, and was the first head of government of a dialogue partner to do so. During the visit he announced the inauguration of the second phase of the ASEAN–Australia Development Cooperation Program through which Australia would provide high-level policy advice, research and implementation support to assist ASEAN in key areas of its economic cooperation, including harmonisation of standards, elimination of tariffs and reduction of non-tariff barriers. This assistance was a significant support for development of the ASEAN Economic Community, a key goal for the Association.[11] In July 2008, the Minister for Foreign Affairs Stephen Smith announced that Australia would upgrade relations by nominating an ambassador to ASEAN. The ambassador would be a senior, Canberra-based diplomat whose duties would include participating in meetings at the ASEAN Secretariat and in other regional ASEAN meetings.[12]

The Rudd Government finalised the process begun under the Howard Government of negotiation of a trade agreement to link the ASEAN Free Trade Area with the Australia–New Zealand Closer Economic Relations (CER) and this was announced on 28 August 2008. The ASEAN–Australia–New Zealand Free Trade Agreement (AANZFTA) was introduced with an enthusiastic statement by the 12 trade ministers involved: 'The Ministers noted that the Agreement is an important milestone in the long-standing ASEAN–CER comprehensive partnership. As a living document, the Agreement

---

10   Kathleen G. Southwick, 'Bumpy Road to the ASEAN Human Rights Declaration', *Asia-Pacific Bulletin*, No. 197, Washington, DC: East–West Center, 22 January 2013; Mathew Davies, 'The ASEAN Synthesis: Human Rights, Non-Intervention, and the ASEAN Human Rights Declaration', *Georgetown Journal of International Affairs*, 14(2) 2013.

11   Kevin Rudd, 'Joint Press Statement with Ausaid: ASEAN and Australian Advances Cooperation in Economic Integration', media release, Jakarta, 13 June 2008.

12   Mark Dodd, 'Canberra to Assign an Envoy to ASEAN', *The Australian*, 25 July 2008. On 5 September, the government announced that Gillian Bird, a deputy secretary in the Department of Foreign Affairs and Trade, had been appointed to the post. See Stephen Smith, 'Diplomatic Appointment – Ambassador to ASEAN', media release, 5 September 2008.

brings to a new height the level of cooperation and relationship between the governments of ASEAN, Australia and New Zealand as well as its [sic] peoples.'[13]

The Australian Government saw substantial benefits for Australian traders, including extensive tariff reductions, regional rules of origin that could provide new opportunities for Australian exporters to tap into production networks in the region, promotion of greater certainty for Australian service suppliers and investors including through enhanced protection for Australian investors in ASEAN members, and additional economic cooperation and business outreach programs.[14]

The AANZFTA came into force in January 2010.[15] Its potential impact on trade varied, essentially because ASEAN had made more progress on liberalising trade in goods than in services. The agreement would also come into effect gradually, because some ASEAN members needed time to adjust their domestic frameworks of laws and regulations and because some areas of liberalisation would not be implemented fully until at least 2020. It was difficult to assess the likely long-term impact of the agreement, but it marked a major advance in the institutional relationship.[16]

Australia's 'Asia Pacific Community' proposal

Other aspects of the Rudd Government's approach proved controversial. As discussed in previous chapters, Australia's relations with ASEAN have had tensions stemming from Australia's interest in cooperation on a broader regional basis that can involve participation by ASEAN and the major powers (including Australia's ally the United States).

---

13   ASEAN, 'Joint Media Statement of the Thirteenth AEM–CER Consultations', Singapore, 28 August 2008.
14   Australian Department of Foreign Affairs and Trade, 'Overview and Key Outcomes of the ASEAN–Australia–New Zealand Free Trade Agreement', Department of Foreign Affairs and Trade Speaking Notes for Presentation at Austrade's ASEAN Now seminars, 15–30 October 2009; Minter Ellison Lawyers, 'The ASEAN Australia New Zealand Free Trade Agreement: Our Overview and Assessment', April 2009.
15   The parties to the AANZFTA signed a protocol in August 2014 to provide improved administrative efficiency for customs authorities and to encourage enhanced business utilisation of the agreement; see Australian Department of Foreign Affairs and Trade, 'Signature of AANZFTA Protocol', media release, 27 August 2014.
16   Ibid. See also Razeen Sally, 'ASEAN FTAs: State of Play and Outlook for ASEAN's Regional and Global Integration', in Sanchita Basu Das et al., eds, *The ASEAN Economic Community: A Work in Progress,* Singapore: ISEAS Publishing, 2013, pp. 357–62.

Some early tension was evident in 1973 and 1974 when Gough Whitlam's government proposed an Asia-Pacific forum (as discussed in Chapter 1). ASEAN sensitivity about its identity and position were also issues in the negotiations that led to the advent of the Asia-Pacific Economic Cooperation (APEC) grouping and the ASEAN Regional Forum (ARF) in the period 1989–94 (discussed in Chapter 3). In 2008, Australian interests in regional institutional design again produced a contest with ASEAN.

Rudd had come to office with a particular interest in relations among the major powers, especially the US and China, and in the potential for multilateral cooperation to help manage and stabilise regional and international relationships. In 2005, Australia had gained membership in the new East Asia Summit with the 10 ASEAN members, plus Japan, China, South Korea, India and New Zealand. On 4 June 2008, Rudd put forward a further ambitious proposal for multilateral cooperation. In a speech to the Asia Society AustralAsia Centre, he argued that it was desirable to review the long-term vision for the 'architecture' for the Asia-Pacific region.[17] Strong and effective regional institutions, he suggested, were needed 'that will underpin an open, peaceful, stable, prosperous and sustainable region'. Rudd said that 'we need to have a vision for an Asia Pacific Community', which he suggested should be achieved by 2020. This vision needed to embrace '[a] regional institution that spans the entire Asia-Pacific region − including the United States, Japan, China, India, Indonesia and the other states of the region', and '[a] regional institution which is able to engage in the full spectrum of dialogue, cooperation and action on economic and political matters and future challenges related to security'. Rudd argued that '[a]t present none of our existing regional mechanisms as currently configured are capable of achieving these purposes' and proposed 'a regional debate about where we want to be in 2020'.[18]

On the sensitive issue of how such a concept might affect existing regional institutions, Rudd said:

> Such a debate does not of itself mean the diminution of any of the existing regional bodies. APEC, the ASEAN Regional Forum, the East Asia Summit, ASEAN Plus Three and ASEAN itself will continue

---

17   Kevin Rudd, 'It's Time to Build an Asia Pacific Community', Address to the Asia Society AustralAsia Centre, Sydney, 4 June 2008.
18   Ibid.

to play important roles, and longer-term may continue in their own right or embody the building blocks of an Asia Pacific Community. There will be wide ranging views about this across the region – some more supportive than others. New bodies and new ideas will continue to emerge.[19]

Rudd mentioned the example of the European Union (EU), saying that while it was not an 'identikit model', the European case showed that it was necessary to take the first step. ASEAN, Rudd argued, was an example of the benefits of a long-term vision. 'In a diverse region, ASEAN has brought together a varied group and forged a common outlook on many questions. ASEAN has built habits of cooperation and dialogue. And ASEAN has played a critical role in building and maintaining peace in the region through its work.'[20]

In this speech, Rudd had recognised and praised ASEAN. However, his speech could also be seen as an implicit criticism of ASEAN's efforts so far in sponsoring the ARF and the East Asia Summit as useful but inadequate bases for longer-term institutional development.[21] Rudd's comment that regional groupings, including ASEAN, would 'continue to play important roles', might 'continue in their own right', or indeed even 'embody the building blocks of an Asia Pacific Community', could be seen as a surprisingly casual reference to East Asia's leading regional group, whose members might well not have welcomed the idea of their Association being considered as a building block for a wider community that they had not proposed.

Rudd announced that he had appointed Richard Woolcott (former secretary of the Department of Foreign Affairs and Trade (DFAT) who had been Prime Minister Bob Hawke's envoy during the development of APEC) as his special envoy to consult on the proposal. Woolcott later confirmed that he had less than one day's advance notice about the speech and his own nomination as special envoy.[22]

---

19   Ibid.

20   Ibid.

21   See Seng Tan, *Multilateral Asian Security Architecture: Non-ASEAN Stakeholders*, Abingdon: Routledge, 2016, pp. 48–53; See Seng Tan, 'Hobnobbing with Giants: Australia's Approach to Asian Regionalism', in Sally Percival Wood and Baogang He, eds, *The Australia–ASEAN Dialogue: Tracing 40 Years of Partnership*, New York: Palgrave Macmillan, 2014.

22   Richard Woolcott, interview with Graeme Dobell, Sydney, October 2010 (used with the permission of Mr Dobell).

Early comments in the Australian media noted that the Asia Pacific Community proposal had been announced with little advanced preparation or consultation and at an early stage in the Rudd Government's term in office. Michelle Grattan described the announcement as 'breathtaking' but added that '[r]egional countries might see Rudd's initiative as the new boy on the block getting above himself. Best to wait awhile before you throw your weight around'.[23]

Some initial reactions in the ASEAN region were favourable. A senior Indonesian analyst, Hadi Soesastro, indicated support for the principles and vision underlying the proposal and said that Indonesia should back Australia on it:

> Australian critics of Prime Minister Rudd's Asia Pacific Community initiative have got it wrong about the idea not being well thought out. Kevin Rudd's initiative should be seen as an invitation to other leaders, policy makers, and thinkers in the region to join … in a serious discussion about how best the Asia Pacific region could be organized. If Rudd had come up with a fully-baked proposal, the exercise could be self-defeating. Evolving regionalism in Asia Pacific requires that all parties concerned should have an active part in the process, especially in the shaping of a new vision for the region … Indonesia should support Rudd's initiative and the process of deliberations that will follow from it.[24]

In early July 2008, Thailand's Foreign Minister Noppadon Pattama expressed his country's willingness to discuss the proposal: 'Any idea that brings peace and stability to the region, we can't see any reason why we shouldn't study or deliberate the issue.'[25]

However, most reactions in ASEAN were critical. In July 2008, Prime Minister Abdullah Badawi of Malaysia suggested that it would be desirable to develop the existing regional institutions: '[w]e already have a forum, the ASEAN Regional Forum. We can continue with the existing institutions'. The Indonesian Government was also not supportive: Vice President Yusuf Kalla commented that '[f]or me, it's not necessary to make a new body. We already have ASEAN and

---

23   Michelle Grattan, 'The Danger of Taking on Too Much', *The Age*, 6 June 2008; see also Paul Kelly, 'Time May Not Be Ripe for Brave New Forum', *The Australian*, 9 July 2008.
24   Hadi Soesastro, 'Kevin Rudd's Architecture for the Asia Pacific', *East Asia Forum*, 9 June 2008.
25   ABC News, 'Thailand Shows Interest in Rudd's Asia-Pac Community', 4 July 2008.

APEC. There is no need for all countries in Asia Pacific to make one objective.'[26] Indonesia's official attitude was clearly notable given that country's central role in ASEAN and its significance for Australia in collaboration on regional cooperation. In the same month Barry Desker, a Singaporean analyst and former senior official, said about Rudd's proposal that 'I would think it is dead in the water right from the very beginning. It would have been much more useful if it had been thought through before and conceptualised with regional leaders before it was presented as a bright new idea from Australia.'[27]

At the time of ASEAN's ministerial meetings in Singapore in late July 2008, the official spokesman for the meetings, Andrew Tan, commented that:

> On this subject of a pan-Asian regional forum, or whatever name it is to be called, I think ASEAN countries have said that they are still waiting for more details of this proposal. The region itself is already quite complex so if there can be another regional process that can help us better manage this, there is no reason why we should stop it from being developed, but it also has to take into account the region's view as well as regional sensitivities and regional circumstance.[28]

The United States' reaction was also cool.[29] John Negroponte, Deputy Secretary of State in the George W. Bush administration, commented in late June 2008 that the US did not have details of the Rudd proposal, but emphasised the importance to the US of its major bilateral relations in the Asia-Pacific region and that '[i]t makes sense to aspire towards more meaningful region-wide institutions, but I think we're very much at the beginning of that process in historic terms'.[30] Diplomatic cables released by WikiLeaks in late 2010 revealed that US officials in Canberra had been critical about the Rudd proposal; they were reported to have complained that the proposal reflected Rudd's tendency to be 'obsessed with managing the media cycle rather than engaging in collaborative decision-making'.[31]

---

26   Angus Grigg, 'Blow to Rudd's Asia Plan', *Australian Financial Review*, 23 July 2008.
27   Patrick Walters, 'Rudd Asia Plan "Dead in Water"', *The Australian*, 4 July 2008.
28   Katrina Nicholas, 'Smith Still Keen on New Regional Group', *Australian Financial Review*, 24 July 2008.
29   Baogang He, 'The Awkwardness of Australian Engagement with Asia: The Dilemmas of Australian Idea of Regionalism', *Japanese Journal of Political Science*, 12(2) 2011: 272–3.
30   Daniel Flitton, 'US Diplomat Wary of Rudd's Big Idea', *The Age*, 30 June 2008.
31   Philip Dorling, 'Rudd's Man Criticised Hasty Asia-Pacific Community Plan', *Sydney Morning Herald*, 24 December 2010.

In subsequent statements, Rudd continued to advance his proposal, but with more explicit recognition of ASEAN's contribution to regional cooperation. Speaking in Singapore in August 2008, Rudd placed strong emphasis on the contribution that had been made towards regional cooperation by ASEAN, which he called 'an outstanding essay in institutional success'.[32] In the latter part of 2008 and in 2009, Woolcott conducted a series of consultations in 21 countries to explore attitudes towards the Asia Pacific Community (the consultations included all ASEAN countries except Myanmar).[33]

In an address to the Shangri-la Dialogue in Singapore in May 2009, Rudd presented preliminary findings from Woolcott's consultations and argued that there had been broad agreement on the value of a focused discussion about how regional architecture should develop, and that there was recognition that there was at present no single forum for leaders to discuss the full range of political, strategic and economic challenges for the future. However, there was 'no appetite for additional institutions'. He said that he would brief leaders at the forthcoming East Asia Summit and APEC meetings and that Australia would invite 'key government officials, academics and opinion makers from around the region' to attend 'a one and a half track conference to further explore the idea of an Asia-Pacific community'. The speech marked the moment when the government made a symbolic change in the way they referred to the proposal; the 'large C' Community became a 'small c' community.[34]

At the 'one and half track' meeting in Sydney on 3–5 December 2009, Rudd said that 'ASEAN should be at the core of any future Asia Pacific community'. He sought to reassure Southeast Asian leaders that Australia's diplomacy was not a threat to their regional significance: 'Our ambition in Australia has been to open paths to dialogue rather than to close them off, to listen as much as to speak, to encourage

---

32   Kevin Rudd, 'The Singapore Lecture: Building on ASEAN's Success: Towards an Asia Pacific Century', Singapore, 12 August 2008.

33   Woolcott visited Brunei, Cambodia, Canada, Chile, China, India, Indonesia, Japan, Laos, Malaysia, Mexico, New Zealand, Papua New Guinea, Peru, Philippines, Russia, Singapore, South Korea, Thailand, the US, and Vietnam. See John Faulkner, 'Questions on Notice: Mr Richard Woolcott (Question No. 2123)', in *Commonwealth of Australia Parliamentary Debates*, Senate, Official Hansard, No. 13, 17 November 2009, p. 8091.

34   Kevin Rudd, 'Address at Shangri-La Dialogue', Singapore, 29 May 2009. The use of a capital 'C' was discontinued partly because it was considered that it might produce some confusion between Rudd's concept and cooperation patterns in Europe.

conversation rather than to dominate it.'[35] One or more of the existing regional institutions might evolve in mission and composition to adapt to the needs of the region.

At the Sydney meeting, there was considerable interest in reviewing existing institutional arrangements and a former prime minister of South Korea, Han Seung-soo, proposed setting up an eminent persons' group 'capable of devising a concrete plan for the eventual creation of an Asia-Pacific community'.[36] The meeting, however, did not arrive at a consensus. Controversy arose over a summing up presentation by Michael Wesley, the Australian co-chair, in which he referred to the concept of a 'concert of powers' as a means to manage relations in the Asia-Pacific. Wesley said just after the conference that 'I believe people misinterpreted what I was saying. I think while the great powers in the region need to come together, the smaller powers also must be involved'.[37] Some delegates, however, saw the comments as a challenge to ASEAN's identity and role.[38] In particular, a senior Singaporean figure, Professor Tommy Koh, in a critical account published shortly after the meeting, strongly reasserted ASEAN's claim to a primary role in regional diplomacy and institutional development:

> ASEAN is acceptable to all the stakeholders as the region's convenor and facilitator because it is neutral, pragmatic and welcoming. We in ASEAN feel the grouping's long-term goal of peace and stability and the dividends obtained to date should not be minimised or marginalised. The conference in Sydney did not provide us with the clarity or reassurance we had hoped for.[39]

---

35   Kevin Rudd, 'Address to the Asia Pacific Community Conference', Sydney, 4 December 2009.
36   Peter Hartcher, 'Rudd Puts Lesson in Rat Cunning to Use', *Sydney Morning Herald*, 8 December 2009.
37   Paul Kelly, 'Diplomatic Activist Reshapes Region', *The Australian*, 12 December 2009; Michael Wesley, interview with the author, Canberra, July 2015. The term 'concert of powers' reflects assessments of the state of international relations in Europe between the Congress of Vienna in 1815 and the advent of the First World War in 1914. Key elements of a 'concert of powers' are a commitment by the powers involved to maintain the status quo, an agreement not to use war (or its threat) to solve problems (or to contain and minimise any conflict that does develop), and agreement that a concert is an informal arrangement based on enlightened self-interest rather than formalised norms; see Sandy Gordon, 'The Quest for a Concert of Powers in Asia', *Security Challenges*, 8(4) 2012: 36.
38   Tan, *Multilateral Asian Security Architecture*, pp. 50–3; see also Kelly, 'Diplomatic Activist Reshapes Region'.
39   Tommy Koh, 'Rudd's Reckless Regional Rush', *The Australian*, 18 December 2009.

In the following months, Australia's ideas continued to be discussed, but the eminent persons' group proposal did not eventuate. It was notable that Indonesia continued to be unenthusiastic about the proposal. During a visit to Australia in March 2010, President Susilo Bambang Yudhoyono told Rudd that while the Asia Pacific community was 'an intriguing idea to explore', Jakarta's priority was to strengthen ASEAN and he suggested that the matter should be discussed at foreign minister level.[40] By June 2010, when Singapore's Foreign Minister George Yeo visited Australia, Rudd said that he was now quite happy to leave ASEAN to discuss how the original concept should evolve.[41] ASEAN was indeed moving to consider how to associate the US and Russia more closely with its multilateral cooperation. Yeo said that while Singapore had differed with aspects of Rudd's initial proposal, the two countries were now 'almost in complete agreement':

> There was some question in the original proposal over whether [ASEAN] was central to [Rudd's vision for an Asia-Pacific community] and we were naturally worried about that. But that was quickly clarified and I think Australia's happy to leave it to ASEAN to discuss how that original configuration should evolve.[42]

Having challenged ASEAN's role as the arbiter of regional institutional building, Australia had accepted the Association's central role in this area. Australia had shifted from a Community concept to a community conversation conducted by ASEAN.

Rudd's proposal for a new mode of regional cooperation encountered problems and resistance for several reasons. Rudd and the government had not prepared the ground among regional governments and opinion leaders for the advancement of new ideas and proposals and the abrupt announcement left many in the region bemused and sceptical. The use of the term 'community' was problematic because there was no common and agreed concept of how a regional 'community' should be defined and sought, and whether it might evolve on either an East Asian or an Asia-Pacific basis. Sheryn Lee and Anthony Milner have argued that many in East Asia considered that a 'community' should be pursued more appropriately among East Asian states rather than

---

40   Mark Dodd, 'SBY Cold on Rudd's Asia Plan', *The Australian*, 10 March 2010.
41   Rowan Callick, 'Rudd's Asian Vision Quietly Buried', *The Australian*, 21 June 2010.
42   John Kerin, 'Singapore Backs Rudd's Regional Vision', *Australian Financial Review*, 17 June 2010.

in a broader Asia-Pacific grouping. It was therefore problematic for Rudd to have appeared to assume that a constituency already existed for considering development of a 'community' in the Asia-Pacific.[43]

An additional issue was that Australia did not have collaborators within ASEAN willing to give diplomatic support and to join in advancing the proposal. Instead, Australia encountered opposition. Indonesia, whose support for and collaboration with Australia in previous regional initiatives (including the Cambodian peace process and the development of APEC and the ARF) had been vital, was not enthusiastic about the Rudd concept (as Yudhoyono had indicated). In public discussions on the Rudd proposal, Singapore was a prominent critic, possibly because it saw a wider regional grouping not clearly identified with and led by ASEAN as a challenge to its own influence in ASEAN and Southeast Asia.[44] In the debate about the Asia Pacific community, it had been reaffirmed that ASEAN's prime role in sponsoring regional dialogues and institutions had to be acknowledged and recognised by Australia.

ASEAN and changing US approaches to multilateral cooperation

By mid-2010, it was clear that the Rudd Government's attempted initiative on institutional adaptation had not been accepted by ASEAN. However, by that time, the context for discussions about regional dialogue had changed, particularly because of developments in the approach of the United States under Barack Obama's administration to Southeast Asia and to ASEAN. These developments led to an important expansion of the membership of the East Asia Summit to include the US and Russia.

The Obama administration had come to office in January 2009 wanting to upgrade the US's profile in East Asia and to take a more active role in multilateral cooperation.[45] During the period of the Bush administration, the US had been preoccupied heavily by

---

43   See Sheryn Lee and Anthony Milner, 'Practical vs. Identity Regionalism: Australia's APC Initiative, a Case Study', *Contemporary Politics*, 20(2) 2014.
44   Woolcott, interview with Dobell.
45   Jeffrey A. Bader, *Obama and China's Rise: An Insider's Account of America's Asia Strategy*, Washington, DC: Brookings Institution Press, 2012, pp. 1–8.

the impact of the terrorist attacks in September 2001 and then by military involvements in Afghanistan and Iraq. After 2001, the US had expanded its bilateral linkages and cooperation with a number of members of ASEAN. However the Bush administration had shown comparatively less interest in Asian multilateral cooperation; for example, Secretary of State Condoleezza Rice had to miss two meetings of the ARF (in 2005! and 2007) because of other commitments. At the same time, China had been advancing its relations in Southeast Asia, both bilaterally and through cooperation with ASEAN, including through the China–ASEAN Free Trade Agreement. While the US was preoccupied in the Middle East, China was seen to be enhancing its position in Southeast Asia.[46] The US accordingly pursued an increased diplomatic involvement in Southeast Asia, and from 2011 announced a 'pivot' (subsequently termed a 'rebalance') towards the Asia-Pacific that would insulate US defence commitments to the region from budget cuts, increase the presence of US forces, including on a rotational basis, and enhance the US's economic ties with the region through a multilateral economic agreement, the Trans-Pacific Partnership (TPP).[47]

These developments had important implications for US approaches towards multilateral cooperation and ASEAN. In February 2009, Hillary Clinton became the first US secretary of state to visit ASEAN headquarters in Jakarta. In an important step, the US acceded to the ASEAN Treaty of Amity and Cooperation (TAC) in July 2009. This opened the way for US participation in the East Asia Summit, since ASEAN had made accession to the treaty a prerequisite for such membership.[48] The US's capacity for discussions with all ASEAN members was facilitated by the opening of direct dialogue between the US Government and Myanmar, which included a visit to the country by US Deputy Secretary of State Kurt Campbell in early November 2009.[49] US presidents had previously been unwilling to

---

46   Ian Storey, *Southeast Asia and the Rise of China: The Search for Security*, London: Routledge, 2011, pp. 64–98.
47   Carlyle A. Thayer, 'Deference/Defiance: Southeast Asia, China and the South China Sea', Paper prepared for International Studies Association Annual Convention, Hilton San Francisco, Union Square, 5 April 2013, pp. 26–7.
48   Bader, *Obama and China's Rise*, pp. 13–15; Sheldon Simon, 'US–Southeast Asia Relations: The United States is Back!' *Comparative Connections: A Quarterly E-Journal on East Asian Bilateral Relations*, 11(3) 2009.
49   Associated Press, 'Top US Officials Meet Myanmar Junta, Suu Kyi', 4 November 2009.

meet with ASEAN leaders on a joint basis because of the unpopularity of the Myanmar regime, which had recently been exacerbated by that regime's repression of demonstrations in 2007. During his visit to East Asia in November 2009, President Obama held the first summit meeting between the US and all ASEAN members in Singapore. In his speech on US regional policies in Tokyo, Obama stated that:

> As an Asia-Pacific nation, the United States expects to be involved in the discussions that shape the future of this region, and to participate fully in appropriate organizations as they are established and evolve … And the United States looks forward to engaging with the East Asia Summit more formally as it plays a role in addressing the challenges of our time.[50]

Japan's Prime Minister Hatoyama Yukio (September 2009 – June 2010) added to the debate about regional cooperation by raising the concept of an 'East Asia Community'.[51] Hatoyama suggested an informal and staged approach towards a regional community. He proposed to follow a phased path, starting with economic ties and then moving through issues-based cooperation towards eventual institutionalisation. Hatoyama did not make clear exactly what membership was envisaged: he initially did not appear to envisage US participation, although he later did assure the US that it would not be excluded.[52] While Hatoyama's concept did not move beyond the proposal stage before he left office, his suggestion added to reassessments of institutional consultation in East Asia and the Asia-Pacific.[53]

In this climate of debate and reconsideration, ASEAN began to consider ways of including the US and also Russia in regular discussions with the Association and its other dialogue partners. At the 16th ASEAN Summit in Hanoi in April 2010, Clinton made it clear that the US wanted to join the East Asia Summit. There was debate within ASEAN on whether it would be best to include the US in the Summit or whether it would be desirable to pursue a separate

50   Barack Obama, 'Remarks by President Barack Obama at Suntory Hall', Tokyo, Office of the Press Secretary, The White House, 14 November 2009.
51   Yukio Hatoyama, 'A New Path for Japan', *New York Times*, 26 August 2009; Aurelia George Mulgan, 'Is There a "Japanese" Concept of an East Asia Community?' *East Asia Forum*, 6 November 2009.
52   Rikki Kersten and William T. Tow, 'Evolving Australian Approaches to Security Architecture in the Asia-Pacific', Tokyo Foundation, 22 April 2011.
53   Ibid.; Woolcott, interview with Dobell.

meeting with the 16 members of the Summit and the US and Russia in an ASEAN Plus Eight forum. This forum, it was suggested, could be held every two years, alongside the APEC leaders' meeting when that was being held in an ASEAN country (given that the annual meetings of APEC alternate between ASEAN and non-ASEAN members). This arrangement would maximise the likelihood of regular participation by the US president, given that he/she would be able on the same visit to attend APEC and also the mooted 'ASEAN Plus' gathering. Singapore was a strong advocate of the ASEAN Plus Eight formula but other members (including Indonesia, Malaysia, Laos and Vietnam) preferred the option of inviting the US and Russia into the East Asia Summit. This was adopted as ASEAN's approach and the US and Russia duly joined the Summit in November 2010.[54]

Many questions remained on how the expanded East Asia Summit might develop. However, the concept of a leaders' dialogue forum with a membership including ASEAN, the Northeast Asian states, India, the US, Russia, Australia, and New Zealand had been realised. Looking back on his role as special envoy, Woolcott felt that the changing major power environment – and particularly the interest of China, Russia and the US in participating in a dialogue through the East Asia Summit – had been relevant to Rudd's policy goals. He commented in October 2010 that 'the times have worked quite well for Rudd ... because they are three of the major powers' and India had also wanted to join the Summit.[55]

In a speech in December 2010, Rudd (now foreign minister in the Gillard Government) expressed his satisfaction at the expansion of the East Asia Summit. He stated that:

> This was our core objective in proposing the concept of an Asia Pacific community ... a regional institution with sufficient membership and mandate, and meeting at summit level, to begin to carve out a rules-based order for the future ... [W]ith the EAS' [East Asia Summit] expansion, we achieved the core of that objective. The challenge now is to build this emerging institution's agenda.[56]

---

54   Kersten and Tow, 'Evolving Australian Approaches'.
55   Woolcott, interview with Dobell.
56   Kevin Rudd, 'Future Stability and Security in the Asia Pacific Region', Address to the Brisbane Institute, 8 December 2010.

The question remained, however, as to whether the climate of relations among the East Asia Summit members, particularly between the major powers, would enable the Summit to begin in Rudd's words to 'carve out a rules-based order' for East Asia and the Asia-Pacific and the outlook for this was uncertain.

ASEAN relations 2010–13: Consolidation and caution

Gillard replaced Rudd as prime minister on 24 June 2010 and led the government for the next three years. In a comment in early July on her policy approach, Gillard said that she did not envisage major changes in foreign relations and that her government would not be emphasising Rudd's recent pursuit of an Asia Pacific community.[57] The Gillard Government, however, continued to focus heavily on major power relationships and the implications of these for the Asia-Pacific and East Asia. The government supported strongly the US recommitment through its 'rebalance' to the Asia-Pacific and welcomed Obama's announcement in November 2011 in Canberra of an increased presence of US forces in Australia, including the rotation of US Marines through Darwin. Gillard also sought to consolidate relations with China and achieved an annual high-level strategic and economic dialogue with that country (announced in April 2013).[58]

In the period from 2010, the Australian Government made another adaptation in Australia's approach towards defining its interest in relation to regions. Alongside ongoing references to the Asia-Pacific, there was increasing discussion of the 'Indo-Pacific' as a frame of regional reference. Reference to the Indo-Pacific reflected the growing profile of India both for Australia's bilateral relationships and as a factor in Asia overall. Rudd, foreign minister in the Gillard Government from June 2010 to February 2012, noted in November 2010 that 'we have long looked east across the Pacific to our long-standing allies the United States … equally now Australia must now look west to the great challenges and opportunities that now present

---

57   Peter Hartcher, 'Gillard Rejects Rudd's Asia Vision', *Sydney Morning Herald*, 5 July 2010.
58   Carlyle A. Thayer, 'Australia, the ANZUS Alliance and US Rebalancing to the Asia-Pacific', Keynote Paper presented to the International Conference on Australia–Asia Relations under Prime Minister Tony Abbott, National Cheng Chi University, Taipei, 31 March – 1 April 2015.

themselves across the Indian Ocean region'.[59] The government's 2013 Defence White Paper gave extensive emphasis to the Indo-Pacific as a regional reference, stating that:

> [A] new Indo-Pacific strategic arc is beginning to emerge, connecting the Indian and Pacific oceans through Southeast Asia. This new strategic construct ... is being forged by a range of factors. Notably, India is emerging as an important strategic, diplomatic and economic actor, 'looking East', and becoming more engaged in regional frameworks. Growing trade, investment and energy flows across the broader region are strengthening economic and security interdependencies. These two factors combined are also increasingly attracting international attention to the Indian Ocean, through which some of the world's busiest and most strategically significant trade routes pass.[60]

While the concept of 'Indo-Pacific' was still being debated, this discussion suggested that Australia's ASEAN relations would be pursued alongside regional contexts that now extended to the Indian Ocean as well as the Western Pacific.[61]

Institutional relations and economic cooperation

The Gillard Government from 2010 continued to build on relationships with ASEAN. While Australia itself did not seek institutional innovation, it joined two new ASEAN-sponsored ministerial-level dialogues – the negotiations for RCEP and the ADMM-Plus process, and a new dialogue at senior official level on maritime issues. Australia faced some significant issues in its ASEAN relations, including the impact of increasing major power competition, which was clearly evident in relation to the South China Sea, and the process of change in Myanmar. The dilemma of people movements and irregular migration, a highly contentious issue in Australian domestic politics, also saw some strain in key Australian bilateral relations in the ASEAN region.

---

59   Quoted in David Scott, 'Australia's Embrace of the "Indo-Pacific": New Term, New Region, New Strategy?' *International Relations of the Asia-Pacific*, 13(3) 2013: 430.
60   Australian Department of Defence, *2013 Defence White Paper*, Canberra: Commonwealth of Australia, 2013, p. 7.
61   Rory Medcalf, 'Reimagining Asia: From Asia-Pacific to Indo-Pacific', *Asan Forum*, 26 June 2015; Trevor Wilson, 'The "Indo-Pacific": Absent Policy Behind Meaningless Words', *East Asia Forum*, 19 September 2014.

In engagement with ASEAN after 2010, another milestone in interactions was reached in Hanoi on 30 October 2010 with the holding of a further ASEAN–Australia summit at leadership level. This was only the third such heads of government summit between Australia and ASEAN, after those held in 1977 and (along with New Zealand) in 2004. The meeting's joint statement expressed ASEAN's appreciation for Australia's 'steadfast friendship' since 1974. After a period of some controversy in relations, the statement affirmed that 'ASEAN Leaders appreciated Australia's continued support for ASEAN's institutional strengthening' and for ASEAN's 'central role in the regional architecture in responding to regional and global challenges'.[62]

The meeting reviewed and reaffirmed the wide areas of ongoing cooperation between the parties. Prime Minister Gillard announced three initiatives: aid to the Greater Mekong Sub-Region 'to assist in connecting the rural poor to new markets, including by upgrading, rehabilitating and maintaining roads, bridges and rail links in the region'; support for the International Labour Organization to protect migrant workers; and aid for the ASEAN Intergovernmental Commission on Human Rights that had been established the previous year.[63] The Gillard Government made a further commitment to advance relations in its October 2012 White Paper, which announced the establishment of a position of resident Australian ambassador to ASEAN who would be based in Jakarta to facilitate close liaison with the ASEAN Secretariat.[64]

In a further institutional linkage, Australia joined with ASEAN in negotiations for a new economic cooperation enterprise, RCEP, which was designed to be a regional free trade agreement to include the 10 ASEAN members along with the countries that currently had free trade agreements with ASEAN – Australia, China, India, Japan, South Korea and New Zealand. RCEP's vision was to be a 'high-quality' and mutually beneficial economic partnership agreement that would broaden and deepen current free trade agreement arrangements. The RCEP concept grew out of two previous proposals for regional trade agreements

---

62 ASEAN, 'ASEAN and Australia: An Enduring Connection', Joint Statement of the ASEAN–Australia Summit, Hanoi, 30 October 2010.
63 Ibid.
64 Australian Government, *Australia in the Asian Century: White Paper*, Canberra: Commonwealth of Australia, October 2012, p. 257.

based around the 13 ASEAN Plus Three members and also the original 16 members of the East Asia Summit (that is, the membership before the US and Russia joined). As an ASEAN process, RCEP was to be guided by the 'ASEAN way' of consensus and voluntary adherence to agreements. It would also likely seek to accommodate the varying levels of economic development of the participants by avoiding commitments that the less-developed economies would find hard to meet.[65] By sponsoring RCEP, ASEAN sought to bolster its centrality in regional economic integration although at the time of writing it was not clear how the negotiations would evolve and how effective the negotiations would be in producing significant liberalisation.[66]

By participating in RCEP, Australia continued its long-term support for ASEAN's economic goals. In a joint statement on 20 November 2012 while in Phnom Penh for ASEAN-sponsored meetings, Prime Minister Gillard and the Minister for Trade Craig Emerson congratulated ASEAN on the initiative. They noted that RCEP participating countries include nine of Australia's top 12 trading partners and account for almost 60 per cent of Australia's two-way trade and 70 per cent of exports.[67]

As Gillard and Emerson also noted, Australia was participating in RCEP alongside bilateral trade agreements and also an additional negotiation, the US-sponsored TPP. The TPP is a multilateral negotiation that is intended to achieve a process of liberalisation more ambitious in scope than RCEP.[68] The Obama administration was an active supporter of the TPP, which it saw as a key part of its rebalance towards the Asia-Pacific that could bolster US economic ties after a period when US trade interests had been affected adversely by the development of bilateral and regional free trade agreements.[69]

---

65   Sanchita Basu Das, 'RCEP and TPP: Comparisons and Concerns', *ISEAS Perspective*, 7 January 2013.
66   Sanchita Basu Das and Reema B. Jagtiani, 'The Regional Comprehensive Economic Partnership: New Paradigm or Old Wine in a New Bottle?' ISEAS Economics Working Paper No. 2014–3, Singapore: Institute of Southeast Asian Studies, November 2014.
67   'Australia Joins Launch of Massive Asian Regional Trade Agreement', joint media release, Prime Minister and Minister for Trade and Competitiveness, Phnom Penh, 20 November 2012.
68   The TPP in 2015 included Australia, Brunei, Canada, Chile, Japan, Malaysia, Mexico, New Zealand, Peru, Singapore, the United States and Vietnam. See Ian F. Fergusson, Mark A. McMinimy and Brock R. Williams, 'The Trans-Pacific Partnership (TPP): Negotiations and Issues for Congress', Washington, DC: Congressional Research Service, 20 March 2015.
69   Michael Wesley, 'Trade Agreements and Strategic Rivalry in Asia', *Australian Journal of International Affairs*, 69(5) 2015.

The pursuit in parallel of both RCEP and the TPP was yet another example of the pluralism and competition in regionalism in East Asia and the Asia-Pacific with groupings with differing memberships pursuing cooperation goals in parallel.[70] In this case, in 2015 RCEP included China but not the US (because it did not have a multilateral free trade agreement with ASEAN), while the TPP process included the US but not China (although other countries in the Asia-Pacific can join the process with the agreement by consensus of the existing participants).[71] Australia was one of a number of countries participating in both processes, along with Japan, New Zealand and four ASEAN members (Brunei, Malaysia, Singapore and Vietnam). Gillard and Emerson suggested in November 2012 that Australia saw value in both parallel processes: 'Australia's participation in each of these negotiations will add momentum to the process of competitive trade liberalisation.'[72] However, at the time of writing, neither process had been completed so their contribution to trade and economic interactions had not yet become clear.[73]

Security dialogue and the East Asia Summit

After 2010, ASEAN initiated a further ministerial-level cooperation dialogue in the area of defence and security. The ADMM-Plus process brought together the defence ministers of the same 18 countries who meet in the East Asia Summit. Australia took part in the inaugural meeting in Hanoi in October 2010 and took up the role of co-chair (with Malaysia) of the ADMM-Plus Maritime Security Experts Group that examined maritime cooperation and subsequently co-chaired (with Singapore) an Experts Working Group on counter-terrorism.[74]

---

70   Ibid.

71   Das, 'RCEP and TPP'.

72   'Australia Joins Launch'.

73   On 6 October 2015, it was announced that agreement had been reached on the terms of the TPP after talks in Atlanta; the TPP agreement now needed to be ratified by the participants in the negotiations before it could come into force and be implemented. See Malcolm Turnbull, 'Historic Asia-Pacific Trade Agreement Opens New Era of Opportunities', media release, Canberra, 6 October 2015; Peter Drysdale and Shiro Armstrong, 'What Comes After the Atlanta Deal on the Trans-Pacific Partnership?' *East Asia Forum*, 19 October 2015.

74   See Stephen Smith, 'Paper Presented by Minister for Defence Stephen Smith to the ADMM-Plus Maritime Security Experts' Working Group Inaugural Meeting', Perth, 21 July 2011.

The ADMM-Plus process was considered to be a promising new dialogue that could potentially foster some useful practical cooperation among defence ministers and senior officers.[75] Australia's ambassador to ASEAN, Simon Merrifield, commented that:

> [w]ith disputed territories in our region giving rise to the risk of miscalculation, the ADMM+'s fostering of mil-mil [military-to-military] cooperation at the operational level is of immense value – its efforts on building relationships and familiarity between services has a vital role to play in regional security, complementing both the ARF and the EAS.[76]

The premier security dialogue continued to be the East Asia Summit, and its profile was enhanced when the United States and Russia participated for the first time in 2011. The Summit was continuing to develop areas of dialogue in a cautious manner. The key event was the annual meeting, of about three hours duration. The Summit was pursuing working groups and projects in six priority areas: regional economic and financial integration, education, regional disaster response, energy and environment, health, and connectivity. The Summit was supported in its economic and financial areas from 2008 by the Economic Research Institute for ASEAN and East Asia, established with backing from Japan. However, the Summit remained very limited in institutional terms; it had no secretariat of its own and relied on assistance from ASEAN's Secretariat, and it had no annual membership fees or budget to support its agenda and to ensure coherence and continuity. The Summit therefore remained very much a work in progress.[77]

---

75   Ron Huisken, 'ADMM Plus Cooperates on Security and Defence Issues', *East Asia Forum*, 19 October 2010.

76   Simon Merrifield, 'Australia and ASEAN: Past, Present and Future', Remarks by Australian Ambassador to ASEAN, Foreign Service Institute, Manila, 27 March 2015. A further dialogue was initiated at senior official level among the same 18 countries participating in the ADMM-Plus, the Expanded ASEAN Maritime Forum, to develop additional avenues for cooperation in areas including maritime search and rescue; the forum met for the first time in 2012, with Australian participation.

77   David Camroux, 'The East Asia Summit: Pan-Asian Multilateralism Rather than Intra-Asian Regionalism', in Mark Beeson and Richard Stubbs, eds, *Routledge Handbook of Asian Regionalism*, London: Routledge, 2012; Nick Bisley and Malcolm Cook, 'How the East Asia Summit Can Achieve its Potential', *ISEAS Perspective*, 28 October 2014; Avery Poole, 'The East Asia Summit: Navigating ASEAN Multilateralism', in Sally Percival Wood and Baogang He, eds, *The Australia–ASEAN Dialogue: Tracing 40 Years of Partnership*, New York: Palgrave Macmillan, 2014.

Australia made several proposals for East Asia Summit cooperation in 'non-traditional security' areas. At the sixth East Asia Summit on 19 November 2011, agreement was reached to endorse a joint proposal by Australia and Indonesia to strengthen regional responses to natural disasters, working with other regional groupings. Minister for Foreign Affairs Senator Bob Carr commented that '[t]his is a major priority for our region, as well as an important area of potential soft security cooperation between the emergency services and the armed forces of the region'.[78] At the seventh East Asia Summit in Phnom Penh (20 November 2012), Gillard announced additional cooperative measures to combat trafficking in persons and a contribution to the Asia-Pacific Leaders' Malaria Alliance for action to combat the disease.[79]

Carr discussed in measured terms the potential long-term value of the East Asia Summit in an article in July 2012: 'The concept of common security is as much a habit as it is a concrete doctrine guiding specific actions. The habits of regular leaders-led dialogue on an agenda that includes security policy is [sic] itself inherently normalising.'[80] The question remained, however, as to whether a 'normalising' process could progress very far amid continuing major power tensions and competition, for example in the South China Sea.

ASEAN and the South China Sea

The need for greater coordination and dialogue among the major powers and regional states, and also the obstacles to pursuing this goal, were highlighted by the increasing contestation over the South China Sea.

---

78   Bob Carr, 'The East Asia Summit: Building our Regional Architecture for the 21st Century', *Strategic Review* (Jakarta), July 2012.
79   Australian Department of Foreign Affairs and Trade, 'East Asia Summit', dfat.gov.au/international-relations/regional-architecture/eas/Pages/east-asia-summit-eas.aspx (accessed 1 October 2015).
80   Carr, 'The East Asia Summit'.

The South China Sea has been a focus for close attention in ASEAN since the 1990s and this intensified after 2009.[81] Six littoral parties have claims in the South China Sea: China and Taiwan and four ASEAN members – Brunei, Malaysia, the Philippines and Vietnam. In 1992 China reasserted its claim to most of the area of the sea by passing its 'Law of the Territorial Sea and Contiguous Zone of the People's Republic of China': China's claims conflicted with those of the four ASEAN member state claimants.[82] After clashes between China and Vietnam over disputed areas in the sea, ASEAN in the same year issued a 'Declaration on the South China Sea', which called for restraint and urged the parties to pursue cooperation without prejudicing matters of sovereignty. The declaration called on all parties to respect ASEAN's TAC and to develop a 'code of international conduct' for the sea.[83] ASEAN's declaration, however, did not deter China from expanding its presence by assuming effective control of Mischief Reef in 1995 (in an area also claimed by the Philippines). After 1995, ASEAN's capacity to maintain a unified position on the South China Sea issue declined after its expansion in membership (because the new members included Cambodia, Laos and Myanmar, who were not claimants, and were comparatively less concerned with South China Sea issues).[84]

After 1992, ASEAN tried to develop its proposal for a formal code of conduct but did not secure China's participation.[85] ASEAN was compromised by the fact that its own claimant members had overlapping claims in the South China Sea. In place of a formal code of conduct, ASEAN and China in 2002 signed a non-binding Declaration on the Conduct of Parties in the South China Sea. The declaration advocated the building of trust and confidence among and between the signatories; the parties also reaffirmed 'that the adoption of a code

81   On the South China Sea overall, see Leszek Buszynski and Christopher B. Roberts, eds, *The South China Sea Maritime Dispute: Political, Legal and Regional Perspectives*, Abingdon: Routledge, 2015; Bill Hayton, *The South China Sea: The Struggle for Power in Asia*, New Haven, CT: Yale University Press, 2014.

82   On the competing claims, see Leszek Buszynski, 'The Origins and Development of the South China Sea Maritime Dispute', in Leszek Buszynski and Christopher B. Roberts, eds, *The South China Sea Maritime Dispute: Political, Legal and Regional Perspectives*, Abingdon: Routledge, 2015.

83   Christopher B. Roberts, 'ASEAN: The Challenge of Unity in Diversity', in Leszek Buszynski and Christopher B. Roberts, eds, *The South China Sea Maritime Dispute: Political, Legal and Regional Perspectives*, Abingdon: Routledge, 2015; Ian Storey, 'Disputes in the South China Sea: Southeast Asia's Troubled Waters', *politique étrangère*, 3, 2014.

84   Roberts, 'ASEAN', pp. 131–2.

85   Carlyle A. Thayer, 'ASEAN, China and the Code of Conduct in the South China Sea', *SAIS Review of International Affairs*, 33(2) 2013.

of conduct in the South China Sea would further promote peace and stability in the region and agree to work, on the basis of consensus, towards the eventual attainment of this objective'.[86] The declaration did not deal with sovereignty questions and did not attempt to establish any sanctions for breach of its terms. ASEAN subsequently had great difficulty in trying to move beyond this non-binding declaration. A key factor has been that China has consistently wished to deal with the issue of competing claims on a bilateral basis and as Christopher Roberts has written, 'China has mustered the potential to splinter any sense of collective identity in ASEAN's elite-level strategic identity'.[87]

Tensions over the South China Sea were fuelled after 2009 by increasing attention on competing claims, rising nationalist sentiments among claimants, and an increase in interest in the area by major powers including the US and Japan. ASEAN sought support for a code of conduct but faced challenges stemming from the differing perceptions among its members, including between the claimant and non-claimant members. As Ian Storey argued in 2013:

> Lack of progress on the South China Sea is not only due to intransigence on China's part, but also the lack of consensus within ASEAN on how to deal with the problem. This lack of consensus stems from differing national interests and their varied relationships with China. The ten members of ASEAN have differing interests in and positions on the South China Sea: Vietnam and the Philippines view the problem as a major national security concern; fellow claimants Malaysia and Brunei tend to downplay tensions; Indonesia and Singapore have both called on China to clarify its claims; the four non-claimants in mainland Southeast Asia – Thailand, Myanmar, Cambodia and Laos – do not perceive a direct stake in the dispute and in any case wish to avoid jeopardizing close economic and political links with China by taking positions inimical to China's interests.[88]

Internal tensions within ASEAN were evident in 2012 when ASEAN was unable to agree on a joint communiqué after its annual meeting of foreign ministers in Phnom Penh in July. Cambodia, the chair of ASEAN for that year, prevented the explicit mention of South China

---

86   Cited in ibid., p. 77.
87   Christopher B. Roberts, *ASEAN Regionalism: Cooperation, Values and Institutionalization*, Abingdon: Routledge, 2012, p. 81.
88   Ian Storey, 'Can the South China Sea Dispute Be Resolved or Better Managed?' Paper presented at 27th Asia-Pacific Roundtable, Kuala Lumpur, 3–4 June 2013, pp. 3–4.

Sea issues in the draft communiqué and for the first time in ASEAN's 45-year history, no joint foreign ministers' meeting communiqué was issued. Cambodia was seen to have been serving China's preferences. ASEAN subsequently settled on a set of agreed principles on the South China Sea but continued to make no effective progress towards a code of conduct.[89]

The Australian Government maintained a position that emphasised the desirability of dialogue and negotiation, supported development of a code of conduct and supported second track discussion on maritime confidence-building measures.[90] However, the government saw little scope for further initiatives in relation to the South China Sea. Carr said in July 2012 that:

> I don't think it is in Australia's interest to take on for itself a brokering role in territorial disputes in the South China Sea. I don't think that is remotely in our interest. I think we should adhere to the policy we have got of not supporting any one of the nations making competing territorial claims and reminding them all that we want it settled, because we have a stake in it – 60 percent of our trade goes through the South China Sea.[91]

ASEAN and Myanmar

Australia in this period was closely interested in another of ASEAN's most important concerns: the situation in Myanmar. After joining ASEAN in 1997, Myanmar's government had continued to remain largely aloof from the rest of Southeast Asia. The regime's repressive policies had been a source of criticism among some of ASEAN's dialogue partners, particularly the US and the EU, and ASEAN's relations with those partners had as a result been affected adversely.[92] The regime had repressed demonstrations in 2007 and had been reluctant to accept external assistance after the devastation caused by Cyclone

---

89   For a detailed account of this meeting, see Carlyle A. Thayer, 'ASEAN's Code of Conduct in the South China Sea: A Litmus Test For Community Building?' *Asia-Pacific Journal: Japan Focus*, 10(34) 20 August 2012.

90   See Australian Strategic Policy Institute, 'Maritime Confidence Building Measures in the South China Sea Conference', Special Report, Canberra: ASPI, September 2013.

91   ABC Radio Australia, 'Australia Should Stay out of South China Sea Dispute says Carr', Transcript, 30 July 2012.

92   For a detailed discussion of Myanmar and ASEAN up to 2010, see Christopher Roberts, *ASEAN's Myanmar Crisis: Challenges to the Pursuit of a Security Community*, Singapore: Institute of Southeast Asian Studies, 2010.

Nargis in early 2008. ASEAN had subsequently played a mediating role in facilitating the transfer of much needed aid to the country. The Myanmar Government had produced a new constitution that retained a strong role for the long-dominant military and announced elections. The elections in November 2010 resulted in a thoroughly predominant position for the ruling party, the military-aligned Union Solidarity and Development Party.[93] However in the period after the elections a process of liberalisation developed in which political restrictions eased. The prominent opposition leader Aung San Suu Kyi was released from home detention and was then able to run successfully for parliament in April 2012. ASEAN was keen to see the liberalisation proceed and for this to be recognised and supported internationally.[94]

In an area of significant interest to ASEAN, Australia gave strong support to change in Myanmar after the 2010 elections. The Australian Government welcomed the reforms implemented after the inauguration of the new Myanmar Government in March 2011. Carr visited Myanmar on 5–8 June 2012 to assess what more Australia could do. During the visit, Carr announced that Australia would lift its travel and financial sanctions on Myanmar (a decision that took effect on 3 July 2012) although an embargo on arms sales or transfers was maintained; he also announced a doubling of Australia's bilateral aid to A$100 million.[95]

Australia also supported ASEAN by pressing the EU to lift permanently its sanctions on Myanmar. Australia's effort included discussions with the US, the UK, Canada, France, Germany and Holland. Greg Sheridan wrote in February 2013 that 'Senator Carr's activism has won strong support among ASEAN officials'.[96] When the EU lifted its sanctions in April 2013, Carr noted his satisfaction, while also expressing concern about incidences of inter-ethnic violence involving the minority Rohingya people.[97]

---

93   Amitav Acharya, 'ASEAN and Burma/Myanmar: Past and Prologue', Policy Brief, Washington, DC: Sigur Center for Asian Studies, George Washington University, April 2012.

94   Moe Thuzar, 'Myanmar and the 2014 ASEAN Chairmanship', ISEAS Perspective, 18 March 2013.

95   Australian Department of Foreign Affairs and Trade, 'Burma Country Brief', dfat.gov.au/geo/burma/pages/burma-country-brief.aspx (accessed 1 October 2015).

96   Greg Sheridan, 'Carr Goes All Out to Bring Myanmar in From the Cold', The Australian, 7 February 2013.

97   Bob Carr, 'European Union Lifts Myanmar Sanctions', media release, 24 April 2013.

In an address on Australia's foreign policy priorities to the National Press Club in Canberra in June 2013, Carr commented on Australia's policy on Myanmar as an illustration of the Labor Government's current overall approach towards ASEAN:

> I've said to ASEAN foreign ministers when I've met them in various forums: that's an example of Australia moving its policy in alignment with the policy struck with the ten nations of ASEAN, that's habits of consultation. And it's an ingrained habit. And it means that you don't lecture them. You don't harass them. You speak to them, taking account of their concern for ASEAN centrality. And we've been doing that. But it's something that will have a cumulative effect as we go on. And Myanmar is a good working example of an Australian policy settled on after consultation, and after recognition of what the ten nations of ASEAN were doing.[98]

Carr's comments could clearly be seen as an implicit recognition of criticism of some recent Australian policy emphases in regional relations, including the Asia Pacific community proposal.

Irregular migration and Australia's regional relations

While Australia pursued many areas of cooperation with Southeast Asia and ASEAN in this period, the issue of approaches towards irregular migration was, under the Rudd and Gillard governments, a source of both intense domestic controversy within Australia and of discord with some key regional states.

The Howard Government's policies of tightening border controls and pursuing regional cooperation on irregular migration through the Bali process had by 2003 contained the flows of people to Australian territory by boat.[99] In 2001, 5,516 people had arrived in Australia by boat, but in the next six years, only 288 people arrived in this way. However, while the Howard policies had been successful in reducing the numbers of arrivals by boat, aspects of the policies (including offshore processing of asylum-seekers) were the subject of criticism and controversy in Australia. When the Rudd Government came to office at the end of 2007, it modified and loosened the control regime

---

98   Bob Carr, 'Australia's Foreign Policy Directions', Address to the National Press Club, Canberra, 26 June 2013.
99   Andrew Carr, *Winning the Peace: Australia's Campaign to Change the Asia-Pacific*, Carlton, Vic.: Melbourne University Press, 2015, pp. 103–23.

of the previous government, particularly by ending the transfer of irregular migrants to processing centres offshore (the 'Pacific Solution') and by increasing the rights of asylum-seekers. These moves coincided with an upsurge in people seeking to travel by boat to Australia, particularly among those fleeing from Afghanistan and Sri Lanka (after the traumatic end of the civil war in May 2009). In 2009, 2,726 people arrived by boat and from 2010 to 2013 the number was 48,911.[100]

The Rudd Government did not succeed in managing or containing the rise in flows of irregular arrivals by boat. The issue played a significant role in a loss of public support for the Rudd Government, and, as mentioned earlier, Rudd was replaced as prime minister by Gillard in June 2010.[101] The Gillard Government from June 2010 sought an increased emphasis on regional cooperation on irregular migration, particularly through the Bali process (discussed in Chapter 4), which had been downplayed by Rudd. Progress was made in early 2011 on a new Regional Cooperation Framework through the Bali process (a grouping that included Australia and all the ASEAN members but whose membership and scope went well beyond ASEAN to include states in the South Pacific, South Asia and the Middle East, along with China and the US).[102] The Gillard Government also renewed emphasis on offshore processing but it encountered major setbacks in these efforts. A suggestion that East Timor might accept asylum-seekers for processing was rejected by that government. The Australian Government then reached an agreement with Malaysia under which Malaysia would accept 800 persons who had arrived in Australia in return for Australia accepting from Malaysia 4,000 people who had been determined to be refugees. The Gillard Government considered that this agreement would be a valuable additional measure to deter boat arrivals (in that the 800 people would be seen to have been denied asylum in Australia) but the agreement was declared to be invalid by

100 Ibid., pp. 124–5; Janet Phillips, 'Boat Arrivals and Boat "Turnbacks" in Australia since 1976: A Quick Guide to Statistics', Parliamentary Library Research Paper Series 2015–2016, Canberra: Department of Parliamentary Services, 11 September 2015.
101 Paul Kelly, *Triumph and Demise: The Broken Promise of a Labor Generation*, Carlton, Vic.: Melbourne University Press, 2014, pp. 175–88.
102 See 'The Bali Process on People Smuggling, Trafficking in Persons and Related Transnational Crime', www.baliprocess.net/ (accessed 1 October 2015).

the Australian High Court. The incidence of arrivals by boat remained a highly contentious issue up until the time the Labor Government lost office in September 2013.[103]

The Australian Government in this period discussed the issue of irregular migration with ASEAN (for example, through dialogue with the heads of the ASEAN members' departments of immigration and with the ASEAN Immigration Intelligence Forum), but the main avenue for multilateral discussion and negotiation was through the wider Bali process.[104] While Australia had been able to cooperate with ASEAN on the outflows of people from Indochina in the 1970s (outflows that had originated within Southeast Asia), the sources of asylum-seekers after the late 1990s were primarily outside Southeast Asia and cooperation on the issues accordingly needed to encompass a wider grouping of countries. The discord over policies towards irregular migrants clearly had the potential to impact adversely on some of Australia's relations with ASEAN members, for example when the proposed agreement with Malaysia was debated in acrimonious terms in Australia.[105] The issue was a further example of how Australian domestic political debates could impact on regional relations in Southeast Asia.

In overall terms, the Gillard Government had thus been less ambitious in approaching regional and ASEAN relations than its predecessor, the Rudd Government. It had not sought to initiate any new institution and had accepted ASEAN's role as sponsor of institutional development. In line with this approach, Australia had welcomed ASEAN's move to widen the membership of the East Asia Summit, had joined new ASEAN-sponsored dialogues in both economic and security areas and had supported ASEAN diplomatic goals, for example in relation to Myanmar.

---

103 Kelly, *Triumph and Demise*, pp. 387–402; Carr, *Winning the Peace*, pp. 128–36.
104 Joint Standing Committee on Foreign Affairs, Defence and Trade, *Inquiry into Australia's Relationship with ASEAN*, Canberra: Commonwealth of Australia, June 2009, pp. 18–20.
105 Carr, *Winning the Peace*, pp. 130–1; Kelly, *Triumph and Demise*, pp. 390–1.

The Abbott Government and the 2014 Commemorative Summit

The Labor Government (led again by Rudd from June 2013) was replaced in elections on 7 September 2013 by a new Liberal–National Party Coalition administration led by Tony Abbott. The Liberal–National Party policy statement issued before the elections asserted the importance of relations with Australia's allies, regional partners and major trading associates. On regional policy approaches overall, the Coalition document declared: '[t]he Coalition will work cooperatively within our neighbourhood to make existing institutions work better to serve the national interest and the interests of our region rather than creating new ones.' The Coalition also reaffirmed recent Australian official interest in the regional concept of the 'Indo-Pacific' by saying that 'Australia's neighbourhood will be defined as the Asia Pacific-Indian Ocean region. We will focus diplomatic, development, trade and security efforts in parts of the Indian Ocean rim that have the capacity to advance Australia's interests.'[106]

The Abbott Government in office reaffirmed the broad directions of Australian foreign policy, including commitment to the US alliance and an endorsement of the US 'rebalance' towards the Asia-Pacific. Strong emphasis was placed on Japan, which Abbott declared early in his term to be Australia's 'best friend in Asia' and relations were advanced by a visit by Prime Minister Abe Shinzo in July 2014 and by agreements to enhance defence cooperation.[107] The government continued to pursue close relations with China and with the other key Northeast Asian states and during 2014 achieved success in completing negotiations on bilateral trade agreements with South Korea, Japan and China.[108]

The new government maintained emphasis on engagement with Southeast Asia and with ASEAN, with a focus on the lead-up to the fortieth anniversary of multilateral relations in 2014, to which the

---

106 Australian Liberal Party and National Party, 'The Coalition's Policy for Foreign Affairs', Canberra, September 2013, p. 3.
107 Graeme Dobell, 'Australia–East Asia/US Relations: China Bumps, Indonesia Breach, Japan as Ally', *Comparative Connections: A Triannual E-Journal on East Asian Bilateral Relations*, 16(2) 2014.
108 Ibid.

government gave considerable attention. Minister for Foreign Affairs Julie Bishop affirmed the value placed on the ASEAN connection in comments at the time of the anniversary in April 2014 and pursued a commitment to visit all member states in the lead-up to the planned Commemorative Leaders' Summit in November 2014.[109] The government added a new element to Australian education policies and to ASEAN relations with its New Colombo Plan designed to increase greatly the numbers of young Australians who could live and study in Asian countries. The program was notable as a concrete indication that interactions with neighbouring countries would involve an increased emphasis on learning by Australians about Asia. The program would cover many Asian countries including all the members of ASEAN and was expected to have a strong impact on enhancing personal connections between Australia and the ASEAN countries.[110]

Progress was made in some key bilateral relations with ASEAN members. Australia's relations with Malaysia were enhanced by the extensive role that Australia played in leading efforts to locate Malaysian Airlines flight MH370 after its disappearance in March 2014.[111] Australia and Vietnam reviewed and agreed to enhance further their relationship during the visit of Prime Minister Nguyen Tan Dung to Australia in March 2015.[112] Relations with Singapore were reaffirmed and extended by an agreement in June 2015 to establish a Comprehensive Strategic Partnership between the two countries.[113] Australia, however, experienced another phase of tension in its often sensitive relationship with Indonesia. Abbott in Opposition had been intensely critical of the former Labor Government over border control and the influx of irregular migrants by boat; one of his key pledges was to 'stop the boats', including by if necessary turning boats approaching Australia back to Indonesia. The government implemented 'Operation

---

109 Julie Bishop, 'Australia's Prospering Partnership with ASEAN', op-ed article, 17 April 2014.
110 See Australian Department of Foreign Affairs and Trade, 'New Colombo Plan', www.dfat.gov.au/people-to-people/new-colombo-plan/pages/new-colombo-plan.aspx (accessed 11 March 2015).
111 Adam Davies, 'Australia Spent $100 Million to MH 370 Search So Far', *The Northern Star*, 7 August 2015.
112 Carl Thayer, 'Australia and Vietnam Enhance their Comprehensive Partnership', *The Diplomat*, 17 March 2015.
113 Daniel Wei Boon Chua, 'Fifty Years of Singapore-Australian Relations: An Enduring Strategic Partnership – Analysis', *Eurasia Review*, 26 August 2015; Graeme Dobell, 'Singapore and Oz: Mismatched Mates', *The Strategist*, 24 August 2015.

Sovereign Borders' in late 2013 and this included a willingness to tow boats back to Indonesian waters, a policy that resulted in criticism both from UN representatives and from Indonesia.[114] The government's approach effectively halted the flow of vessels towards Australia, but the tow-back policy produced substantial criticism in Indonesia.[115]

An additional area of bilateral sensitivity with Indonesia was opened up when a major release of US intelligence material by Edward Snowden in late 2013 included revelations that Australian intelligence had sought to intercept the telephone of Indonesia's President Yudhoyono in August 2009: interceptions were also pursued on the phone of the president's wife.[116] Abbott in Parliament refused to detail Australian intelligence operations or to apologise for them. In response, Indonesia suspended military and intelligence cooperation and withdrew its ambassador from Canberra. A process of negotiations followed on the development of a code of conduct on intelligence issues and agreement was reached by October 2014, before President Yudhoyono left office. The two sides agreed not to use surveillance capacities to harm the interests of either party and resolved to promote intelligence cooperation in accordance with their laws and regulations.[117] The agreement appeared to resolve this issue and Abbott attended the inauguration of Yudhoyono's successor, Joko Widodo, in October 2014 (continuing the practice of his predecessors as prime minister, in 2004 and 2009).[118] The potential for discord in relations nonetheless persisted and was illustrated again by the disagreement between the two governments in early 2015 over the execution of two convicted Australian drug traffickers. After the executions, Australia withdrew its ambassador in protest for one month, but the need to maintain and consolidate relations was also clear.[119]

---

114 Michael Bachelard and Sarah Whyte, 'UN Representatives Criticise Abbott Government's Boat Tow-Back Policy', *Sydney Morning Herald*, 23 April 2014.

115 AAP, 'The Way Is Closed, Abbott Declares on Asylum-Seeker Boats', *The Australian*, 29 March 2014; Ken Ward, *Condemned to Crisis? A Lowy Institute Paper*, Melbourne: Penguin, 2015, pp. 67–79.

116 Cameron Stewart, 'Why Did Australia's Spy Agencies Listen in on the Indonesian First Lady?' *The Australian*, 14 December 2013.

117 Dobell, 'Australia-East Asia/US Relations: China Bumps, Indonesia Breach, Japan as Ally'.

118 Dan Harrison, 'Tony Abbott Heads to Jakarta for Inauguration of Indonesian President Joko Widodo', *Sydney Morning Herald*, 19 October 2014.

119 Peter Jennings, 'Australia and Indonesia: No Way Out', *The Strategist*, 18 March 2015; Felicity Norman, 'Looking Ahead: Australia–Indonesia Relations', *New Mandela*, 15 May 2015; Ward, *Condemned to Crisis?* pp. 94–121.

The fortieth anniversary Commemorative Summit: November 2014

The celebrations of the fortieth anniversary of Australia's multilateral relations with ASEAN culminated in a fortieth anniversary Commemorative Summit on 12 November 2014 in Nay Pyi Taw, Myanmar. In the joint ASEAN–Australia leaders' statement, the two sides 'agreed to elevate our comprehensive partnership to a strategic level, founded on common interests in regional peace and prosperity' and affirmed a number of areas of common engagement and cooperation. Australia and ASEAN agreed to support the realisation of the ASEAN Community by 2015, to 'support ASEAN's centrality in the evolving regional architecture and strengthen all ASEAN-led mechanisms' and to work to strengthen the East Asia Summit. The leaders endorsed other areas of cooperation including in counter-terrorism, good governance and human rights, maritime cooperation, combating transnational crime, promotion of economic integration through the AANZFTA and RCEP, and continuing efforts to support reduction of development gaps within ASEAN and to combat infectious diseases. These statements were very much an affirmation of established policies. The statement declared that the parties would 'hold regular leaders summits in the future' although detailed arrangements were not announced.[120]

In comments on 13 November 2014, the day after the summit, Abbott said:

> Australia has been a partner to the countries of our region in every way. We've been an economic partner, obviously. We've been a security partner and we've been almost a spiritual partner given the increasing links, the increasing understanding, between the countries of our region and ourselves. It was interesting that in the summit I attended, almost every ASEAN nation mentioned the New Colombo Plan, which is already sending hundreds of Australians to the universities of our region and in the years to come we'll be sending thousands, perhaps tens of thousands, of Australians into our region ... I'm very proud of

---

120 ASEAN, 'Towards a Strategic Partnership for Mutual Benefit', Joint ASEAN–Australia Leaders' Statement on the 40th Anniversary of ASEAN–Australia Dialogue Relations, Nay Pyi Taw, Myanmar, 12 November 2014.

this initiative, it's very much a signature initiative of this Government and it was something that was very much talked about yesterday at the Australia ASEAN Summit.[121]

In the period after the Commemorative Summit, the two sides moved to follow through the key areas of agreement. They discussed the implementation of the Strategic Partnership announced at the summit, although this was expected to consolidate rather than substantially change relations. At the ASEAN Post-Ministerial Conference in Kuala Lumpur on 5 August 2015, Australia and ASEAN reaffirmed a number of major areas of cooperation including responding to natural disasters. ASEAN welcomed Australia's continuation of support for the ASEAN Coordinating Centre for Humanitarian Assistance. The ministers also followed up on the agreement at the Commemorative Summit by announcing that meetings at heads of government level would now be held on a regular basis, every two years, with the first of the new series to be held in Vientiane in late 2016. This was expected to add further profile to the relationship overall.[122]

In the lead-up to ASEAN's declaration of the inauguration of the ASEAN Community at the end of 2015, the Australian Government issued a report in August 2015 on the economic significance for Australia of the ASEAN economies and of the ASEAN Economic Community (AEC).[123] The report highlighted the status of the ASEAN economies as collectively Australia's second largest trading partner (15 per cent of trade overall), surpassed only by China (23 per cent). If economic growth continued to follow recent trends, the ASEAN market would grow substantially, and the numbers of households defined as 'middle class' (with an annual household income of over US$7,500 in 2005 in terms of purchasing power parity) could be expected to increase from 80 million in 2015 to 160 million by 2030.[124] The report identified a number of areas in which Australian business can participate in 'regional value chains' involving business activities and production networks operating in multiple countries across ASEAN. This created

---

121 Tony Abbott, 'Doorstop Interview, Naypyidaw, Myanmar', Transcript, 13 November 2014.
122 ASEAN, 'Chairman's Statement of the ASEAN Post-Ministerial Conference (10+1 Sessions) with the Dialogue Partners', Kuala Lumpur, 5 August 2015.
123 Australian Department of Foreign Affairs and Trade and Austrade, 'Why ASEAN and Why Now? Insights for Australian Business', Canberra: Australian Department of Foreign Affairs and Trade and Austrade, August 2015, p. 7.
124 Ibid., p. 9.

the potential for further Australian investment in the ASEAN region although the report noted that while ASEAN investment in Australia had reached US$111 billion in 2015, Australian investment in ASEAN was only US$29 billion: the report noted that 'considering ASEAN's proximity to Australia and the complementarities of our economies, two way investment is much lower than might be expected'.[125] The AEC was a 'work in progress' that would need much further development after its formal inauguration in 2015 but it 'will mean that Australian companies with operations in ASEAN will find it easier to invest, move staff within the region, and to manage and build regional supply chains'.[126]

Major power competition and the South China Sea

While Australia and ASEAN had reaffirmed their partnership, the regional and international context for their relations continued to be challenging. Wesley has commented that:

> The rapid economic growth of China, coupled with its large investments in military modernisation and increasingly assertive actions around its maritime boundaries has triggered competitive responses from the United States and most of its neighbours in Asia ... Clashes between China and its neighbours over territorial disputes in the South China Sea and East China Sea, not to mention bouts of hostility on the Korean Peninsula, have raised the prospect of conflict in Pacific Asia to its highest level since the end of the Vietnam war.[127]

The situation in the South China Sea continued to be a key concern for ASEAN and for Australia. A further stage in the contest for influence in the area developed in 2013. From September 2013, China began to transform seven features in the Spratlys into artificial islands and developed civilian and military infrastructure including harbours, radar and surveillance systems, buildings and airfields. China was not the first country to reclaim land and develop facilities in the area; the Philippines had pursued such activities in the 1970s, Malaysia in the 1980s and both Vietnam and Taiwan after 2013. However, China's

---

125 Ibid., p. 14.
126 Ibid.
127 Wesley, 'Trade Agreements', p. 480.

reclamation program was by far the most extensive; by mid-2015 it was estimated to have involved over 800 hectares of land. These projects were expected to assist China to enforce its South China Sea territorial and jurisdictional claims. China argued that it was acting within its sovereign rights and was merely catching up with the activities of other claimants.[128]

The Philippines and Vietnam criticised China's actions (with the former being the most vocal).[129] ASEAN also expressed criticism: at the 26th ASEAN Summit in April 2015, the chairman's statement did not refer to China specifically but expressed 'serious concern' that the land reclamations had 'eroded trust and confidence and may undermine peace, security and stability in the South China Sea'. The pressures facing ASEAN from South China Sea issues were again evident at its ministerial meetings in Kuala Lumpur in August 2015. The release of the annual foreign ministers statement was delayed for two days amid reports of internal differences over the issues.[130] In the statement, the ASEAN foreign ministers said: '[w]e took note of the serious concerns expressed by some ministers on the land reclamations in the South China Sea, which have eroded trust and confidence, increased tensions, and may undermine peace, security and stability in the South China Sea.'[131] At the meeting, China declared that its reclamation program had been completed but China's position in the area had clearly already been enhanced.[132]

The Australian Government continued to express its concern about the tensions in the South China Sea, for example in comments in June 2015 by the Minister for Defence, Kevin Andrews, and by Prime Minister Abbott.[133] During ASEAN's August 2015 ministerial meetings, Foreign Minister Bishop reaffirmed the government's position:

128 Ian Storey, 'China's "Terraforming" in the Spratlys: A Game Changer in the South China Sea?' *ISEAS Perspective*, 23 June 2015.
129 Ibid.
130 AFP, 'Beijing Dilutes ASEAN: Ministers Wrangled Over Islands Disputes', *The Australian*, 7 August 2015.
131 ASEAN, 'Joint Communique, 48th ASEAN Foreign Ministers Meeting', Kuala Lumpur, 4 August 2015.
132 AFP, 'Beijing Dilutes ASEAN'.
133 David Wroe and Philip Wen, 'South China Sea Dispute: Strong Indications Australia Will Join Push Back On China's Island-Building', *Sydney Morning Herald*, 1 June 2015; James Massola and John Garnaut, 'Australia "Deplores" Unilateral Action in South China Sea: Tony Abbott', *Sydney Morning Herald*, 29 June 2015.

> I made it plain that Australia does not take sides in territorial claims, but we urge all nations to halt reclamation work … We are deeply concerned that there may be militarisation of artificial reefs and structures and we called [for] a halt to that as well … [W]e call on the countries of South East Asia and China to respect freedom of navigation, freedom of over-flight and to reject any coercive or unilateral behaviour that can lead to increased tensions.[134]

However the prospects for alleviation of tensions and for productive negotiations remained very uncertain and the potential for increased strain and clashes among contending parties continued.

The Liberal–National Party led by Abbott had therefore reaffirmed established patterns of the ASEAN relationship.[135] The New Colombo Plan had added a new element to relations by promising to contribute to the depth and breadth of personal interactions and knowledge in the Australian community about the ASEAN members. The foreshadowed more regular leadership meetings would help give ASEAN a greater profile in the Australian Government and community. Relations, however, were continuing to be influenced by the shadow of serious major power tensions.

Australia: A possible future member of ASEAN?

A further and speculative question that during the period after 2007 received some discussion (in 2012) was whether Australia might at some future point be considered (and consider itself) as a possible member of ASEAN. Given the obvious differences in societies, economic structures and political systems between Australia and ASEAN members, this has not been a question that has generally gained much attention in discussions about the relationship. As noted in Chapter 3, the issue of Australian membership had been mentioned as a long-term possibility by President Fidel Ramos of the Philippines in 1994. In 1996, Prime Minister Goh Chok Tong of Singapore raised the issue of Australia as a possible ASEAN member during a visit to

---

134 Julie Bishop, 'Doorstop Interview: East Asia Summit, Kuala Lumpur', Transcript, 5 August 2015.
135 The Abbott Government's term in office concluded with the replacement of Abbott as prime minister by Malcolm Turnbull on 14 September 2015.

Singapore by Prime Minister Keating, but Goh made it clear that he had been thinking in a very long-term manner and that there had been no proposal advanced, and no discussions had been held on the matter.

In 2012, several figures in Australia mentioned the concept of Australian membership as a possibility, including former Prime Minister Keating and a former senior Australian ambassador with extensive regional experience, John McCarthy. Keating stated in November 2012 that '[t]his grouping represents the security architecture of south-east Asia, the one with which we can have real dialogue and add substance. In the longer run we should be a member of it — formalising the trade, commercial and political interests we already share'.[136] The potential of Australia to become an ASEAN member was also referred to in a presentation in Australia in August 2012 by the senior Singaporean analyst Kishore Mahbubani, who argued that while membership at present seemed 'unthinkable' to Australia's elite, in the long-term such an approach would strengthen Australia's position in relation to Asia.[137]

Minister for Foreign Affairs Carr in late 2012 indicated that membership of ASEAN was not on the agenda for Australia. In an interview on 25 November 2012, Carr was asked whether he endorsed Keating's suggestion that Australia should seek to join ASEAN and he said: '[i]t's fair enough as a vision', but added:

> It's fair enough to be out there floating as an incentive but in the meantime the practical work is to be done on trade relations involving Australia, New Zealand and others with ASEAN and on the coordination of foreign policy ... if I said today or the Prime Minister said we want to be in ASEAN the chances are we would be rebuffed and ASEAN would say 'that doesn't fit our vision'. The point is to work at it and work on trade, on foreign policy alignment, on consultation, so that when it happens it's an organic thing, a natural thing.[138]

---

136 Paul Keating, 'Forget the West, our Future is to the North', *The Age*, 15 November 2012; John McCarthy, 'Let's Aim to Be More than US Surrogate', *Australian Financial Review*, 21 November 2012.
137 Kishore Mahbubani, 'Australia's Destiny in the Asian Century: Pain or No Pain?' Paper prepared for Emerging Asia and the Future of the Australia–US Alliance, the US–Australia 21st Century Alliance Project, United States Studies Centre, University of Sydney, 31 July 2012, p. 18.
138 'Transcript of Interview with Peter van Onselen and Paul Kelly', *Australian Agenda*, Sky News, 25 November 2012.

Carr later wrote that DFAT in a submission had made clear that they did not consider membership as a realistic or feasible goal for Australia. The department had suggested that the minister should clarify that 'Australia has no plans to seek or even consider membership even in the long term and that doing so is not necessary to pursuing closer engagement with the region'. DFAT argued that membership in ASEAN would

> subordinate aspects of Australian foreign policy to ASEAN. It would require Australia to refrain from any real criticism of ASEAN governments (e.g. on human-rights issues) and from putting forward alternatives to ASEAN positions. It would require Australia to accept other ASEAN countries, notably the ASEAN Chair, representing Australia in discussions with external parties such as the United States, China and international organisations.

The submission also warned that ASEAN members would be strongly opposed to Australia joining the Association.[139]

While the discussion in 2012 of the concept of Australian membership in ASEAN was interesting, it was clearly in the realm of long-term speculation. Since there are a number of policy areas and institutional means through which closer Australian interests with ASEAN can be and are being pursued, an ongoing process of cooperation and closer coordination seemed for the foreseeable future the best path for Australia and its ASEAN partners to pursue.

Conclusion

Relations after 2007 illustrated that closeness can produce partnership but can cause discord and contest. The Rudd proposal for an Asia Pacific Community met substantial resistance. The concept was seen as a challenge to ASEAN's corporate interests and was not supported by Indonesia, often a key partner for Australia in its regional engagements. However in a climate of increased major power competition and contest for influence in Southeast Asia (including in relation to the South China Sea), the Rudd proposal was followed from 2009 by a rise in interest in regional multilateral associations by the US. ASEAN

---

139 Bob Carr, *Diary of a Foreign Minister*, Sydney: NewSouth Publishing, 2014, p. 275.

was able to capitalise on rising interest in wider and more inclusive dialogues by inviting the US and Russia to join the existing East Asia Summit.

With disagreement over the Asia Pacific Community proposal resolved by mid-2010, Australia continued to develop its multilateral ASEAN relations with a further leadership summit meeting in 2010 and participation in new ASEAN-sponsored forums, the ADMM-Plus process and the negotiations for RCEP. This phase in relations culminated in the 2014 Commemorative Summit that reaffirmed key areas of cooperation and foreshadowed more regular dialogues at leadership level, which were announced in August 2015. It was notable in the summit's joint statement that both sides endorsed ASEAN's 'centrality' in regional architecture and committed themselves to 'strengthen all ASEAN-led mechanisms'. This was closeness expressed as agreement and partnership. A key question, however, continued to be whether and how ASEAN and Australia could cooperate to develop the role of ASEAN's dialogues, particularly the expanded East Asia Summit.

6

Australia and ASEAN: Issues, themes and future prospects

Over more than four decades, the Association of Southeast Asian Nations (ASEAN) has been a substantial focus for Australia and the two sides have established many areas of dialogue and cooperation. Australia reaffirmed its commitment to ASEAN in the Commemorative Summit in November 2014. There are, nonetheless, significant questions about the character and likely future course of the relationship. This chapter reviews major themes and lessons that may be drawn from assessing the relationship since 1974, and discusses factors that are likely to be important for the future.

Themes and lessons

Australia has benefited greatly from ASEAN's contribution towards maintaining peace and enhancing stability in relations among its own members, arguably ASEAN's single greatest achievement. Southeast Asia was in a highly unstable position in 1967 in the aftermath of *Konfrontasi* and with the conflicts in Indochina involving intense Cold War competition and massive violence. ASEAN provided a framework for communication and confidence-building that stabilised relations among the original founding members. ASEAN's consensus-based style of cooperation enabled it to encompass Brunei (in 1984) and then four states in mainland Southeast Asia, when this became possible from the mid-1990s. ASEAN's model of cooperation continues to have appeal and Timor-Leste wishes to become the Association's eleventh member.[1] When the highly unstable environment of the mid-1960s is recalled, it is clear that Australia's security has been bolstered by ASEAN's confidence-building within Southeast Asia and its creation of diplomatic habits of mind and behaviour that have had wider Asian applications.

Australia has been able to cooperate with ASEAN in areas of major mutual interest. Early interactions from the mid-1970s produced some significant disagreement over trade relations that were not at that time resolved to ASEAN's satisfaction. However, dialogue on economic policies was increased and a challenge by ASEAN to Australia's policies on civil aviation from 1978 – an early example of ASEAN's capacity to bargain as a group – produced compromises that provided some satisfaction to the ASEAN side, particularly to Singapore. Further cooperation was pursued to deal with the outflows of people from Indochina after 1975. ASEAN's capacity to communicate and coordinate responses to a major political and humanitarian challenge gained greater international attention and assistance, and increased commitments of resettlement places. Coordination between Australia and ASEAN played a crucial role in the development of policies to help Australia manage the intake of refugees and gain cooperation to minimise unregulated flows of people directly to Australia by boat.[2]

Cooperation with ASEAN, along with some policy disagreement, was a key part of the diplomacy pursued by Australia over Cambodia in the 1980s and early 1990s. Australia's approach initially involved some discord with ASEAN as Malcolm Fraser's government in 1980 withdrew recognition from the Democratic Kampuchea (Khmer Rouge) regime. Bob Hawke's government from 1983 then sought to explore avenues for additional dialogue at a time when ASEAN and the major powers were resistant to alternative approaches. However, from 1989, close coordination with ASEAN and with Indonesia in particular was integral to Australia's capacity to help make

---

1   At the time of writing, it was expected widely that Timor-Leste would be accepted as a member by 2017; see Termsak Chalermpalanupap, 'Timor-Leste's Quest to Join ASEAN: The Process and the Pace', *ASEAN Focus*, 1/2015, August 2015.
2   As noted in Chapter 5, in the later phase of people movements from the late 1990s (where most of those seeking asylum came from outside Southeast Asia), the major multilateral effort at coordination was pursued through the Bali process rather than with ASEAN.

a contribution to the development of a peace process that led to the Paris Agreements, United Nations involvement and the redevelopment of an internationally accepted Cambodian state.

Australia's interactions with ASEAN were a key issue in new avenues of cooperation in the wider East Asian and Asia-Pacific regions from the late 1980s. With the Asia-Pacific Economic Cooperation (APEC) grouping, Australia, acting with Japan, was able to develop a proposal for dialogue after gaining ASEAN's acceptance of the concept, albeit with markedly less support from Malaysia. The decline of Cold War tensions after the demise of the Soviet Union facilitated cooperation between Australia and ASEAN on the development of a new security dialogue. In this case, ASEAN took the lead in developing what became the ASEAN Regional Forum (ARF). Australia went on to become a founding member with ASEAN of the East Asia Summit, after formally acceding to ASEAN's Treaty of Amity and Cooperation.

In considering the themes and patterns in the relationship that were outlined in the Introduction, four stand out. First, the climate of relations among the major powers in Southeast and East Asia has clearly and understandably been a key influence on the character of Australia's interactions with ASEAN. ASEAN was established in 1967 at a time of intense conflict in Indochina and there seemed little prospect of alleviation of major power confrontation. The period from 1972, however, was one where the advent of increased communication between the US and China and the withdrawal of US forces from Vietnam stimulated reassessments about how security in Southeast Asia could best be enhanced and about how Australia could seek to support this. In this period, Australia's greater interest in ASEAN and the inauguration of multilateral relations under Gough Whitlam's government was a significant part of this process. The climate of ASEAN relations was influenced strongly by the reassertion of Cold War tensions in the late 1970s as intensified competition between the Soviet Union and China ushered in 15 years of regional and international confrontation over Cambodia. Southeast Asia was again affected profoundly by the decline of Cold War tensions at the end of the 1980s, which opened up new opportunities for détente between the states of Indochina and ASEAN and between China and the members of ASEAN. The changed and comparatively more cooperative state of major power relations then facilitated initiatives by Australia with ASEAN over Cambodia and in the development of APEC and the ARF.

The climate of major power competition has continued to be a central issue and challenge for Australia–ASEAN relations as the discussion below suggests.

A second long-term theme in Australia's approaches towards ASEAN since the 1970s has been an interest by successive Australian governments in fostering cooperation and reconciliation among all the states of the Southeast Asian region and in particular between the founding members and the states of Indochina, which could both enhance the security environment of Southeast Asia and reduce the avenues for major power interference and competition. In the early phase of its multilateral association with ASEAN, Australia from 1975 expressed interest in the potential for détente between the original ASEAN five and the regimes in Indochina. This interest was expressed by both the Whitlam and Fraser governments up to 1978, and was a significant motivation for the approaches towards the Cambodian conflict advanced by the Hawke Government after 1983. A further instance of this strand in Australia's interactions with ASEAN can be seen in the case of ASEAN's policies of encouraging wider international relationships for Myanmar after the 2010 elections and for the phasing down of the sanctions previously pursued by many Western governments: Australia supported ASEAN by using its diplomatic capacities to help advance ASEAN's policies of supporting wider relationships for Myanmar both regionally and internationally.

A third long-term theme has been the diversity, pluralism and at times competition, in both Australia and Southeast Asia, in relation to conceptions of 'region' in which to pursue cooperation. Successive Australian governments have expressed strong interest in Southeast Asia, and since the 1970s ASEAN has been an obvious focus for this interest. However Australia has wanted to define other 'regions' as being of relevance and concern. The major wider focus pursued has been the conception of the 'Asia-Pacific', extending beyond Southeast Asia to encompass Northeast Asia and Australia's ally, the United States (and potentially other parties in the Americas): APEC was a notable reflection of this focus. In the years since 2010, Australian policymakers have also discussed an additional regional identity, the 'Indo-Pacific', a conception that seeks to take account of the rising prominence of India and the Indian Ocean, although the coherence and relevance of this 'region' is still in the process of being established.[3]

Pluralism in defining regions appropriate for cooperation has also been evident in ASEAN and East Asia. ASEAN's initial and principal focus has by design been Southeast Asia. ASEAN, however, has wanted to bolster its economic and security interests by engaging major external powers in dialogue. In the early 1990s, ASEAN sponsored the ARF whose regional scope included a wide range of nations across the Asia-Pacific, including the United States and India. ASEAN however has also at times pursued additional and different conceptions of 'region' for the purposes of cooperation. Many in ASEAN have supported a conception of 'East Asia' as a basis for cooperation and community-building; this concept was associated particularly with Malaysian Prime Minister Mahathir Mohamad from the early 1990s and was expressed after 1997 in the advent of the ASEAN Plus Three group, joining ASEAN with China, Japan and South Korea. The East Asia Summit was a proposal that emerged from the ASEAN Plus Three grouping and this initially also reflected an East Asia-focused conception of 'region'. However, in the process of developing the East Asia Summit, amid contestation for influence between China and Japan, a majority of ASEAN members supported a wider membership than ASEAN Plus Three, to include India, Australia and New Zealand in 2005, and then in 2011 to include also the US and Russia.

This pluralism in conceptions of 'region' reflects the challenges of an environment of overlapping and competitive interests and at times of severe tensions among the major powers. In this environment, no individual major power would be acceptable to others as a sponsor or leader in regional institutions, especially in relation to security issues. Indeed, regional states and major powers have been prepared to see different groups with differing memberships operating in parallel, in patterns of 'competitive regionalism'. This institutional pluralism has reflected the diversity of states and interests in East Asia and

---

3   Rory Medcalf, 'Reimagining Asia: From Asia-Pacific to Indo-Pacific', *Asan Forum*, 26 June 2015; Trevor Wilson, 'The "Indo-Pacific": Absent Policy Behind Meaningless Words', *East Asia Forum*, 19 September 2014.

the Asia-Pacific and has been a long-standing feature of regional cooperation, even if these arrangements can sometimes look 'messy' to other observers.[4]

The pursuit of differing conceptions of region has at times caused debate and tension in Australia–ASEAN relations. Australia has been closely interested in cooperation with ASEAN but has approached this both as an ally of the United States and as a country with deep economic and strategic interests in Northeast Asia, a perspective encouraging an orientation towards an 'Asia-Pacific' focus. Australia's interests in Asia-Pacific cooperation have, however, sometimes not been welcomed by ASEAN members, sensitive about their hard-won regional identity being challenged or even supplanted by wider groupings. When Prime Minister Whitlam advanced his concept of an 'Asia-Pacific forum' in 1973, ASEAN responses were cool and Indonesian President Suharto was quick to indicate opposition to it in talks with Whitlam in February 1973. Even before Australia had a formal multilateral linkage with ASEAN, the Association was able to exercise an effective veto over an Australian policy initiative. When Australia was interested in advancing proposals for wider groupings at the end of the 1980s, ASEAN's sensitivity about its corporate identity was again a significant issue and ASEAN exerted a major influence on how the new institutions developed. ASEAN's concurrence and participation were vital to the successful inauguration of APEC and ASEAN itself assumed the leadership role for the ARF. In 2008, Prime Minister Kevin Rudd's proposal for discussion about an 'Asia Pacific Community' was seen widely as a challenge to ASEAN's profile and position. It was the East Asia Summit, an ASEAN-initiated grouping, which became the vehicle for bringing the US and Russia into an institutional leadership dialogue with ASEAN and Asian states. ASEAN has therefore been active in asserting and protecting its identity and Australia has needed to recognise this.

A fourth long-term theme in Australia's ASEAN relations is that cooperation has worked best when Australia has been able to operate in collaboration with key members of ASEAN in developing policy initiatives. This has been understandably and particularly

---

4   William T. Tow and Brendan Taylor, 'Emerging Regional Security Architecture: An Australian Perspective', in William T. Tow and Chin Kin Wah, eds, *ASEAN India Australia: Towards Closer Engagement in a New Asia*, Singapore: Institute of Southeast Asian Studies, 2009.

important in relation to Indonesia. Because of its size and capacity for influence and leadership in Southeast Asia, Indonesia is an essential partner for Australia. Cooperation with Indonesia was at the centre of the Cambodian peace process diplomacy in 1989 and 1990. Indonesia played a major role with Australia in the advent and initial development of APEC and the ARF. Indonesia was a key supporter for Australia in gaining membership in the East Asia Summit. By contrast, when Australia has sought to pursue regional initiatives without Indonesia's collaboration, or at least its acceptance, as in the case of Whitlam's Asia-Pacific forum concept and Rudd's Asia Pacific Community proposal, success has been less likely. The viability and health of the Indonesian relationship and Indonesia's preparedness to collaborate with Australia have thus been vital for Australia's capacity for multilateral access and cooperation.

In reviewing the pattern of Australia's ASEAN relations since 1974, a further issue should be noted. Since the 1970s while there has been a change in the relative economic size and weight of Australia vis-à-vis the ASEAN members there has also been a very great broadening of Australia's interactions with those members. In 1974, when multilateral relations were inaugurated, Australia's economy was clearly larger than the aggregate of the then five members of ASEAN: Australia's gross national product was assessed by the World Bank at around US$71 billion and the ASEAN aggregate was estimated at around US$61 billion.[5] In 2014, ASEAN's combined gross domestic product was significantly greater than that of Australia's (Australian Government figures for 2014 were approximately US$1.5 trillion for Australia and US$2.5 trillion for ASEAN).[6] While ASEAN's membership has increased since the 1970s, this relative change is primarily a reflection of the successful advance of economic growth in the ASEAN region, a development that has been very much in Australia's interests.

At the same time, the scale and breadth of interactions have expanded greatly. While relations were ushered in on a government-to-government level in 1974 by a small number of political leaders and

---

5   Figures on gross national product at market prices from World Bank, *World Bank Atlas: Population, Per Capita Product, and Growth Rates*, Washington, DC: World Bank, 1976, pp. 26–8.
6   Australian Department of Foreign Affairs and Trade and Austrade, 'Why ASEAN and Why Now? Insights for Australian Business', Canberra: Australian Department of Foreign Affairs and Trade and Austrade, August 2015, p. 7; 'The G20 Economies Explained in 12 Charts', *The Conversation*, 12 November 2014.

officials, interactions are now very wide. Immigration has brought large communities of peoples to Australia from Southeast Asia, with the 2011 census indicating that over 650,000 people claim Southeast Asian heritage. Links in education have meant there are deep connections across many sectors. Merchandise trade has increased 107 times since 1973–74 to reach a level of over A$100 billion in 2013–14 and trade with the ASEAN members has increased in relative significance for Australia.[7] Relations that were initiated by a small number of officials and political leaders have also been advanced by non-governmental actors including academics, business groups and 'second track' dialogues such as those sponsored by the Council for Security and Cooperation in the Asia Pacific (CSCAP) and Asialink (University of Melbourne).[8] Thus, while Australia's relative economic size in relation to ASEAN has declined since the 1970s, interlinkages with ASEAN are far wider and deeper and the relationship matters more than ever.

Future issues and prospects

ASEAN, as we have argued, has been valuable to Australia for its contribution to stability in Southeast Asia, as a partner in areas of common interest and as a convenor of forums that have provided regular dialogues for Australia with both regional states and major powers that it would not otherwise have. Australia at the Commemorative Summit in November 2014 reaffirmed its commitment to the relationship and its support for ASEAN's 'centrality' in regional dialogues and

---

7   In the period 1976–77, ASEAN members took 6.6 per cent of Australia's exports and were the source of 4.1 per cent of imports, while in 2014, the figures were 11.4 per cent of Australia's exports and 19.2 per cent of imports; see Clive T. Edwards, 'Current Issues in Australian–ASEAN Trade Relations', *Southeast Asian Affairs 1979*, Singapore: Institute of Southeast Asian Studies, 1979, pp. 30–1; and Australian Department of Foreign Affairs and Trade, 'Association of Southeast Asian Nations (ASEAN)', dfat.gov.au/international-relations/regional-architecture/asean/Pages/association-of-southeast-asian-nations-asean.aspx (accessed 1 October 2015).

8   Since 2008, Asialink has collaborated with the Institute for Strategic and International Studies Malaysia (ISIS-Malaysia) and the Asia New Zealand Foundation to organise the annual ASEAN–Australia–New Zealand Dialogue. The Dialogue provides a 'second track' discussion and review of the ASEAN–Australia and ASEAN–New Zealand relationships by participants from the 12 countries; see Asialink, 'ASEAN–Australia–New Zealand Dialogue', asialink.unimelb.edu.au/asialink_diplomacy/dialogues/asean-australia-new_zealand_dialogue (accessed 14 January 2016). Asialink also sponsors discussions between ASEAN and Australian representatives on specific economic, social and political areas of common interest and concern in the Asialink Conversations. See Asialink, 'Asialink Conversations', asialink.unimelb.edu.au/asialink_diplomacy/dialogues/asialink_conversations2 (accessed 14 January 2016).

institutional development. However, ASEAN's ongoing success – and the potential for Australia's relations with it – should not be taken for granted. In the future development of Australia's relations with ASEAN, five factors are likely to be of particular significance.

First, ASEAN's progress towards its declared goals for economic integration and security cooperation will be crucial. As noted in Chapter 4, the Association has committed itself to developing an ASEAN Community, which was inaugurated formally at the end of 2015, but whose goals are expected widely to need to be pursued well beyond that date. Considerable progress has been made in economic cooperation through the ASEAN Economic Community (AEC) project. Tariff barriers among members have been reduced substantially, customs procedures have been streamlined, cross-border flows of skilled labour in some sectors have been facilitated, the Master Plan on ASEAN Connectivity is in place and should help improve infrastructure and reduce business transaction costs, and disparities in income levels between richer and poorer members have been reduced. A number of businesses increasingly look at the ASEAN area as a regional market. However, the AEC project faces the persistence of many non-tariff barriers and of obstacles to services and investment liberalisation. While it was clear at the time of writing that all the goals of the AEC could not be met by the end of 2015, ASEAN would be able to declare that significant progress had been achieved and efforts at economic integration were set to continue beyond 2015.[9]

ASEAN's Political-Security and Socio-Cultural Communities will be even longer-term endeavours. The Socio-Cultural Community can broaden and deepen interconnections across the immensely diverse ASEAN societies, but its goals cannot be realised rapidly.[10] In the realm of security, ASEAN has been crucial in advancing communication and accord among its members and overt sustained conflict has never occurred. The Political-Security Community seeks to extend this

---

9 See Siow Yue Chia, 'The ASEAN Economic Community: Progress, Challenges, and Prospects', ADBI Working Paper 440, Tokyo: Asian Development Bank Institute, October 2013; Jayant Menon and Anna Cassandra Melendez, 'Realizing an ASEAN Economic Community: Progress and Remaining Challenges', ADB Economics Working Paper 432, Metro Manila: Asian Development Bank, May 2015; Stephen Groff, 'Overcoming Southeast Asia's Barriers to Trade', *Wall Street Journal Asia*, 30 June 2015; Tham Siew Yean and Sanchita Basu Das, 'Domestic Consensus Vital for ASEAN Economic Integration Beyond 2015', *ISEAS Perspective*, 24 September 2015.

10 Julio S. Amador III, 'ASEAN Socio-Cultural Community: An Assessment of its Institutional Prospects', Foreign Service Institute, Pasay City, The Philippines, 28 February 2011.

process, but ASEAN members will continue to face challenges in maintaining regional order. Insurgent and separatist conflicts confront Myanmar, Thailand and the Philippines, despite efforts towards resolution. There has been sensitivity and tension in some inter-state relations (for example, between Thailand and Cambodia, and Cambodia and Vietnam). ASEAN's desire for a stable and manageable regional order will also be challenged by major power competition, for example in relation to activities in the South China Sea.[11] The pursuit of a political and security community will thus need to extend well into the future.[12]

The ASEAN Community project is significant for Australia, which has benefited greatly from ASEAN's success in dampening the bases for inter-state conflict. Further political and security cooperation in ASEAN would consolidate these benefits. Economic integration can enhance ASEAN's value as a trade partner by making the market across the 10 countries both larger and easier to relate to. ASEAN's claims to maintain 'centrality' in regional dialogue will be stronger if its progress towards its goals of integration is seen to be effective and this will be important for all its dialogue partners, including Australia.[13]

A second and related issue for the future of Australia–ASEAN relations will be the climate and evolution of interactions among the major powers. ASEAN was established at a time of Cold War-era competition in Southeast Asia; the pattern of major power relations has been a key factor for ASEAN's subsequent development and continues to exert pressure on the Association. This has been evident in relations among the three most important of these powers in East Asia – the US, China and Japan – where there has been both great economic cooperation and significant strategic tensions, especially between the US and China, and between China and Japan. These tensions deepened from 2009, and by 2015 pressures were if anything intensifying. China was

---

11   Christopher B. Roberts, *ASEAN Regionalism: Cooperation, Values and Institutionalization*, Abingdon: Routledge, 2012, pp. 147–87; Donald E. Weatherbee, *Indonesia in ASEAN: Vision and Reality*, Singapore: ISEAS Publishing, 2013, pp. 59–82.

12   Roberts, *ASEAN Regionalism*, pp. 174–87.

13   Mely Caballero-Anthony, 'Understanding ASEAN's Centrality: Bases and Prospects in an Evolving Regional Architecture', *Pacific Review*, 27(4), 2014. See also the valuable discussion of 'ASEAN centrality' in See Seng Tan, *Multilateral Asian Security Architecture: Non-ASEAN Stakeholders*, Abingdon: Routledge, 2016, pp. 18–40.

continuing its military modernisation and assertiveness on territorial issues while the US was pursuing its rebalance towards East Asia. Relations between Japan and China, a long-term focus for competition in East Asia and in regional cooperative efforts, continued to involve discord over the unresolved legacies of the Second World War and more recent strategic confrontation, notably in the East China Sea.[14]

Major power competition has also contributed to tensions in the South China Sea, where, as noted in Chapter 5, the pattern of disputes intensified after 2009. ASEAN has had great difficulty in responding. The open divisions at the Phnom Penh foreign ministers' meeting in July 2012 illustrated the pressures ASEAN has faced. ASEAN in 2015 was continuing to pursue multilateral discussions with China about a possible code of conduct, but it was not clear if any progress could be made. The South China Sea issue has challenged ASEAN as a political community, given the differing strategic interests of members. Claimant states (particularly the Philippines and Vietnam) were much more affected by, and involved in, the issue than the non-claimants.[15]

Increasing major power competition could undermine ASEAN's capacity as a diplomatic actor. ASEAN has been able to claim a central place in regional dialogue and cooperation because no one major power has been in a position to lead and the competitive climate of major power relations has enabled ASEAN to operate and be accepted as sponsor and convenor of East Asian and Asia Pacific security dialogues.[16] However, heightened major power competition could damage ASEAN's cohesion and reduce its room for manoeuvre. In particular, rivalry between the US and China will exert continuing

---

14 International Crisis Group, 'Old Scores and New Grudges: Evolving Sino-Japanese Tensions', Asia Report No. 258, Brussels: International Crisis Group, 24 July 2014; Ron Huisken, 'Security in the Asia Pacific: Growing Turbulence or a Gathering Storm?' *CSCAP Regional Security Outlook 2015*, Canberra: Council for Security Cooperation in the Asia Pacific, 2015. See also Michael Wesley, *Restless Continent: Wealth, Rivalry and Asia's New Geopolitics*, Collingwood, Vic.: Black Inc., 2015, pp. 93–174.

15 Ian Storey, 'Disputes in the South China Sea: Southeast Asia's Troubled Waters', *politique étrangère*, 3, 2014; International Crisis Group, 'Stirring up the South China Sea (III): A Fleeting Opportunity for Calm', Asia Report No. 267, Brussels: International Crisis Group, 7 May 2015; Ian Storey, 'ASEAN's Failing Grade in the South China Sea', *Asan Forum*, 31 July 2015.

16 Caballero-Anthony, 'Understanding ASEAN's Centrality'.

pressure on the states of Southeast Asia and could circumscribe ASEAN's capacity to maintain an effective common strategic outlook and to operate independently between these powers.[17]

A third and related key issue for Australia and ASEAN will be the prospects for wider multilateral dialogues to make substantive contributions to cooperation and security in East Asia. States in Southeast and East Asia have pursued cooperation through multiple groupings and this pluralism seems set to continue, as will contest between different conceptions of regional dialogues. ASEAN Plus Three, for example, is likely to continue to operate alongside the East Asia Summit. Economic and trade negotiations, as outlined in Chapter 5, have been conducted by different groups with differing memberships, notably through the ASEAN-sponsored Regional Comprehensive Economic Partnership (RCEP) and through the Trans-Pacific Partnership (TPP). China has, in addition, contributed to the array of multilateral cooperation avenues. In 2015, China established a new regional economic institution, the Asian Infrastructure Investment Bank, which will operate alongside the Asian Development Bank.[18]

While pluralism in the range of institutions and cooperation dialogues seems set to continue, there may be potential for rationalisation among some of the major regional dialogues.[19] A key issue is the character and role of the East Asia Summit and its relationships with other major dialogues. Australia for the past two decades has been involved in the development of ASEAN-sponsored forums beginning with the ARF and extending most recently to the ASEAN Defence Ministers' Meeting (ADMM) Plus process. Australia has been a strong proponent of the highest profile of these groupings, the East Asia Summit, which has proceeded cautiously since its inauguration in 2005 and has operated with its expanded membership (with the US and Russia) only

---

17 Donald K. Emmerson, 'Challenging ASEAN: The American Pivot in Southeast Asia', *East Asia Forum*, 13 January 2013; Huisken, 'Security in the Asia Pacific'; Amitav Acharya, 'Is ASEAN Losing its Way?' *YaleGlobal online*, 24 September 2015.
18 See David Arase, 'What to Make of the Asian Infrastructure Investment Bank', *Asan Forum*, 26 June 2015.
19 See Nick Bisley and Malcolm Cook, 'How the East Asia Summit Can Achieve its Potential', *ISEAS Perspective*, 28 October 2014.

since 2011.[20] A significant question for both ASEAN and Australia is whether the East Asia Summit may be able to develop a more substantive role in promoting cooperation and security.

There are inter-related political and institutional questions about the East Asia Summit. As noted in Chapter 5, the Summit has begun to develop an identity and has pursued a range of cooperative projects, but the annual leaders' meeting – the keystone of the Summit – is short and has had little organised institutional backup to support it or to help it pursue follow-up activities. The Australian Government has hoped to see the East Asia Summit advance its identity and role as a leaders' meeting. Ideas for enhancing the role and capacity of the East Asia Summit have been proposed, notably in a memorandum issued by CSCAP in June 2014.

The CSCAP report (which was endorsed by a multinational panel of experts) advocated both strengthening the East Asia Summit and rationalising its roles, along with those of the ARF and ADMM-Plus. CSCAP suggested that the Summit could expand from its current limited duration (about three hours) to a full day. ASEAN could consider joint chairmanship of the Summit with non-ASEAN members, which would help give those members an increased sense of involvement in the Summit. Additional support could be provided to the Summit by an expanded ASEAN Secretariat. Communication and connectivity among the dialogues, CSCAP argued, could be improved, so that the Summit could focus on strategic direction, the ARF on structured security dialogue and the ADMM-Plus on practical security cooperation.[21] The CSCAP proposals were a valuable contribution to the debate on regional institutions, especially given their endorsement by representatives from the Council's membership across the Asia-Pacific region. At the time of writing, the proposals were being considered within ASEAN under Malaysia's chairmanship in 2015 and were another notable example of the contribution to regional cooperation that have been made by non-official individuals and groups and in which Australians have been able to take part.[22]

---

20   Ibid.
21   CSCAP, 'Towards an Effective Regional Security Architecture for the Asia Pacific', CSCAP Memorandum No. 26, June 2014.
22   Ron Huisken and Anthony Milner, 'On a Track to Regional Peace with CSCAP', *The Australian*, 2 July 2014.

The East Asia Summit could be better organised and supported. However its viability will still depend on the commitment of the participating states to help make it work. A further and highly significant issue for the Summit therefore is that its potential will be affected and constrained by the state of major power relations. In 2015, interactions among the major power members of the East Asia Summit were not propitious for the development of common endeavours. Relationships among the US and China and China and Japan were uneasy and levels of strategic communication and trust were not high. Relations between the US and Russia had also deteriorated in the wake of the political crisis in Ukraine from the first part of 2014 and by Russia's annexation of the territory of Crimea, a step criticised sharply by the US.[23] These issues posed major questions about the potential for the effective advancement of the East Asia Summit. Multilateral forums can provide valuable venues for building additional communication, alongside bilateral relations. However, without a greater degree of strategic accord among the major powers, the potential for substantive cooperation in multilateral forums like the Summit is likely to remain limited.[24] As a founding member of the East Asia Summit, Australia has a strong interest in how the debates about the Summit develop and whether a consensus can emerge for adaptation and change.

A fourth key issue for the future of Australia–ASEAN relations is the character and evolution of Australia's interactions with ASEAN as an institution. Australia is pursuing its ASEAN relations in an environment where other dialogue partners are active in their own multilateral relations with the Association, including China, Japan, South Korea and India. In this context it is important that Australia should maximise its efforts to bolster the profile of its engagement both within Australia and in ASEAN. By 2015, Australia was interacting regularly with ASEAN in many venues, headed by the annual Post-Ministerial Conference of foreign ministers. At heads of government level, ASEAN's profile for Australia has been less prominent. The two sides up to 2015 held four leaders' summit meetings (1977, 2004,

---

23   Huisken, 'Security in the Asia Pacific'; See Seng Tan and Oleg Korovin, 'Seeking Stability in Turbulent Times: Southeast Asia's New Normal?' in Daljit Singh, ed., *Southeast Asian Affairs 2015*, Singapore: Institute of Southeast Asian Studies, 2015.

24   William T. Tow, 'Great Powers and Multilateralism: The Politics of Security Architectures in Southeast Asia', in Ralf Emmers, ed., *ASEAN and the Institutionalization of East Asia*, London: Routledge, 2012; Evelyn Goh, 'ASEAN-led Multilateralism and Regional Order: The Great Power Bargain Deficit', *Asan Forum*, May–June 2014.

2010 and 2014). The holding of more frequent leaders' meeting (every two years), which was foreshadowed at the 2014 Commemorative Summit, was agreed upon in August 2015, with the first of the regular meetings to be held in Vientiane in late 2016. This should advance the profile of relations on both sides and be a significant way of visibly increasing cooperation.

Australia's relationship with ASEAN's institutional structures is also important. A centrepiece of the institutional relationship, as noted in Chapter 5, is Australia's multilateral assistance program with ASEAN (the Australia–ASEAN Development Cooperation Program), which is focused on the ASEAN Secretariat and has a particular emphasis on supporting the Association's capacities for economic integration. This aspect of the Australia–ASEAN relationship is appreciated and valued by the ASEAN side. This is particularly the case because the Secretariat in Jakarta has operated with a limited funding base in which individual ASEAN members have paid the same annual contribution (towards the annual budget that in 2014 was under US$20 million) despite the obvious differences in wealth among them. The relatively small Secretariat has to manage hundreds of meetings annually and many complex cooperative programs. It has been argued that ASEAN will need considerably expanded resources for the Secretariat if it is to pursue its ASEAN Community cooperative plans effectively.[25] ASEAN has been considering its own structures and how they may be enhanced through a high-level task force. A significant question will be whether a consensus will develop to give the Secretariat more resources, when there has been a long-standing tendency within ASEAN to maintain the Secretariat at a relatively modest size and to retain the principle of equality of the size of contributions. Australia can continue to develop ways of enhancing its assistance to the ASEAN Secretariat and to the Association's integration projects and this can provide further relevant support to ASEAN when its administrative resources are stretched and add further depth to the Australian relationship.

There are additional steps that Australia could take to maximise the potential for the ASEAN relationship. The New Colombo Plan is a positive addition to Australia's basis for interaction with ASEAN and

---

25   Chia, 'The ASEAN Economic Community'; Asian Development Bank Institute, *ASEAN 2030: Toward a Borderless Economic Community*, Tokyo: Asian Development Bank Institute, 2014, pp. 272–5.

with Asia overall. The long-term benefits of this plan can be enhanced by further support in Australia to the education sector to encourage language and non-language studies of the ASEAN members.[26] Australia could also raise its own profile in the ASEAN region through expanded use of the Special Overseas Visitors Program to increase dialogue between public and private sector policymakers from ASEAN and relevant sectors in Australia. In addition, Australia could make a more concerted effort to raise the attention given to ASEAN in Australia; the Australia–ASEAN Council, which was inaugurated on 8 September 2015 with the goal of initiating and supporting activities designed to enhance awareness, understanding and links between people and institutions in Australia and the 10 ASEAN countries, can make a valuable contribution to this process.[27]

A fifth key issue is Australia's relationship with Indonesia. While all of the bilateral relationships support the multilateral association, the Indonesia connection has been integral to Australia's interactions with ASEAN. Indonesia's support has been crucial on a number of occasions in assisting Australia to gain acceptance in regional dialogues and to facilitate Australian policy initiatives, including the particularly close cooperation during the Cambodian peace process, and the development of APEC, the ARF and the East Asia Summit. It was noted in Chapter 4 that the improved climate in bilateral relations after 2002 (in which cooperation on counter-terrorism issues was a central element) played a major role in the revival of progress in Australia's multilateral relations with ASEAN.

While relations developed substantially in the decade of the Susilo Bambang Yudhoyono administration (2004–14), the potential for discord continues.[28] There are ongoing problems of comparative lack of trust on both sides and the efforts made in advancing official dialogues has not been matched by the development of accord at the

26   Anthony Milner and Sally Percival Wood, eds, 'Our Place in the Asian Century: Southeast Asia as "The Third Way"', Melbourne: Asialink, University of Melbourne, 2012, pp. 20–4.
27   Australian Department of Foreign Affairs and Trade, 'The Australia–ASEAN Council', 17 July 2015, dfat.gov.au/people-to-people/foundations-councils-institutes/Pages/the-australia-asean-council.aspx (accessed 1 October 2015).
28   See Ken Ward, *Condemned to Crisis? A Lowy Institute Paper*, Melbourne: Penguin, 2015.

level of popular opinion.[29] The health and viability of this bilateral relationship will remain crucial for productive Australian interactions with ASEAN.[30]

Since the 1970s Australia has gained great benefits from ASEAN's contribution to stability in Southeast Asia. Australia and ASEAN have been able to work together on many problems of common concern to advance security. Australia has supported strongly ASEAN's dialogue processes involving the major powers in East Asia and its associated groups including the ARF and the East Asia Summit. Economic growth has broadened the basis for Australia's engagement with the ASEAN region. ASEAN's programs for deeper integration can add to the basis for Australia's regional political and economic involvements. Australia therefore has a major stake in ASEAN's capacity to achieve its declared goals and in the contribution that the relationship can make to enhancing prosperity and security for all.

---

29   See Peter Varghese, 'The 50th Anniversary of the Indonesia Project', Speech, Canberra, 30 July 2015, dfat.gov.au/news/speeches/Pages/50th-anniversary-dinner-indonesia-project.aspx (accessed 1 October 2015).

30   Christopher B. Roberts and Ahmad D. Habir, 'Indonesia–Australia Relations: Progress, Challenges and Potential', in Christopher B. Roberts, Ahmad D. Habir and Leonard C. Sebastian, eds, *Indonesia's Ascent: Power, Leadership, and the Regional Order*, Basingstoke: Palgrave Macmillan, 2015.

Bibliography

'$5m. to Aid Asian Ties', *Courier Mail*, 17 April 1974.

AAP, 'The Way Is Closed, Abbott Declares on Asylum-Seeker Boats', *The Australian*, 29 March 2014.

Abbott, Tony, 'Doorstop Interview, Naypyidaw, Myanmar', Transcript, 13 November 2014.

ABC News, 'Thailand Shows Interest in Rudd's Asia-Pac Community', 4 July 2008.

ABC Radio Australia, 'Australia Should Stay out of South China Sea Dispute says Carr', Transcript, 30 July 2012.

Acharya, Amitav, 'ASEAN and Burma/Myanmar: Past and Prologue', Policy Brief, Washington, DC: Sigur Center for Asian Studies, George Washington University, April 2012.

Acharya, Amitav, *Constructing a Security Community in Southeast Asia: ASEAN and the Problem of Regional Order*, 3rd edn, Abingdon: Routledge, 2014.

Acharya, Amitav, 'Is ASEAN Losing its Way?' *YaleGlobal online*, 24 September 2015.

Acharya, Amitav, *The Making of Southeast Asia: International Relations of a Region*, Singapore: ISEAS Publishing, 2012.

Acharya, Amitav and See Seng Tan, 'The Normative Relevance of the Bandung Conference for Contemporary Asian and International Order', in See Seng Tan and Amitav Acharya, eds, *Bandung Revisited: The Legacy of the 1955 Asian–African Conference for International Order*, Singapore: NUS Press, 2008, pp. 2–16.

AFP, 'Beijing Dilutes ASEAN: Ministers Wrangled Over Islands Disputes', *The Australian*, 7 August 2015.

Albinski, Henry S., *Australia in Southeast Asia: Interests, Capacity, and Acceptability*, Springfield, VA: National Technical Information Service, December 1970.

Albinski, Henry S., *Australian External Policy under Labor: Content, Process and the National Debate,* St Lucia: University of Queensland Press, 1977.

Allard, Tom, 'Economic Powerhouse Attracts Howard's Eye', *Sydney Morning Herald*, 1 December 2004.

Amador III, Julio S., 'ASEAN Socio-Cultural Community: An Assessment of its Institutional Prospects', Foreign Service Institute, Pasay City, The Philippines, 28 February 2011.

Ang Cheng Guan, *Singapore, ASEAN and the Cambodian Conflict 1978–1991*, Singapore: NUS Press, 2013.

'Anti-Pol Pot "Group Grows"', *The Herald* (Melbourne), 27 August 1980.

Arase, David, 'What to Make of the Asian Infrastructure Investment Bank', *Asan Forum*, 26 June 2015.

ASEAN, 'ASEAN and Australia: An Enduring Connection', Joint Statement of the ASEAN–Australia Summit, Hanoi, 30 October 2010.

ASEAN, 'Chairman's Statement of the 10th ASEAN Summit', Vientiane, 29 November 2004.

ASEAN, 'Chairman's Statement of the ASEAN–Australia and New Zealand Commemorative Summit', Vientiane, 30 November 2004.

ASEAN, 'Chairman's Statement of the ASEAN Post-Ministerial Conference (10+1 Sessions) with the Dialogue Partners', Kuala Lumpur, 5 August 2015.

ASEAN, 'Declaration of ASEAN Concord II (Bali Concord II)', Bali, 7 October 2003.

ASEAN, 'Joint Communique, 48th ASEAN Foreign Ministers Meeting', Kuala Lumpur, 4 August 2015.

ASEAN, 'Joint Media Statement of the Thirteenth AEM–CER Consultations', Singapore, 28 August 2008.

ASEAN, 'Joint Press Statement of the ASEAN Heads of Government and the Prime Minister of Australia', Kuala Lumpur, 7 August 1977.

ASEAN, 'Kuala Lumpur Declaration on the East Asia Summit', Kuala Lumpur, 14 December 2005.

ASEAN, 'The Declaration of ASEAN Concord', Bali, Indonesia, February 1976.

ASEAN, 'The Special ASEAN Economic Ministers Meeting', Kuala Lumpur, 22 February 1979.

ASEAN, 'Towards a Strategic Partnership for Mutual Benefit', Joint ASEAN–Australia Leaders' Statement on the 40th Anniversary of ASEAN–Australia Dialogue Relations, Nay Pyi Taw, Myanmar, 12 November 2014.

ASEAN, 'Treaty of Amity and Cooperation in Southeast Asia', Indonesia, 24 February 1976.

'A.S.E.A.N.', *Canberra Times*, 20 December 1973.

'ASEAN Opens up on Security', *Canberra Times*, 21 July 1991.

ASEAN Secretariat, 'The ASEAN Declaration (Bangkok Declaration)', Bangkok, 8 August 1967.

'ASEAN: Sign the Pact or Stay Away', *The Australian*, 12 April 2005.

'ASEAN Talks End in Trade Pact', *The Age*, 22 June 1978.

'ASEAN Wary of Pacific Security Plan', *The Australian*, 8 October 1990.

Asialink, 'ASEAN–Australia–New Zealand Dialogue', asialink.unimelb. edu.au/asialink_diplomacy/dialogues/asean-australia-new_ zealand_dialogue (accessed 14 January 2016).

Asialink, 'Asialink Conversations', asialink.unimelb.edu.au/asialink_ diplomacy/dialogues/asialink_conversations2 (accessed 14 January 2016).

'Asian and Pacific Council: Joint Communiqué on Establishment of Asian and Pacific Council', *International Legal Materials*, 5(5) 1966: 985–6.

Asian Development Bank Institute, *ASEAN 2030: Toward a Borderless Economic Community*, Tokyo: Asian Development Bank Institute, 2014.

Associated Press, 'Top US Officials Meet Myanmar Junta, Suu Kyi', 4 November 2009.

'Australia Joins Launch of Massive Asian Regional Trade Agreement', joint media release, Prime Minister and Minister for Trade and Competitiveness, Phnom Penh, 20 November 2012.

'Australia to Sign ASEAN Treaty', *The World Today*, ABC Radio, 22 July 2005.

Australian Department of Defence, *2013 Defence White Paper*, Canberra: Commonwealth of Australia, 2013.

Australian Department of Defence, *Review of Australia's Defence Capabilities: Report to the Minister for Defence*, Canberra: Australian Government Publishing Service, 1986.

Australian Department of Defence, *The Defence of Australia*, Canberra: Australian Government Publishing Service, 1987.

Australian Department of Foreign Affairs and Trade, *Advancing the National Interest: Australia's Foreign and Trade Policy White Paper*, Canberra: Commonwealth of Australia, 2003.

Australian Department of Foreign Affairs and Trade, 'Association of Southeast Asian Nations (ASEAN)', dfat.gov.au/international-relations/regional-architecture/asean/Pages/association-of-southeast-asian-nations-asean.aspx (accessed 1 October 2015).

Australian Department of Foreign Affairs and Trade, 'Burma Country Brief', dfat.gov.au/geo/burma/pages/burma-country-brief.aspx (accessed 1 October 2015).

Australian Department of Foreign Affairs and Trade, *Cambodia: An Australian Peace Proposal*, working papers prepared for the Informal Meeting on Cambodia, Jakarta, 26–28 February 1990, Canberra: Australian Government Publishing Service for the Australian Department of Foreign Affairs and Trade, 1990.

Australian Department of Foreign Affairs and Trade, 'East Asia Summit', dfat.gov.au/international-relations/regional-architecture/eas/Pages/east-asia-summit-eas.aspx (accessed 1 October 2015).

Australian Department of Foreign Affairs and Trade, *East Timor in Transition 1998–2000: An Australian Policy Challenge*, Canberra: Australian Department of Foreign Affairs and Trade, 2001.

Australian Department of Foreign Affairs and Trade, *In the National Interest: Australia's Foreign and Trade Policy White Paper*, Canberra: Commonwealth of Australia, 1997.

Australian Department of Foreign Affairs and Trade, 'New Colombo Plan', www.dfat.gov.au/people-to-people/new-colombo-plan/pages/new-colombo-plan.aspx (accessed 11 March 2015).

Australian Department of Foreign Affairs and Trade, 'Overview and Key Outcomes of the ASEAN–Australia–New Zealand Free Trade Agreement', Department of Foreign Affairs and Trade Speaking Notes for Presentation at Austrade's ASEAN Now Seminars, 15–30 October 2009.

Australian Department of Foreign Affairs and Trade, 'Signature of AANZFTA Protocol', media release, 27 August 2014.

Australian Department of Foreign Affairs and Trade, 'The Australia–ASEAN Council', 17 July 2015, dfat.gov.au/people-to-people/foundations-councils-institutes/Pages/the-australia-asean-council.aspx (accessed 1 October 2015).

Australian Department of Foreign Affairs and Trade, 'Where We Give Aid', dfat.gov.au/aid/where-we-give-aid/Pages/where-we-give-aid.aspx (accessed 1 October 2015).

Australian Department of Foreign Affairs and Trade and Austrade, 'Why ASEAN and Why Now? Insights for Australian Business', Canberra: Australian Department of Foreign Affairs and Trade and Austrade, August 2015.

Australian Government, *Australia in the Asian Century: White Paper*, Canberra: Commonwealth of Australia, October 2012.

Australian Labor Party, *Platform, Constitution and Rules as Approved by the 35th National Conference*, Canberra: Australian Labor Party, 1982.

Australian Liberal Party and National Party, 'The Coalition's Policy for Foreign Affairs', Canberra, September 2013.

Australian Strategic Policy Institute, 'Maritime Confidence Building Measures in the South China Sea Conference', Special Report, Canberra: ASPI, September 2013.

Ayres, Philip, *Malcolm Fraser: A Biography*, Richmond, Vic.: William Heinemann Australia, 1987.

Bachelard, Michael and Sarah Whyte, 'UN Representatives Criticise Abbott Government's Boat Tow-Back Policy', *Sydney Morning Herald,* 23 April 2014.

Bader, Jeffrey A., *Obama and China's Rise: An Insider's Account of America's Asia Strategy*, Washington, DC: Brookings Institution Press, 2012.

Baker, Mark, 'ASEAN Leaders Resist Push to Isolate Burma', *The Age*, 16 December 1995.

Baker, Mark, 'Australia Drops Bid to Join Summit', *The Age*, 7 October 2003.

Baker, Mark, 'Beyond the Pale', *Sydney Morning Herald*, 9 November 2002.

Baker, Mark, 'Hun Sen Defies His Critics', *The Age*, 11 July 1997.

Baker, Mark, 'Malaysia's New PM Leaves Mahathir's Acrimonious Legacy at the 19th Hole', *The Age*, 12 June 2004.

Ball, Desmond and Pauline Kerr, *Presumptive Engagement: Australia's Asia-Pacific Security Policy in the 1990s,* St Leonards, NSW: Allen & Unwin, in association with the Department of International Relations, The Australian National University, 1996.

Bathurst, Peter, 'Common Denominator: Captured Guns', *Far Eastern Economic Review,* 4 July 1975.

Berry, Ken, *Cambodia from Red to Blue: Australia's Initiative for Peace,* St Leonards, NSW: Allen & Unwin, in association with the Department of International Relations, The Australian National University, 1997.

Berry, Ken, 'UNTAC as a Paradigm: A Flawed Success', *Pacifica Review,* 7(2) 1995: 87–101.

Bersick, Sebastian, 'Europe's Role in Asia: Distant but Involved', in David Shambaugh and Michael Yahuda, eds, *International Relations of Asia,* 2nd edn, New York: Rowman & Littlefield, 2014, pp. 115–44.

Bishop, Julie, 'Australia's Prospering Partnership with ASEAN', op-ed article, 17 April 2014.

Bishop, Julie, 'Doorstop Interview: East Asia Summit, Kuala Lumpur', Transcript, 5 August 2015.

Bisley, Nick and Malcolm Cook, 'How the East Asia Summit Can Achieve its Potential', *ISEAS Perspective,* 28 October 2014.

Blaxland, John, 'Australia, Indonesia and Southeast Asia', in Peter J. Dean, Stephan Frühling and Brendan Taylor, eds, *Australia's Defence: Towards A New Era?,* Carlton, Vic.: Melbourne University Press, 2014, pp. 107–39.

Bloomfield, Alan, 'To Balance or to Bandwagon? Adjusting to China's Rise during Australia's Rudd–Gillard Era', *Pacific Review,* published online, 16 March 2015.

Boyd, Alan, 'Proposal for Asian Trading Bloc Gets Lukewarm Reception', *The Australian,* 8 February 1991.

Braddick, C. W., 'Japan, Australia and ASPAC: The Rise and Fall of an Asia-Pacific Cooperative Security Framework', in Brad Williams and Andrew Newman, eds, *Japan, Australia and Asia-Pacific Security*, Abingdon: Routledge, 2006, pp. 30–46.

Brenchley, Fred, 'The Howard Defence Doctrine', *The Bulletin*, 28 September 1999.

'Britain Drops Kampuchea's Pol Pot Government', *Sydney Morning Herald*, 8 December 1979.

Brown, MacAlister and Joseph J. Zasloff, *Cambodia Confounds the Peacemakers, 1979–1998*, Ithaca, NY: Cornell University Press, 1998.

Bryant, John, 'Australian Support Canvassed', *Canberra Times*, 2 October 1982.

'Building Trust with ASEAN', *Daily Telegraph*, 14 August 2004.

Burrell, Andrew, 'Downer Enjoys a Warmer North', *Australian Financial Review*, 8 December 2004.

Burrell, Andrew, 'PM Hails Stronger Ties with Jakarta', *Australian Financial Review*, 21 October 2004.

Burrell, Steve, 'APEC Takes Off as EAEG Nose-Dives', *Australian Financial Review*, 18 November 1991.

Buszynski, Leszek, *SEATO – The Failure of an Alliance Strategy*, Singapore: Singapore University Press, 1983.

Buszynski, Leszek, 'The Origins and Development of the South China Sea Maritime Dispute', in Leszek Buszynski and Christopher B. Roberts, eds, *The South China Sea Maritime Dispute: Political, Legal and Regional Perspectives*, Abingdon: Routledge, 2015, pp. 1–23.

Buszynski, Leszek and Christopher B. Roberts, eds, *The South China Sea Maritime Dispute: Political, Legal and Regional Perspectives*, Abingdon: Routledge, 2015.

Caballero-Anthony, Mely, 'The ASEAN Charter: An Opportunity Missed or One that *Cannot* be Missed', *Southeast Asian Affairs 2008*, Singapore: Institute of Southeast Asian Studies, 2008, pp. 71–85.

Caballero-Anthony, Mely, 'Understanding ASEAN's Centrality: Bases and Prospects in an Evolving Regional Architecture', *Pacific Review*, 27(4) 2014: 563–84.

Callick, Rowan, 'Beijing Attacks Curbs on N Korea', *The Australian*, 21 September 2006.

Callick, Rowan, 'Rudd's Asian Vision Quietly Buried', *The Australian*, 21 June 2010.

Camilleri, Joseph A., *Regionalism in the New Asia-Pacific Order: The Political Economy of the Asia-Pacific Region, Volume II*, Cheltenham: Edward Elgar, 2003.

Camroux, David, 'The East Asia Summit: Pan-Asian Multilateralism Rather than Intra-Asian Regionalism', in Mark Beeson and Richard Stubbs, eds, *Routledge Handbook of Asian Regionalism*, London: Routledge, 2012, pp. 375–83.

Carr, Andrew, *Winning the Peace: Australia's Campaign to Change the Asia-Pacific*, Carlton, Vic.: Melbourne University Press, 2015.

Carr, Bob, 'Australia's Foreign Policy Directions', Address to the National Press Club, Canberra, 26 June 2013.

Carr, Bob, *Diary of a Foreign Minister*, Sydney: NewSouth Publishing, 2014.

Carr, Bob, 'European Union Lifts Myanmar Sanctions', media release, 24 April 2013.

Carr, Bob, 'Southeast Asia: At the Crossroads of the Asian Century', IISS-Fullerton Lecture, Singapore, 9 July 2013.

Carr, Bob, 'The East Asia Summit: Building our Regional Architecture for the 21st Century', *Strategic Review* (Jakarta), July 2012.

Chalermpalanupap, Termsak, 'Timor-Leste's Quest to Join ASEAN: The Process and the Pace', *ASEAN Focus*, 1/2015, August 2015, pp. 9–10.

Chanda, Nayan, *Brother Enemy: The War After the War*, New York: Free Press, 1988.

Chia, Siow Yue, 'The ASEAN Economic Community: Progress, Challenges, and Prospects', ADBI Working Paper 440, Tokyo: Asian Development Bank Institute, October 2013.

Chin Kin Wah, 'Background to an Evolving ASEAN–ANZ Relationship', in Michael Richardson and Chin Kin Wah, *Australia–New Zealand & Southeast Asia Relations: An Agenda for Closer Cooperation*, Singapore: ISEAS Publications, 2004, pp. 14–24.

Chua, Daniel Wei Boon, 'Fifty Years of Singapore-Australian Relations: An Enduring Strategic Partnership – Analysis', *Eurasia Review*, 26 August 2015.

Chung, Chien-Peng, 'China and Japan in "ASEAN Plus" Multilateral Arrangements: Raining on the Other Guy's Parade', *Asian Survey*, 53(5) 2013: 801–24.

Cole-Adams, Peter, 'PM Looks to Join ASEAN Trade Bloc', *Canberra Times*, 8 April 1994.

Colebatch, Tim, 'Australia May Be Alone On Treaty', *The Age*, 30 November 2004.

Conley Tyler, Melissa and Eric Lerais, 'Australia and ASEM: The First Two Years', Working Paper 2013/1, Caulfield East, Vic.: Monash University European and EU Centre, May 2013.

Costello, Michael, 'Cambodia: A Diplomatic Memoir', *Sydney Papers*, 6(3) 1994: 98–108.

Cotton, James, 'Asian Regionalism and the Australian Policy Response in the Howard Era', *Journal of Australian Studies*, 32(1) 2008: 115–34.

Cotton, James, *East Timor, Australia and Regional Order: Intervention and its Aftermath in Southeast Asia*, London: Routledge, 2004.

Courtland-Robinson, W., *Terms of Refuge: The Indochinese Exodus and the International Response*, London: Zed Books, 1998.

Cromie, Ali, 'Peacock Queries Policy on Pol Pot', *The Age*, 14 July 1980.

Crone, Donald, 'The Politics of Emerging Pacific Cooperation', *Pacific Affairs*, 65(1) 1992: 68–83.

Crouch, Harold, 'Understanding Malaysia', in Anthony Milner and Mary Quilty, eds, *Australia in Asia: Episodes*, Melbourne: Oxford University Press, 1998, pp. 37–60.

CSCAP (Council for Security Cooperation in the Asia Pacific), 'Towards an Effective Regional Security Architecture for the Asia Pacific', CSCAP Memorandum No. 26, June 2014.

Curran, James, *Unholy Fury: Whitlam and Nixon at War*, Carlton, Vic.: Melbourne University Press, 2015.

Dalrymple, Rawdon, *Continental Drift: Australia's Search for a Regional Identity*, Aldershot: Ashgate, 2003.

Das, Sanchita Basu, 'RCEP and TPP: Comparisons and Concerns', *ISEAS Perspective,* 7 January 2013.

Das, Sanchita Basu and Reema B. Jagtiani, 'The Regional Comprehensive Economic Partnership: New Paradigm or Old Wine in a New Bottle?' ISEAS Economics Working Paper No. 2014–3, Singapore: Institute of Southeast Asian Studies, November 2014.

Davies, Adam, 'Australia Spent $100 Million to MH 370 Search So Far', *The Northern Star*, 7 August 2015.

Davies, Mathew, 'The ASEAN Synthesis: Human Rights, Non-Intervention, and the ASEAN Human Rights Declaration', *Georgetown Journal of International Affairs*, 14(2) 2013: 51–8.

Dee, Moreen and Frank Frost, 'Indochina', in Peter Edwards and David Goldsworthy, eds, *Facing North: A Century of Australian Engagement with Asia, Volume 2: 1970s to 2000*, Carlton, Vic.: Melbourne University Press, 2003, pp. 178–215.

Desker, Barry, 'Why the East Asian Summit Matters', *PacNet*, No. 55B, Pacific Forum/CSIS, Hawaii, 19 December 2005.

Dobell, Graeme, 'Australia–East Asia/US Relations: Australia Adjusts to New Realities', *Comparative Connections: A Quarterly E-Journal on East Asian Bilateral Relations*, 11(3) 2009.

Dobell, Graeme, 'Australia–East Asia/US Relations: China Bumps, Indonesia Breach, Japan as Ally', *Comparative Connections: A Triannual E-Journal on East Asian Bilateral Relations*, 16(2) 2014: 143–55.

Dobell, Graeme, *Australia Finds Home: The Choices and Chances of an Asia Pacific Journey*, Sydney: ABC Books, 2000.

Dobell, Graeme, 'Singapore and Oz: Mismatched Mates', *The Strategist*, 24 August 2015.

Dodd, Mark, 'Canberra to Assign an Envoy to ASEAN', *The Australian*, 25 July 2008.

Dodd, Mark, 'SBY Cold on Rudd's Asia Plan', *The Australian*, 10 March 2010.

Dodd, Tim, 'ASEAN Stifles New Merger Deal', *Weekend Australian Financial Review*, 7–8 October 2000.

Dorling, Philip, 'Rudd's Man Criticised Hasty Asia-Pacific Community Plan', *Sydney Morning Herald*, 24 December 2010.

Downer, Alexander, 'Australia's Engagement with Asia', Speech to the Asialink Chairman's Dinner, Melbourne, 1 December 2005.

Downer, Alexander, 'Association of Southeast Asian Nations', Question, in *Commonwealth of Australia Parliamentary Debates*, House of Representatives, Official Hansard, No. 2, 29 November 2004, pp. 32–3.

Downer, Alexander, 'What Australia Wishes for ASEAN', Speech to the Singapore Institute for International Affairs, Singapore, 23 July 2001.

Drysdale, Peter and Shiro Armstrong, 'What Comes After the Atlanta Deal on the Trans-Pacific Partnership?' *East Asia Forum*, 19 October 2015.

Dupont, Alan, 'ASEAN's Response to the East Timor Crisis', *Australian Journal of International Affairs*, 54(2) 2000: 163–70.

Dwyer, Michael, 'Downer Calls for ARF to Arbitrate Regional Disputes', *Australian Financial Review*, 3 May 1996.

Earl, Greg, 'Asian Trade Club Opens Up to Aust', *Australian Financial Review*, 26 November 1993.

Earl, Greg, 'Malaysian Rebuff Fails to Dent Evans' Confidence', *Australian Financial Review*, 26 July 1994.

Edwards, Clive T., 'Current Issues in Australian–ASEAN Trade Relations', *Southeast Asian Affairs 1979*, Singapore: Institute of Southeast Asian Studies, 1979, pp. 30–44.

Ellis, Eric, 'Goh: Australian Role in ASEAN', *Australian Financial Review*, 16 January 1996.

Ellis, Eric, 'Ramos to Australia: Join Us in ASEAN', *Australian Financial Review*, 23 February 1994.

Emmers, Ralf, Joseph Chinyong Liow and See Seng Tan, *The East Asia Summit and the Regional Security Architecture*, Maryland Series in Contemporary Asian Studies, No. 3, Baltimore, MD: School of Law, University of Maryland, 2010.

Emmerson, Donald K., 'Challenging ASEAN: The American Pivot in Southeast Asia', *East Asia Forum*, 13 January 2013.

'Evans Endorses Defence Forum', *Canberra Times*, 26 July 1993.

Evans, Gareth, 'An Idea Whose Time Has Come', *Australian Foreign Affairs Record,* 60(5) 1989: 183–6.

Evans, Gareth, 'Australia and Northeast Asia', Address by the Minister for Foreign Affairs and Trade, Senator Gareth Evans, to the Committee for the Economic Development of Australia (CEDA), Melbourne, 22 March 1990.

Evans, Gareth, 'Australia's Regional Security', Ministerial Statement, Canberra: Australian Department of Foreign Affairs and Trade, 1989.

Evans, Gareth, 'Prospects for a Cambodian Peace Settlement', Ministerial Statement, in *Commonwealth of Australia Parliamentary Debates*, Senate, Official Hansard, No. 142, 6 December 1990, pp. 5164–75.

Evans, Gareth, 'Statement by Senator Gareth Evans, the Minister for Foreign Affairs and Trade, to the 6+6 Session, 23rd ASEAN Post-Ministerial Conference, Jakarta', news release, 27 July 1990.

Evans, Gareth and Bruce Grant, *Australia's Foreign Relations in the World of the 1990s*, 2nd edn, Carlton, Vic.: Melbourne University Press, 1995.

Faulkner, John, 'Questions on Notice: Mr Richard Woolcott (Question No. 2123)', in *Commonwealth of Australia Parliamentary Debates*, Senate, Official Hansard, No. 13, 17 November 2009, pp. 8091–2.

Fergusson, Ian F., Mark A. McMinimy and Brock R. Williams, 'The Trans-Pacific Partnership (TPP): Negotiations and Issues for Congress', Washington, DC: Congressional Research Service, 20 March 2015.

Firth, Stewart, *Australia in International Politics: An Introduction to Australian Foreign Policy*, 3rd edn, Crows Nest, NSW: Allen & Unwin, 2011.

Flitton, Daniel, 'US Diplomat Wary of Rudd's Big Idea', *The Age*, 30 June 2008.

Frame, Tom, *The Life and Death of Harold Holt*, St Leonards, NSW: Allen & Unwin, 2005.

Fraser, Malcolm, 'Address to the Second ASEAN Trade Fair', Melbourne, 4 August 1980.

Fraser, Malcolm, 'Post ASEAN Conference Talks', Ministerial Statement, in *Commonwealth of Australia Parliamentary Debates*, House of Representatives, Official Hansard, No. 33, 17 August 1977, pp. 351–5.

Fraser, Malcolm and Margaret Simons, *Malcolm Fraser: The Political Memoirs*, Carlton, Vic.: Miegunyah Press, 2010.

'Fraser May Get ASEAN Invite', *Canberra Times*, 28 February 1977.

'Fraser "No" to ASEAN Plea on Imports', *Sydney Morning Herald*, 18 January 1978.

Frost, Frank, 'ASEAN and Australia', in Alison Broinowski, ed., *Understanding ASEAN*, London: Macmillan, 1982, pp. 144–68.

Frost, Frank, 'ASEAN and Regional Cooperation: Recent Developments and Australia's Interests', Parliamentary Library Research Paper Series, 2013–14, Canberra: Department of Parliamentary Services, 8 November 2013, www.aph.gov.au/About_Parliament/ Parliamentary_Departments/Parliamentary_Library/pubs/rp/ rp1314/ASEAN (accessed 1 October 2015).

Frost, Frank, 'Labor and Cambodia', in David Lee and Christopher Waters, eds, *Evatt to Evans: The Labor Tradition in Australian Foreign Policy*, St Leonards, NSW: Allen & Unwin, in association with the Department of International Relations, The Australian National University, 1997, pp. 196–218.

Frost, Frank, 'Political Issues in Australia–ASEAN Relations', *Asia Pacific Community* (Tokyo), 7(Winter) 1980: 119–47.

Frost, Frank, 'The Cambodia Conflict: The Path Towards Peace', *Contemporary Southeast Asia*, 13(2) 1991: 119–63.

Frost, Frank, 'The Peace Process in Cambodia: Issues and Prospects', Australia–Asia Paper No. 69, Nathan, Qld: Centre for the Study of Australian–Asian Relations, Griffith University, 1993.

Frost, Frank, 'Vietnam, ASEAN and the Indochina Refugee Crisis', *Southeast Asian Affairs 1980,* Singapore: Institute of Southeast Asian Studies, 1980, pp. 347–67.

Frost, Frank, 'Vietnam's Foreign Relations: Dynamics of Change', Pacific Strategic Paper No. 6, Singapore: Institute of Southeast Asian Studies, 1993.

Funston, John, 'The Legacy of Dr Mahathir', *Australian Financial Review*, 30 July 2004.

Garnaut, Ross, *Australia and the Northeast Asian Ascendancy: Report to the Prime Minister and the Minister for Foreign Affairs and Trade*, Canberra: Australian Government Publishing Service, 1989.

George Mulgan, Aurelia, 'Is There a "Japanese" Concept of an East Asia Community?' *East Asia Forum*, 6 November 2009.

Gilson, Julie, 'The Asia–Europe Meeting (ASEM)', in Mark Beeson and Richard Stubbs, eds, *Routledge Handbook of Asian Regionalism*, London: Routledge, 2012, pp. 394–405.

Goh Chok Tong and Paul Keating, 'Joint Press Conference at the Shangri La Hotel, Singapore, 17 January 1996: Transcript'.

Goh, Evelyn, 'ASEAN-led Multilateralism and Regional Order: The Great Power Bargain Deficit', *Asan Forum*, May–June 2014.

Goh, Evelyn, 'Southeast Asia's Evolving Security Relations and Strategies', in Saadia M. Pekkanen, John Ravenhill and Rosemary Foot, eds, *The Oxford Handbook of the International Relations of Asia*, Oxford: Oxford University Press, 2014, pp. 462–80.

Goldsworthy, David, 'Introduction', in Peter Edwards and David Goldsworthy, eds, *Facing North: A Century of Australian Engagement with Asia, Volume 2: 1970s to 2000*, Carlton, Vic.: Melbourne University Press, 2003, pp. 1–12.

Goldsworthy, David, 'Regional Relations', in Peter Edwards and David Goldsworthy, eds, *Facing North: A Century of Australian Engagement with Asia, Volume 2: 1970s to 2000*, Carlton, Vic.: Melbourne University Press, 2003, pp. 130–77.

Goldsworthy, David, David Dutton, Peter Gifford and Roderic Pitty, 'Reorientation', in David Goldsworthy, ed., *Facing North: A Century of Australian Engagement with Asia, Volume 1: 1901 to the 1970s*, Carlton, Vic.: Melbourne University Press, 2001, pp. 310–71.

Gordon, Sandy, 'The Quest for a Concert of Powers in Asia', *Security Challenges*, 8(4) 2012: 35–55.

Grattan, Michelle, 'PM Resumes Disaster Aid to the Viets', *The Age*, 22 November 1983.

Grattan, Michelle, 'The Danger of Taking on Too Much', *The Age*, 6 June 2008.

Greenlees, Don, 'Downer Assigns Asia Top Priority', *The Australian*, 12 April 1996.

Grigg, Angus, 'Blow to Rudd's Asia Plan', *Australian Financial Review*, 23 July 2008.

Grigson, Paul, 'ASEAN Bid to Absorb the New Conference', *The Age*, 7 November 1989.

Groff, Stephen, 'Overcoming Southeast Asia's Barriers to Trade', *Wall Street Journal Asia,* 30 June 2015.

Gyngell, Allan, 'Ambition: The Emerging Foreign Policy of the Rudd Government', *Analysis*, Sydney: Lowy Institute for International Policy, December 2008.

Gyngell, Allan, 'Emerging Challenges for Australian Foreign Policy', *Australian Journal of International Affairs*, 68(4) 2014: 381–5.

Gyngell, Allan and Michael Wesley, *Making Australian Foreign Policy,* 2nd edn, Cambridge: Cambridge University Press, 2007.

Harries, Owen, *Australia and the Third World: Report of the Committee on Australia's Relations with the Third World*, Canberra: Australian Government Publishing Service, 1979.

Harrison, Dan, 'Tony Abbott Heads to Jakarta for Inauguration of Indonesian President Joko Widodo', *Sydney Morning Herald*, 19 October 2014.

Hartcher, Peter, 'Gillard Rejects Rudd's Asia Vision', *Sydney Morning Herald*, 5 July 2010.

Hartcher, Peter, 'Rudd Puts Lesson in Rat Cunning to Use', *Sydney Morning Herald*, 8 December 2009.

Hartcher, Peter and Cynthia Banham, 'Bush Gives Howard the Nod for Summit', *Sydney Morning Herald*, 21 July 2005.

Hasluck, Paul, 'Statement', in *Current Notes on International Affairs*, 38(8) August 1967: 328–9.

Hastings, Peter, 'Australia Remains Cool on Kampuchea Coalition', *Sydney Morning Herald*, 9 September 1982.

Hastings, Peter, 'Canberra Disappoints Thailand', *Sydney Morning Herald*, 10 August 1982.

Hastings, Peter, 'Price of the "Expel" Policy', *Sydney Morning Herald*, 6 July 1979.

Hatoyama, Yukio, 'A New Path for Japan', *New York Times*, 26 August 2009.

Hawke, Bob, *The Hawke Memoirs*, Port Melbourne, Vic.: William Heinemann Australia, 1994.

Hawke, Robert, 'Speech by the Prime Minister, State Banquet, Seoul – 30 January 1989'.

Hayden, Bill, 'Australia and Indo-China', Ministerial Statement, in *Commonwealth of Australia Parliamentary Debates,* House of Representatives, Official Hansard, No. 134, 7 December 1983, pp. 3404–9.

Hayden, Bill, *Hayden: An Autobiography*, Sydney: Angus & Robertson, 1996.

Hayton, Bill, *The South China Sea: The Struggle for Power in Asia*, New Haven, CT: Yale University Press, 2014.

He, Baogang, 'The Awkwardness of Australian Engagement with Asia: The Dilemmas of Australian Idea of Regionalism', *Japanese Journal of Political Science*, 12(2) 2011: 267–85.

Hoare, Judith, 'Fraser Stops Aid to Vietnam', *Australian Financial Review*, 24 January 1979.

Howard, John, 'Doorstop Interview, Regent Hotel, Kuala Lumpur', Transcript, 14 December 2005.

Howard, John, 'Statement at the Special ASEAN Leaders' Meeting on the Aftermath of the Tsunami, Jakarta Convention Centre, Indonesia', Transcript, 6 January 2005.

Huisken, Ron, 'ADMM Plus Cooperates on Security and Defence Issues', *East Asia Forum*, 19 October 2010.

Huisken, Ron, 'Security in the Asia Pacific: Growing Turbulence or a Gathering Storm?' *CSCAP Regional Security Outlook 2015*, Canberra: Council for Security Cooperation in the Asia Pacific, 2015, pp. 3–6.

Huisken, Ron and Anthony Milner, 'On a Track to Regional Peace with CSCAP', *The Australian*, 2 July 2014.

Hywood, Greg, 'ASEAN Cracks Australia's Air Fare Barriers', *Australian Financial Review*, 8 May 1979.

'Import Quality Control Sought by ASEAN', *Canberra Times*, 18 April 1974.

'Improve Asean Relations – PM', *Courier Mail*, 19 January 1976.

'Indonesia Tells Whitlam, Aust Welcomed in SE-Asian Defence', *Sydney Morning Herald*, 22 February 1973.

Ingleson, John, 'Southeast Asia', in W. J. Hudson, ed., *Australia in World Affairs 1971–1975*, Sydney: Allen & Unwin and Australian Institute of International Affairs, 1980, pp. 283–305.

International Crisis Group, 'Old Scores and New Grudges: Evolving Sino-Japanese Tensions', Asia Report No. 258, Brussels: International Crisis Group, 24 July 2014.

International Crisis Group, 'Stirring up the South China Sea (III): A Fleeting Opportunity for Calm', Asia Report No. 267, Brussels: International Crisis Group, 7 May 2015.

'Japan, China Clash Over E. Asia Summit', *Yomiuri Shimbun*, 25 November 2005.

Jenkins, David, 'After Marcos, Now for the Suharto Billions', *Sydney Morning Herald,* 10 April 1986.

Jennings, Peter, 'Australia and Indonesia: No Way Out', *The Strategist*, 18 March 2015.

Johns, Brian, 'Whitlam: Some Rabbits Out of the Hat', *Sydney Morning Herald*, 25 February 1974.

Joint Committee on Foreign Affairs and Defence, *Australia and ASEAN: Challenges and Opportunities,* Report, Canberra: Australian Government Publishing Service, 1984.

Joint Standing Committee on Foreign Affairs, Defence and Trade, *Inquiry into Australia's Relationship with ASEAN*, Canberra: Commonwealth of Australia, June 2009.

Jones, David Martin and Michael Smith, 'Making Process, not Progress', *International Security*, 32(1) 2007: 148–84.

Jones, David Martin, Nicholas Khoo and M. L. R. Smith, *Asian Security and the Rise of China: International Relations in an Age of Insecurity*, Cheltenham: Edward Elgar, 2013.

Joustra, Wio, 'Zhao Plans Tough Talk on Our Aid to Vietnam', *The Australian*, 15 April 1983.

Keating, Paul, *Engagement: Australia Faces the Asia-Pacific*, Sydney: Pan Macmillan, 2000.

Keating, Paul, 'Forget the West, our Future is to the North', *The Age*, 15 November 2012.

Kelly, Paul, 'Diplomatic Activist Reshapes Region', *The Australian*, 12 December 2009.

Kelly, Paul, 'Howard's Decade: An Australian Foreign Policy Reappraisal', Lowy Institute Paper 15, Sydney: Lowy Institute for International Policy, 2006.

Kelly, Paul, 'One Club We Won't Be Joining', *The Australian*, 26 April 2000.

Kelly, Paul, 'The Day Foreign Policy Won Asia', *Weekend Australian*, 6 August 2005.

Kelly, Paul, *The March of Patriots: The Struggle for Modern Australia*, Carlton, Vic.: Melbourne University Press, 2009.

Kelly, Paul, 'Time May Not Be Ripe for Brave New Forum', *The Australian,* 9 July 2008.

Kelly, Paul, *Triumph and Demise: The Broken Promise of a Labor Generation*, Carlton, Vic.: Melbourne University Press, 2014.

Kerin, John, 'Singapore Backs Rudd's Regional Vision', *Australian Financial Review*, 17 June 2010.

Kersten, Rikki and William T. Tow, 'Evolving Australian Approaches to Security Architectures in the Asia-Pacific', Tokyo Foundation, 22 April 2011.

Khanh, Huynh Kim, 'Into the Third Indochina War', *Southeast Asian Affairs 1980*, Singapore: Institute of Southeast Asian Studies, 1980, pp. 327–46.

Kiernan, Ben, *The Pol Pot Regime: Race, Power, and Genocide in Cambodia under the Khmer Rouge, 1975–79*, 3rd edn, New Haven, CT: Yale University Press, 2008.

Koh, Tommy, 'Rudd's Reckless Regional Rush', *The Australian*, 18 December 2009.

Lachica, Eduardo, 'Australia Suggests Coexistence Talks', *The Australian*, 20 June 1975.

Lawe-Davies, Joanna, 'The Politics of Protection: Australian–ASEAN Economic Relations 1975–1980', Research Paper No. 13, Nathan, Qld: Centre for the Study of Australian–Asian Relations, Griffith University, 1981.

Lee, David, 'Indonesia's Independence', in David Goldsworthy, ed., *Facing North: A Century of Australian Engagement with Asia, Volume 1: 1901 to the 1970s*, Carlton, Vic.: Melbourne University Press, 2001, pp. 134–70.

Lee, David and Moreen Dee, 'Southeast Asian Conflicts', in David Goldsworthy, ed., *Facing North: A Century of Australian Engagement with Asia, Volume 1: 1901 to the 1970s*, Carlton, Vic.: Melbourne University Press, 2001, pp. 262–309.

Lee, Sheryn and Anthony Milner, 'Practical vs. Identity Regionalism: Australia's APC Initiative, a Case Study', *Contemporary Politics*, 20(2) 2014: 209–28.

Lewis, Steve, 'Howard Runs the Gauntlet of Asia', *The Australian*, 2 December 2002.

Lim, Robyn, 'Current Australian–ASEAN Relations', *Southeast Asian Affairs 1980*, Singapore: Institute of Southeast Asian Studies, 1980, pp. 37–53.

MacIntyre, Andrew, T. J. Pempel and John Ravenhill, eds, *Crisis as Catalyst: Asia's Dynamic Political Economy*, Ithaca, NY: Cornell University Press, 2008.

Mackie, J. A. C., *Konfrontasi: The Indonesia–Malaysia Dispute, 1963–1966*, Kuala Lumpur: Oxford University Press, 1974.

Mackie, Jamie, 'Australia and Indonesia: Current Problems, Future Prospects', Lowy Institute Paper 19, Sydney: Lowy Institute for International Policy, 2007.

Mackie, Jamie, *Bandung 1955: Non-Alignment and Afro-Asian Solidarity*, Singapore: Editions Didier Millet, 2005.

Mahbubani, Kishore, 'Australia's Destiny in the Asian Century: Pain or No Pain?' Paper prepared for Emerging Asia and the Future of the Australia–US Alliance, the US–Australia 21st Century Alliance Project, United States Studies Centre, University of Sydney, 31 July 2012.

Malik, Mohan, 'China and the East Asian Summit: More Discord than Accord', Honolulu: Asia-Pacific Center for Security Studies, February 2006.

Malik, Mohan, 'The East Asia Summit: More Discord than Accord', *YaleGlobal Online*, 20 December 2005.

Manyin, Mark E., Michael John Garcia and Wayne M. Morrison, 'US Accession to ASEAN's Treaty of Amity and Cooperation (TAC)', CRS Report for Congress, Washington, DC: Congressional Research Service, 5 May 2009.

Massola, James and John Garnaut, 'Australia "Deplores" Unilateral Action in South China Sea: Tony Abbott', *Sydney Morning Herald*, 29 June 2015.

McCarthy, John, 'Let's Aim to Be More than US Surrogate', *Australian Financial Review*, 21 November 2012.

McDonald, Hamish, 'ASEAN Hostile to "Fly-Over" Air Fares', *Australian Financial Review*, 8 June 1978.

McGregor, Richard and Anna Fifield, 'Divisions Undermine East Asia Summit', *Financial Times* (London), 1 December 2005.

McPhedran, Ian, 'ASEAN Asked to Press Burma Harder Towards Democracy', *Canberra Times*, 4 May 1994.

McPhedran, Ian, 'Underlying Fears as Australia Strengthens Ties with Indonesia', *Adelaide Advertiser*, 18 November 2006.

Medcalf, Rory, 'Reimagining Asia: From Asia-Pacific to Indo-Pacific', *Asan Forum*, 26 June 2015.

Menon, Jayant and Anna Cassandra Melendez, 'Realizing an ASEAN Economic Community: Progress and Remaining Challenges', ADB Economics Working Paper 432, Metro Manila: Asian Development Bank, May 2015.

Merrifield, Simon, 'Australia and ASEAN: Past, Present and Future', Remarks by Australian Ambassador to ASEAN, Foreign Service Institute, Manila, 27 March 2015.

Milner, Anthony, 'Balancing "Asia" Against Australian Values', in James Cotton and John Ravenhill, eds, *The National Interest in a Global Era: Australia in World Affairs 1996–2000*, South Melbourne: Oxford University Press, 2001, pp. 31–50.

Milner, Anthony, 'Regionalism in Asia', in Juliet Love, ed., *The Far East and Australasia 2014*, 45th edn, Abingdon: Routledge, 2013, pp. 65–73.

Milner, Anthony and Sally Percival Wood, eds, 'Our Place in the Asian Century: Southeast Asia as "The Third Way"', Melbourne: Asialink, University of Melbourne, 2012.

Minister for Foreign Affairs, news release, M129, 13 November 1978.

Minister for Foreign Affairs, news release, M35/IEA 94/77, 28 November 1977.

Minister for Foreign Affairs, news release, M58, 28 May 1981.

Minter Ellison Lawyers, 'The ASEAN Australia New Zealand Free Trade Agreement: Our Overview and Assessment', April 2009.

Morada, Noel M., 'The ASEAN Regional Forum: Origins and Evolution', in Jürgen Haacke and Noel M. Morada, eds, *Cooperative Security in the Asia-Pacific: The ASEAN Regional Forum*, London: Routledge, 2010, pp. 13–35.

Murdoch, Lindsay, 'Australia's Hard Line on Burma Softens', *The Age,* 11 October 1993.

Narine, Shaun, 'Asia, ASEAN and the Question of Sovereignty', in Mark Beeson and Richard Stubbs, eds, *Routledge Handbook of Asian Regionalism*, London: Routledge, 2012, pp. 155–65.

Nicholas, Katrina, 'Smith Still Keen on New Regional Group', *Australian Financial Review*, 24 July 2008.

Nixon, Peter, 'International Aviation Policy', Ministerial Statement, in *Commonwealth of Australia Parliamentary Debates*, House of Representatives, Official Hansard, No. 41, 11 October 1978, pp. 1696–709.

Norman, Felicity, 'Looking Ahead: Australia–Indonesia Relations', *New Mandela*, 15 May 2015.

O'Brien, Philip, 'The Making of Australia's Indochina Policies Under the Labor Government (1983–1986): The Politics of Circumspection?' Australia–Asia Papers No. 39, Nathan, Qld: Centre for the Study of Australian–Asian Relations, Griffith University, September 1987.

Obama, Barack, 'Remarks by President Barack Obama at Suntory Hall', Tokyo, Office of the Press Secretary, The White House, 14 November 2009.

Okamoto, Jiro, *Australia's Foreign Economic Policy and ASEAN*, Singapore: Institute of Southeast Asian Studies, 2010.

'Our Stand on Kampuchea Criticised', *The Mercury* (Hobart), 1 June 1981.

Parkinson, Tony, 'ASEAN Ready to Strengthen Australian Ties', *The Age*, 14 April 2004.

Peacock, Andrew, 'Australia–ASEAN Relations', news release, 19 January 1977.

'Peacock Goes to ASEAN Talks on Refugees', *The Australian*, 30 June 1979.

Percival Wood, Sally and Baogang He, eds, *The Australia–ASEAN Dialogue: Tracing 40 Years of Partnership*, New York: Palgrave Macmillan, 2014.

Phillips, Janet, 'Boat Arrivals and Boat "Turnbacks" in Australia since 1976: A Quick Guide to the Statistics', Parliamentary Library Research Paper Series 2015–2016, Canberra: Department of Parliamentary Services, 11 September 2015.

Pillai, M. G. G., 'Viet Hardware Now Going Cheap', *The Nation Review* (Melbourne), 19 June 1975.

Pitty, Roderic, 'Regional Economic Co-operation', in Peter Edwards and David Goldsworthy, eds, *Facing North: A Century of Australian Engagement with Asia, Volume 2: 1970s to 2000*, Carlton, Vic.: Melbourne University Press, 2003, pp. 13–47.

Pitty, Roderic, 'Strategic Engagement', in Peter Edwards and David Goldsworthy, eds, *Facing North: A Century of Australian Engagement With Asia, Volume 2: 1970s to 2000*, Carlton, Vic.: Melbourne University Press, 2003, pp. 48–80.

Poole, Avery, 'The East Asia Summit: Navigating ASEAN Multilateralism', in Sally Percival Wood and Baogang He, eds, *The Australia–ASEAN Dialogue: Tracing 40 Years of Partnership*, New York: Palgrave Macmillan, 2014, pp. 49–64.

Ravenhill, John, *APEC and the Construction of Pacific Rim Regionalism*, Cambridge: Cambridge University Press, 2001.

Razaleigh Hamzah, Tengku, 'Speech', delivered to the first ASEAN–Australia Business Conference, 24 June 1980.

'Refugee Talks Planned Monday', *Canberra Times*, 7 January 1979.

Richardson, Michael, 'Asean Aims to Fight Cheap Air Fares', *The Age*, 18 December 1978.

Richardson, Michael, 'ASEAN Takes Fraser to Task', *Australian Financial Review*, 27 July 1976.

Richardson, Michael, 'Asean Upset By Our Trade Curb', *The Age*, 27 February 1976.

Richardson, Michael, 'Asean Warns of Trade Reprisals', *The Age*, 23 April 1973.

Richardson, Michael, 'ASEAN's Air Fare Threat', *Australian Financial Review*, 19 May 1978.

Richardson, Michael, 'Asians Will Put Fraser to the Test', *The Age*, 14 July 1977.

Richardson, Michael, 'Aust Hand of Friendship to South-East Asia', *Sydney Morning Herald*, 17 November 1973.

Richardson, Michael, 'Canberra Ruffles Asean Feathers over Kampuchea', *The Age*, 19 June 1981.

Richardson, Michael, 'Ease Curbs, Asean Asked', *The Age*, 4 July 1979.

Richardson, Michael, 'Govt Seeks a New Patsy on ASEAN Trade War', *Australian Financial Review*, 11 July 1977.

Richardson, Michael, 'Hayden Rebuffed on Kampuchea Proposal', *The Age*, 14 July 1984.

Richardson, Michael, 'How Mr Fraser Got the Cold Shoulder', *Australian Financial Review*, 27 February 1976.

Richardson, Michael, 'Lee Defines the ASEAN Blueprint', *Far Eastern Economic Review*, 10 June 1977.

Richardson, Michael, 'Move Away from Pol Pot Disappoints Asean', *The Age*, 15 October 1980.

Richardson, Michael, 'PM Sought Invitation from ASEAN', *The Age*, 11 February 1976.

Richardson, Michael, 'Shared Perceptions', in Michael Richardson and Chin Kin Wah, *Australia–New Zealand & Southeast Asia Relations: An Agenda for Closer Cooperation*, Singapore: ISEAS Publications, 2004, pp. 25–43.

Roberts, Christopher, *ASEAN's Myanmar Crisis: Challenges to the Pursuit of a Security Community,* Singapore: Institute of Southeast Asian Studies, 2010.

Roberts, Christopher B., 'ASEAN: The Challenge of Unity in Diversity', in Leszek Buszynski and Christopher B. Roberts, eds, *The South China Sea Maritime Dispute: Political, Legal and Regional Perspectives*, Abingdon: Routledge, 2015, pp. 130–49.

Roberts, Christopher B., *ASEAN Regionalism: Cooperation, Values and Institutionalization*, Abingdon: Routledge, 2012.

Roberts, Christopher B. and Ahmad D. Habir, 'Indonesia–Australia Relations: Progress, Challenges and Potential', in Christopher B. Roberts, Ahmad D. Habir and Leonard C. Sebastian, eds, *Indonesia's Ascent: Power, Leadership, and the Regional* Order, Basingstoke: Palgrave Macmillan, 2015, pp. 195–218.

Rothwell, Nicholas, 'Malaysia Walks Out as Hayden Speaks', *The Australian*, 4 October 1983.

Rowland, John, 'Two Transitions: Indochina 1952–1955, Malaysia, 1969–1972', Australians in Asia Series No. 8, Nathan, Qld: Centre for the Study of Australian–Asian Relations, Griffith University, 1992.

Rudd, Kevin, 'Address at Shangri-La Dialogue', Singapore, 29 May 2009.

Rudd, Kevin, 'Address to the Asia Pacific Community Conference', Sydney, 4 December 2009.

Rudd, Kevin, 'Future Stability and Security in the Asia Pacific Region', Address to the Brisbane Institute, 8 December 2010.

Rudd, Kevin, 'It's Time to Build an Asia Pacific Community', Address to the Asia Society AustralAsia Centre, Sydney, 4 June 2008.

Rudd, Kevin, 'Joint Press Statement with Ausaid: ASEAN and Australian Advances Cooperation in Economic Integration', media release, Jakarta, 13 June 2008.

Rudd, Kevin, 'Smart Power', *The Diplomat*, February–March 2007, pp. 21–5.

Rudd, Kevin, 'National Security', Ministerial Statement, in *Commonwealth of Australia Parliamentary Debates*, House of Representatives, Official Hansard, No. 18, 4 December 2008, pp. 12549–61.

Rudd, Kevin, 'The Singapore Lecture: Building on ASEAN's Success: Towards an Asia Pacific Century', Singapore, 12 August 2008.

Sally, Razeen, 'ASEAN FTAs: State of Play and Outlook for ASEAN's Regional and Global Integration', in Sanchita Basu Das, Jayant Menon, Rodolfo Severino and Omkar Lal Shreshtra, eds, *The ASEAN Economic Community: A Work in Progress,* Singapore: ISEAS Publishing, 2013, pp. 320–81.

Samuel, Peter, 'Labor's Support for Vietnam Aid Sparks ASEAN Outcry', *The Australian,* 17 March 1983.

Sargent, Sarah, 'Region Ministers in Favour of Pact', *Australian Financial Review,* 13 September 1989.

Scott, David, 'Australia's Embrace of the "Indo-Pacific": New Term, New Region, New Strategy?' *International Relations of the Asia-Pacific,* 13(3) 2013: 425–48.

Scott, Keith, *Gareth Evans,* St Leonards, NSW: Allen & Unwin, 1999.

'Security, in Letter and Spirit', *Australian Financial Review,* 2 May 1991.

Selochan, Viberto, 'New Directions and New Thinking in Australia–Southeast Asia Relations', Australia–Asia Papers No. 62, Nathan, Qld: Centre for the Study of Australian–Asian Relations, Griffith University, March 1992.

Senate Standing Committee on Foreign Affairs and Defence, *Australia and ASEAN,* Report, Canberra: Australian Government Publishing Service, 1980.

Severino, Rodolfo C., *Southeast Asia in Search of an ASEAN Community: Insights from the Former ASEAN Secretary-General,* Singapore: Institute of Southeast Asian Studies, 2006.

Sheridan, Greg, 'ASEAN Thumbs Down Caps Our Bad Week in Asia', *The Australian,* 7 November 2002.

Sheridan, Greg, 'Carr Goes All Out to Bring Myanmar in From the Cold', *The Australian,* 7 February 2013.

Sheridan, Greg, 'Inept Downer a Regional Flop', *The Australian,* 28 April 2000.

Short, John, 'ASEAN Hits Aust Policies on Tariffs, Aviation', *Australian Financial Review*, 22 November 1978.

Simon, Sheldon, 'Cambodia and Regional Diplomacy', *Southeast Asian Affairs 1982*, Singapore: Institute of Southeast Asian Studies, 1982, pp. 196–207.

Simon, Sheldon, 'US–Southeast Asia Relations: The United States is Back!' *Comparative Connections: A Quarterly E-Journal on East Asian Bilateral Relations*, 11(3) 2009.

Smith, Stephen, 'Diplomatic Appointment – Ambassador to ASEAN', media release, 5 September 2008.

Smith, Stephen, 'Paper Presented by Minister for Defence Stephen Smith to the ADMM-Plus Maritime Security Experts' Working Group Inaugural Meeting', Perth, 21 July 2011.

Soesastro, Hadi, 'Kevin Rudd's Architecture for the Asia Pacific', *East Asia Forum*, 9 June 2008.

Solingen, Etel, 'ASEAN Cooperation: The Legacy of the Economic Crisis', *International Relations of the Asia-Pacific*, 5(1) 2005: 1–29.

'South-East Asia: The Neutralisation Proposal', *Current Notes on International Affairs*, 43(10) October 1972: 498–504.

Southwick, Kathleen G., 'Bumpy Road to the ASEAN Human Rights Declaration', *Asia-Pacific Bulletin*, No. 197, Washington, DC: East–West Center, 22 January 2013.

Steketee, Mike, 'Timor, Viet Aid: Hawke Goes Alone', *Sydney Morning Herald*, 6 June 1983.

Stewart, Cameron, 'Evans to Urge Tougher ASEAN Stand on Burma', *The Australian*, 25 July 1995.

Stewart, Cameron, 'Why Did Australia's Spy Agencies Listen in on the Indonesian First Lady?' *The Australian*, 14 December 2013.

Stockwin, Harvey, 'The Europeans Lack Vision', *Financial Times* (London), 3 May 1973.

Storey, Ian, 'ASEAN's Failing Grade in the South China Sea', *Asan Forum*, 31 July 2015.

Storey, Ian, 'Can the South China Sea Dispute be Resolved or Better Managed?' Paper presented at 27th Asia-Pacific Roundtable, Kuala Lumpur, 3–4 June 2013.

Storey, Ian, 'China's "Terraforming" in the Spratlys: A Game Changer in the South China Sea?' *ISEAS Perspective*, 23 June 2015.

Storey, Ian, 'Disputes in the South China Sea: Southeast Asia's Troubled Waters', *politique étrangère*, 3, 2014: 1–12.

Storey, Ian, *Southeast Asia and the Rise of China: The Search for Security*, London: Routledge, 2011.

Stubbs, Richard, 'ASEAN Plus Three: Emerging East Asian Regionalism?' *Asian Survey*, 42(3) 2002: 440–55.

Suares, Julie, 'Engaging with Asia: The Chifley Government and the New Delhi Conferences of 1947 and 1949', *Australian Journal of Politics and History*, 57(4) 2011: 495–510.

Sulzberger, C. L., 'New Look, Not New Reality', *New York Times*, 11 March 1973.

Tan, See Seng, 'Hobnobbing with Giants: Australia's Approach to Asian Regionalism', in Sally Percival Wood and Baogang He, eds, *The Australia–ASEAN Dialogue: Tracing 40 Years of Partnership*, New York: Palgrave Macmillan, 2014, pp. 33–48.

Tan, See Seng, *Multilateral Asian Security Architecture: Non-ASEAN Stakeholders*, Abingdon: Routledge, 2016.

Tan, See Seng and Oleg Korovin, 'Seeking Stability in Turbulent Times: Southeast Asia's New Normal?' in Daljit Singh, ed., *Southeast Asian Affairs 2015,* Singapore: Institute of Southeast Asian Studies, 2015, pp. 3–24.

Tarling, Nicholas, *Regionalism in Southeast Asia: To Foster the Political Will*, London: Routledge, 2006.

Tay, Simon S. C., 'Blowing Smoke: Regional Cooperation, Indonesian Democracy, and the Haze', in Donald K. Emmerson, ed., *Hard Choices: Security, Democracy, and Regionalism in Southeast Asia*, Stanford, CA: Walter H. Shorenstein Asia-Pacific Research Center Books, 2008, pp. 219–40.

Thakur, Ramesh, 'Nuclear-Free Dream For Real', *Canberra Times*, 8 April 2010.

Thayer, Carl, 'Australia and Vietnam Enhance their Comprehensive Partnership', *The Diplomat*, 17 March 2015.

Thayer, Carlyle A., 'ASEAN and Indochina: The Dialogue', in Alison Broinoswki, ed., *ASEAN into the 1990s*, London: Macmillan, 1990, pp. 138–61.

Thayer, Carlyle A., 'ASEAN, China and the Code of Conduct in the South China Sea', *SAIS Review of International Affairs*, 33(2) 2013: 75–84.

Thayer, Carlyle A., 'ASEAN's Code of Conduct in the South China Sea: A Litmus Test for Community-Building?' *Asia-Pacific Journal: Japan Focus*, 10(34) 20 August 2012.

Thayer, Carlyle A., 'Australia and Vietnam, 1950–1980, Part II, From Conciliation to Condemnation, 1972–1980', *Dyason House Papers*, 6(3) 1980: 5–12.

Thayer, Carlyle A., 'Australia, the ANZUS Alliance and US Rebalancing to the Asia-Pacific', Keynote Paper presented to the International Conference on Australia–Asia Relations under Prime Minister Tony Abbott, National Cheng Chi University, Taipei, 31 March – 1 April 2015.

Thayer, Carlyle A., 'Deference/Defiance: Southeast Asia, China and the South China Sea', Paper prepared for International Studies Association Annual Convention, Hilton San Francisco, Union Square, 5 April 2013.

'The Bali Process on People Smuggling, Trafficking in Persons and Related Transnational Crime', www.baliprocess.net/ (accessed 1 October 2015).

'The G20 Economies Explained in 12 Charts', *The Conversation*, 12 November 2014.

Thuzar, Moe, 'Myanmar and the 2014 ASEAN Chairmanship', *ISEAS Perspective*, 18 March 2013.

Tow, William T., 'Great Powers and Multilateralism: The Politics of Security Architectures in Southeast Asia', in Ralf Emmers, ed., *ASEAN and the Institutionalization of East Asia*, London: Routledge, 2012, pp. 155–67.

Tow, William T. and Brendan Taylor, 'Emerging Regional Security Architecture: An Australian Perspective', in William T. Tow and Chin Kin Wah, eds, *ASEAN India Australia: Towards Closer Engagement in a New Asia,* Singapore: Institute of Southeast Asian Studies, 2009, pp. 3–21.

'Transcript of Interview with Peter van Onselen and Paul Kelly', *Australian Agenda*, Sky News, 25 November 2012.

Turley, William S., *The Second Indochina War: A Concise Political and Military History*, 2nd edn, Lanham, MD: Rowman & Littlefield, 2009.

Turnbull, Malcolm, 'Historic Asia-Pacific Trade Agreement Opens New Era of Opportunities', media release, Canberra, 6 October 2015.

Varghese, Peter, 'The 50th Anniversary of the Indonesia Project', Speech, Canberra, 30 July 2015, dfat.gov.au/news/speeches/Pages/50th-anniversary-dinner-indonesia-project.aspx (accessed 1 October 2015).

Viviani, Nancy, 'Australia and Southeast Asia', in James Cotton and John Ravenhill, eds, *Seeking Asian Engagement: Australia in World Affairs, 1991–95*, Melbourne: Oxford University Press, 1997, pp. 149–69.

Viviani, Nancy, *The Long Journey: Vietnamese Migration and Settlement in Australia*, Carlton, Vic.: Melbourne University Press, 1984.

Viviani, Nancy, 'The Whitlam Government's Policy Towards Asia', in David Lee and Christopher Waters, eds, *Evatt to Evans: The Labor Tradition in Australian Foreign Policy*, St Leonards, NSW: Allen & Unwin, in association with the Department of International Relations, The Australian National University, 1997, pp. 99–109.

Wain, Barry, *Malaysian Maverick: Mahathir Mohamad in Turbulent Times*, 2nd edn, Basingstoke: Palgrave Macmillan, 2012.

Wain, Barry, *The Refused: The Agony of the Indochina Refugees*, New York: Simon and Schuster, 1982.

Walker, David, 'Nervous Outsiders: Australia and the 1955 Asia–Africa Conference in Bandung', *Australian Historical Studies*, 36(125) 2005: 40–59.

Walker, Tony, 'China Prods Australia Over its Policy on Kampuchea', *Sydney Morning Herald*, 27 June 1981.

Walker, Tony, 'Pol Pot Will Not Get Our Help, PM Tells China', *The Age*, 10 August 1982.

Walters, Patrick, 'Framework for Close Ties First Imperative', *The Australian*, 12 November 2004.

Walters, Patrick, 'Rudd Asia Plan "Dead in Water"', *The Australian*, 4 July 2008.

Walters, Patrick and Roy Ecclestone, 'PM to Fly to Jakarta Summit', *Weekend Australian*, 1 January 2005.

'War Fears Over Flood of S-E Asian Refugees', *The Australian*, 31 July 1979.

Ward, Ken, *Condemned to Crisis? A Lowy Institute Paper*, Melbourne: Penguin, 2015.

Waters, Christopher, 'Creating a Tradition: The Foreign Policy of the Curtin and Chifley Labor Governments', in David Lee and Christopher Waters, eds, *Evatt to Evans: The Labor Tradition in Australian Foreign Policy*, St Leonards, NSW: Allen & Unwin, in association with the Department of International Relations, The Australian National University, 1997, pp. 35–47.

Waters, Christopher, 'Lost Opportunity: Australia and the Bandung Conference', in Derek McDougall and Antonia Finnane, eds, *Bandung 1955: Little Histories*, Caulfield, Vic.: Monash University Press, 2010, pp. 75–87.

Weatherbee, Donald E., *Indonesia in ASEAN: Vision and Reality*, Singapore: ISEAS Publishing, 2013.

Wesley, Michael, 'Australia and the Asian Economic Crisis', in James Cotton and John Ravenhill, eds, *The National Interest in a Global Era: Australia in World Affairs 1996–2000,* South Melbourne: Oxford University Press, 2001, pp. 301–24.

Wesley, Michael, 'Rebuilding Engagement: Australia and South-East Asia', in James Cotton and John Ravenhill, eds, *Trading on Alliance Security: Australia in World Affairs 2001–2005*, South Melbourne: Oxford University Press, 2007, pp. 53–71.

Wesley, Michael, *Restless Continent: Wealth, Rivalry and Asia's New Geopolitics*, Colllingwood, Vic.: Black Inc., 2015.

Wesley, Michael, *The Howard Paradox: Australian Diplomacy in Asia, 1996–2006*, Sydney: ABC Books, 2007.

Wesley, Michael, 'Trade Agreements and Strategic Rivalry in Asia', *Australian Journal of International Affairs*, 69(5) 2015: 479–95.

Westad, Odd Arne and Sophie Quinn-Judge, eds, *The Third Indochina War: Conflict Between China, Vietnam and Cambodia, 1972–79*, London: Routledge, 2006.

Whitlam, Gough, 'Opening Address', delivered to the Australian Institute of Political Science Summer School, Canberra, 27 January 1973.

Whitlam, Gough, in *Commonwealth of Australia Parliamentary Debates*, House of Representatives, Official Hansard, No. 33, 17 August 1967, p. 220.

'Whitlam Sets New Policy on Asia', *The Herald* (Melbourne), 29 January 1973.

Wilson, Trevor, 'The "Indo-Pacific": Absent Policy Behind Meaningless Words', *East Asia Forum*, 19 September 2014.

Woods, Susan, 'Govt Denies Peacock Bypassed on Vietnam Decision', *Australian Financial Review*, 25 January 1979.

Woolcott, Richard, 'Opening Remarks by Mr Richard Woolcott, Deputy Secretary, Department of Foreign Affairs, to Meeting with ASEAN Secretaries General', Canberra, 15 April 1974.

World Bank, *World Bank Atlas: Population, Per Capita Product, and Growth Rates*, Washington, DC: World Bank, 1976.

Wroe, David and Philip Wen, 'South China Sea Dispute: Strong Indications Australia Will Join Push Back On China's Island-Building', *Sydney Morning Herald*, 1 June 2015.

Yahuda, Michael, *Sino-Japanese Relations after the Cold War: Two Tigers Sharing a Mountain*, Abingdon: Routledge, 2014.

Yean, Tham Siew and Sanchita Basu Das, 'Domestic Consensus Vital for ASEAN Economic Integration Beyond 2015', *ISEAS Perspective*, 24 September 2015.

Index

www.ingramcontent.com/pod-product-compliance
Lightning Source LLC
Chambersburg PA
CBHW040142270326
41928CB00023B/3311